THE LETTERS

OF

CHARLES LAMB

THE LETTERS

OF

CHARLES LAMB

Newly Arranged, with Additions

EDITED, WITH INTRODUCTION AND NOTES, BY

ALFRED AINGER

VOL. I.

London

MACMILLAN AND CO., LIMITED

NEW YORK: THE MACMILLAN COMPANY

1904

First Edition, March 1888
Reprinted September 1888, 1891, 1897
Second Edition 1904

TO MY OLD FRIEND

ADOLPHUS WILLIAM WARD
M.A. LITT.D.

OF OWENS COLLEGE, MANCHESTER

THIS EDITION OF

THE WORKS AND CORRESPONDENCE OF CHARLES LAMB

IS

AFFECTIONATELY INSCRIBED

PREFATORY NOTE TO
THE PRESENT EDITION (1904)

THIS new issue in the Eversley Series includes all
the Letters contained in the *Edition de Luxe* of 1900.
But in addition to these, I am now able to add about
twenty, addressed to John Rickman, of the House of
Commons, and now printed for the first time.

All letters not printed in the former Eversley
Edition are marked in the Contents with an asterisk.

TEMPLE,
   October 1903.

CHAPTER III.

1809–1816.

LETTERS TO MANNING, COLERIDGE, WORDSWORTH, AND OTHERS.

SONNET TO ELIA.

THOU gentle Spirit, sweet and pure and kind,
Though strangely witted—''high fantastical"—
Who clothest thy deep feelings in a pall
Of motley hues, that twinkle to the mind,
Half hiding, and yet heightening, what's enshrined
Within ;—who by a power unknown to all
Save thee alone, canst bring up at a call
A thousand seeming opposites, entwined
In wondrous brotherhood—fancy, wild wit,
Quips, cranks, and wanton wiles, with deep sweet thought,
And stinging jests, with honey for the wound ;
All blent in intermixture full and fit,—
A banquet for the choicest souls :—can aught
Repay the solace which from thee I've found ?

J. H. (JOHN HUNTER OF CRAIGCROOK)
From *Friendship's Offering*, 1832.

INTRODUCTION

As I have elsewhere told the story of Charles Lamb's life to the best of my ability, I have not thought it necessary, in editing his Letters, to tell it over again in my own words. The letters themselves contain his story—at least from the year when he came of age and began in earnest the battle of his difficult and lonely life. From the year 1796 to a date preceding his death by only a few days, there are few incidents of that life that are not related or referred to in those letters. When read consecutively, and with the help of such supplementary information as can be provided in notes, they form an almost complete biography.

Material for a larger collection of Lamb's Letters has been gradually accumulating since the appearance of Talfourd's well-known volumes—the *Letters of Charles Lamb, with a Sketch of his Life*, in 1837, and the *Final Memorials* published after the death of Mary Lamb in 1848. It would take long to unfold the complicated history of the various editions of Lamb's correspondence that have since appeared. No change in the form of Talfourd's work would seem to have been made until the year 1868, when an edition of the writings of Lamb was published by Mr. Moxon, preceded by a collection of the Letters, freshly arranged according to the persons to whom they were addressed. This edition was in the first instance prefaced by an "Essay on the Genius of Lamb" from the hand of Mr. G. A. Sala. Two years later the first volume was withdrawn, and re-issued with a substi-

tuted Preface by Mr. Thomas Purnell. This edition was
in its turn replaced in 1875 by another in six volumes,
bearing the name of the same publishers, and under the
editorship of Mr. Percy Fitzgerald. In this last-named
edition the narrative portion of Talfourd's two works
was retained, digested into one continuous narrative,
with additions both in the text and notes. The Letters
were separated from Talfourd's original matter, arranged
(as in the two preceding editions) in groups—the Letters
to Coleridge being followed by those addressed to Southey,
and so forth. Mr. Fitzgerald was able to announce that
he had added forty new letters to the collection.

More than ten years after Mr. Fitzgerald's edition,
Mr. W. C. Hazlitt edited for Mr. George Bell a fresh
Life and Letters, announced as Talfourd's " carefully
revised and greatly enlarged." The edition consists of
Talfourd's text, freely interspersed with original matter,
and the Letters rearranged, with certain additions to
their number. The edition has this advantage over Mr.
Fitzgerald's in that it aims at giving the Letters in
chronological order, and not broken up into groups on any
other plan. But I certainly cannot think that Talfourd's
work, which, whatever be its defects, has long taken its
place as an English Classic, should be re-issued under its
author's name after additions and alterations so extensive
have been introduced into it. I have preferred, therefore,
to omit Talfourd's own narrative altogether, and to print
the Letters only, with such additions to their number as
I have been fortunate in obtaining, and in chronological
order, so far as their dates are discoverable, reserving all
elucidatory matter for the notes at the end of the respective volumes.

The editors of Lamb's Letters who have succeeded
Talfourd have been, I think, unduly severe upon his
methods of procedure. Mr. Fitzgerald, for instance, complains that in Talfourd's hands the Letters were edited " in
accordance with his peculiar views—being cut up, altered,
and dealt with in very summary fashion." This may be

LETTERS OF CHARLES LAMB.

CHAPTER I.

1796–1800.

LETTERS TO COLERIDGE, SOUTHEY, ROBERT LLOYD,
AND MANNING

To SAMUEL TAYLOR COLERIDGE.

LETTER I.]   *May* 27, 1796.

Dear Coleridge—Make yourself perfectly easy about
May. I paid his bill when I sent your clothes. I was
flush of money, and am so still to all the purposes of a
single life; so give yourself no further concern about it.
The money would be superfluous to me if I had it.

When Southey becomes as modest as his predecessor,
Milton, and publishes his Epics in duodecimo, I will read
'em; a guinea a book is somewhat exorbitant, nor have
I the opportunity of borrowing the work. The extracts
from it in the *Monthly Review*, and the short passages in
your *Watchman*, seem to me much superior to any thing
in his partnership account with Lovell. Your poems I
shall procure forthwith. There were noble lines in what
you inserted in one of your Numbers from *Religious
Musings;* but I thought them elaborate. I am somewhat glad you have given up that paper: it must have

VOL. I.   S   B

been dry, unprofitable, and of "dissonant mood" to your disposition. I wish you success in all your undertakings, and am glad to hear you are employed about the *Evidences of Religion*. There is need of multiplying such books a hundredfold in this philosophical age, to *prevent* converts to atheism, for they seem too tough disputants to meddle with afterwards.

Le Grice is gone to make puns in Cornwall. He has got a tutorship to a young boy living with his mother, a widow lady. He will, of course, initiate him quickly in "whatsoever things are honest, lovely, and of good report." He has cut Miss Hunt completely: the poor girl is very ill on the occasion; but he laughs at it, and justifies himself by saying, "she does not see me laugh." Coleridge, I know not what suffering scenes you have gone through at Bristol. My life has been somewhat diversified of late. The six weeks that finished last year and began this, your very humble servant spent very agreeably in a madhouse, at Hoxton. I am got somewhat rational now, and don't bite any one. But mad I was; and many a vagary my imagination played with me, enough to make a volume, if all were told. My Sonnets I have extended to the number of nine since I saw you, and will some day communicate to you. I am beginning a poem in blank verse, which, if I finish, I publish. White is on the eve of publishing (he took the hint from *Vortigern*) "Original letters of Falstaff, Shallow," etc.; a copy you shall have when it comes out. They are without exception the best imitations I ever saw. Coleridge, it may convince you of my regards for you when I tell you my head ran on you in my madness, as much almost as on another person, who I am inclined to think was the more immediate cause of my temporary frenzy.

The Sonnet I send you has small merit as poetry; but you will be curious to read it when I tell you it was written in my prison-house in one of my lucid intervals.

eighth or twenty-ninth, or what you call the "Sigh," I think I hear *you* again. I image to myself the little smoky room at the *Salutation and Cat*, where we have sat together through the winter nights, beguiling the cares of life with Poesy. When you left London I felt a dismal void in my heart. I found myself cut off, at one and the same time, from two most dear to me. "How blest with ye the path could I have trod of quiet life!" In your conversation you had blended so many pleasant fancies that they cheated me of my grief. But in your absence the tide of melancholy rushed in again, and did its worst mischief by overwhelming my reason. I have recovered, but feel a stupor that makes me indifferent to the hopes and fears of this life. I sometimes wish to introduce a religious turn of mind; but habits are strong things, and my religious fervours are confined, alas! to some fleeting moments of occasional solitary devotion. A correspondence, opening with you, has roused me a little from my lethargy, and made me conscious of existence. Indulge me in it: I will not be very troublesome. At some future time I will amuse you with an account, as full as my memory will permit, of the strange turn my frenzy took. I look back upon it at times with a gloomy kind of envy; for, while it lasted, I had many, many hours of pure happiness. Dream not, Coleridge, of having tasted all the grandeur and wildness of fancy till you have gone mad! All now seems to me vapid, comparatively so. Excuse this selfish digression. Your "Monody" is so superlatively excellent, that I can only wish it perfect, which I can't help feeling it is not quite. Indulge me in a few conjectures. What I am going to propose would make it more compressed, and, I think, more energetic, though I am sensible at the expense of many beautiful lines. Let it begin "Is this the land of song-ennobled line?" and proceed to " Otway's famish'd form;" then, "Thee, Chatterton," to " blaze of Seraphim;" then, "clad in Nature's rich array," to "orient day;" then, "but soon the scathing

lightning," to "blighted land;" then, "sublime of
thought," to "his bosom glows;" then

> " But soon upon his poor unshelter'd head
>   Did Penury her sickly mildew shed:
>   Ah! where are fled the charms of vernal Grace,
>   And Joy's wild gleams that lighten'd o'er his face?"

Then "youth of tumultuous soul" to "sigh," as before.
The rest may all stand down to "gaze upon the waves
below." What follows now may come next as detached
verses, suggested by the Monody, rather than a part of
it. They are indeed, in themselves, very sweet:

> " And we, at sober eve, would round thee throng
>   Hanging, enraptured, on thy stately song,"

in particular, perhaps. If I am obscure, you may understand me by counting lines. I have proposed omitting
twenty-four lines. I feel that thus compressed it would
gain energy, but think it most likely you will not agree
with me; for who shall go about to bring opinions to the
bed of Procrustes, and introduce among the sons of men
a monotony of identical feelings? I only propose with
diffidence. Reject, if you please, with as little remorse
as you would the colour of a coat or the pattern of a
buckle, where our fancies differed. The lines "Friend to
the Friendless," etc., which you may think rudely dis-
branched from the Chatterton, will patch in with the
Man of Ross, where they were at once at home, with two
more which I recollect,

> " And o'er the dowried virgin's snowy cheek
>   Bade bridal Love suffuse his blushes meek,"

very beautiful.

The "Pixies" is a perfect thing; and so are the
"Lines on the Spring," page 28. The "Epitaph on an
Infant," like a Jack-o'-lantern, has danced about (or like
Dr. Forster's scholars) out of the *Morning Chronicle* into
the *Watchman*, and thence back into your Collection.
It is very pretty, and you seem to think so; but, may
be, o'erlooked its chief merit, that of filling up a whole

page. I had once deemed Sonnets of unrivalled use that way; but your Epitaphs, I find, are the more diffuse. "Edmund" still holds its place among your best verses. "Ah! fair delights" to "roses round," in your Poem called "Absence," recall (none more forcibly) to my mind the tones in which *you recited it.* I will not notice, in this tedious (to you) manner, verses which have been so long delightful to me, and which you already know my opinion of. Of this kind are Bowles, Priestley, and that most exquisite and most Bowles-like of all, the nineteenth effusion. It would have better ended with "agony of care:" the last two lines are obvious and unnecessary, and you need not now make fourteen lines of it: now it is rechristened from a Sonnet to an Effusion. Schiller might have written the twentieth Effusion: 'tis worthy of him in any sense. I was glad to meet with those lines you sent me, when my sister was so ill: I had lost the copy, and I felt not a little proud at seeing my name in your verse. The "Complaint of Ninathoma" (first stanza in particular) is the best, or only good imitation, of Ossian I ever saw, your "Restless Gale" excepted. "To an Infant" is most sweet. Is not "foodful," though, very harsh? Would not "dulcet" fruit be less harsh, or some other friendly bi-syllable? In "Edmund," "Frenzy, fierce-eyed child," is not so well as "frantic," though that is an epithet adding nothing to the meaning. Slander *couching* was better than "squatting." In the "Man of Ross" it *was* a better line thus:

"If 'neath this roof thy wine-cheer'd moments pass,"

than as it stands now. Time nor nothing can reconcile me to the concluding five lines of "Kosciusko:" call it any thing you will but sublime. In my twelfth effusion I had rather have seen what I wrote myself, though they bear no comparison with your exquisite lines—

"On rose-leaf'd beds, amid your faery bowers," etc.

I love my Sonnets because they are the reflected images

of my own feelings at different times. To instance, in
the thirteenth—

> " How reason reel'd," etc.,

are good lines, but must spoil the whole with me, who
know it is only a fiction of yours, and that the "rude
dashings" did in fact not "rock me to repose." I grant
the same objection applies not to the former Sonnet; but
still I love my own feelings : they are dear to memory,
though they now and then wake a sigh or a tear.
"Thinking on divers things foredone," I charge you,
Coleridge, spare my ewe lambs; and though a gentleman
may borrow six lines in an epic poem (I should have no
objection to borrow five hundred, and without acknowledging), still, in a sonnet, a personal poem, I do not
"ask my friend the aiding verse." I would not wrong
your feelings by proposing any improvements (did I think
myself capable of suggesting 'em) in such personal poems
as "Thou bleedest, my poor heart!"—'od so,—I am
caught—I have already done it; but that simile I propose abridging, would not change the feeling or introduce
any alien ones. Do you understand me ? In the twenty-
eighth, however, and in the "Sigh," and that composed
at Clevedon, things that come from the heart direct, not
by the medium of the fancy, I would not suggest an
alteration. When my blank verse is finished, or any
long fancy-poems, *propino tibi alterandum, cut-up-andum,
abridgandum*, just what you will with it; but spare my
ewe lambs ! That to "Mrs. Siddons," now, you were
welcome to improve, if it had been worth it; but I say
unto you again, Coleridge, spare my ewe lambs ! I must
confess were they mine, I should omit, *in editione secundâ*,
Effusions two and three, because satiric, and below the
dignity of the poet of *Religious Musings*, fifth, seventh,
half of the eighth, that "Written in early youth," as far
as "thousand eyes,"—though I part not unreluctantly
with that lively line—

> " Chaste joyance dancing in her bright blue eyes,"

LETTER V.]   *Tuesday Evening, June* 14, 1796.

I am not quite satisfied now with the Chatterton, and, with your leave, will try my hand at it again. A master joiner, you know, may leave a cabinet to be finished by his journeyman, when his own hands are full.

To your list of illustrative personifications, into which a fine imagination enters, I will take leave to add the following from Beaumont and Fletcher's *Wife for a Month;* 'tis the conclusion of a description of a sea fight: —" The game of *death* was never played so nobly : the meagre thief grew wanton in his mischiefs; and his shrunk, hollow eyes smiled on his ruins." There is fancy in these of a lower order, from *Bonduca;*—" Then did I see these valiant men of Britain, like boding owls creep into tods of ivy, and hoot their fears to one another nightly." Not that it is a personification ; only it just caught my eye in a little extract book I keep, which is full of quotations from Beaumont and Fletcher in particular, in which authors I can't help thinking there is a greater richness of poetical fancy than in any one, Shakspeare excepted. Are you acquainted with Massinger ? At a hazard I will trouble you with a passage from a play of his called *A Very Woman.* The lines are spoken by a lover (disguised) to his faithless mistress. You will remark the fine effect of the double endings. You will by your ear distinguish the lines, for I write 'em as prose. " Not far from where my father lives, *a lady*, a neighbour by, blest with as great a *beauty* as Nature durst bestow without *undoing*, dwelt, and most happily, as I thought then, and blest the house a thousand times she *dwelt* in. This beauty, in the blossom of my youth, when my first fire knew no adulterate *incense*, nor I no way to flatter but my *fondness;* in all the bravery my friends could *show me*, in all the faith my innocence could *give me*, in the best language my true tongue could *tell me*, and all the broken sighs my sick heart *lend me*, I sued and served. Long did I serve this *lady*, long was my travail, long my trade to *win her:* with all the duty of my soul I SERVED HER." "Then she must love." "She did, but never me: she could not *love me;* she would not love, she hated,—more, she *scorn'd me;* and in so poor and base a way *abused me* for all my services, for all my *bounties,* so bold neglects flung on me." "What out of love, and worthy love, I *gave her* (shame to her most unworthy mind!), to fools, to girls, to fiddlers, and her boys she flung, all in disdain of me." One more passage strikes my eye from Beaumont and Fletcher's *Palamon and Arcite.* One of 'em complains in prison:

> " This is all our world :
> We shall know nothing here but one another ;
> Hear nothing but the clock that tells our woes.
> The vine shall grow, but we shall never see it."

Is not the last circumstance exquisite? I mean not to lay myself open by saying they exceed Milton, and perhaps Collins, in sublimity. But don't you conceive all poets, after Shakspeare, yield to 'em in variety of genius? Massinger treads close on their heels ; but you are most probably as well acquainted with his writings as your humble servant. My quotations, in that case, will only serve to show my barrenness of matter. Southey, in simplicity and tenderness, is excelled decidedly only, I think, by Beaumont and Fletcher—in his "Maid's Tragedy" and some parts of "Philaster" in particular, and elsewhere occasionally ; and perhaps by Cowper in his "Crazy Kate," and in parts of his translation, such as the speeches of Hecuba and Andromache. I long to know your opinion of that translation. The Odyssey especially is surely very Homeric. What nobler than the appearance of Phœbus at the beginning of the Iliad—the lines ending with "Dread sounding, bounding on the silver bow !"

I beg you will give me your opinion of the translation ; it afforded me high pleasure. As curious a specimen of translation as ever fell into my hands is a young man's in our office, of a French novel. What in the original was

would not like ; to me 'tis classical ground. Knights-
bridge is a desirable situation for the air of the parks.
St. George's Fields is convenient for its contiguity to the
Bench. Choose! But are you really coming to town?
The hope of it has entirely disarmed my petty disappointment of its nettles ; yet I rejoice so much on my own
account, that I fear I do not feel enough pure satisfaction
on yours. Why, surely, the joint editorship of the
[*Morning*] *Chronicle* must be a very comfortable and
secure living for a man. But should not you read French,
or do you? and can you write with sufficient moderation,
as 'tis called, when one suppresses the one half of what
one feels or could say on a subject, to chime in the better
with popular lukewarmness? White's " Letters " are
near publication. Could you review 'em, or get 'em
reviewed? Are you not connected with the *Critical
Review?* His frontispiece is a good conceit : Sir John
learning to dance to please Madame Page, in dress of
doublet, etc., from the upper half ; and modern pantaloons,
with shoes, etc., of the eighteenth century, from the lower
half ; and the whole work is full of goodly quips and
rare fancies, " all deftly masqued like hoar antiquity "—
much superior to Dr. Kenrick's *Falstaff's Wedding,* which
you may have seen. Allen sometimes laughs at superstition, and religion, and the like. A living fell vacant
lately in the gift of the Hospital : White informed him
that he stood a fair chance for it. He scrupled and
scrupled about it, and at last, to use his own words,
"tampered" with Godwin to know whether the thing
was honest or not. Godwin said nay to it, and Allen
rejected the living ! Could the blindest poor papist have
bowed more servilely to his priest or casuist? Why sleep
the *Watchman's* answers to that Godwin? I beg you
will not delay to alter, if you mean to keep, those last
lines I sent you. Do that, and read these for your
pains :—

TO THE POET COWPER.

Cowper, I thank my God that thou art heal'd !
Thine was the sorest malady of all ;
And I am sad to think that it should light
Upon the worthy head ! But thou art heal'd,
And thou art yet, we trust, the destined man,
Born to reanimate the lyre, whose chords
Have slumber'd, and have idle lain so long ;
To the immortal sounding of whose strings
Did Milton frame the stately-pacèd verse ;
Among whose wires with light finger playing,
Our elder bard, Spenser, a gentle name,
The lady Muses' dearest darling child,
Elicited the deftest tunes yet heard
In hall or bower, taking the delicate ear
Of Sidney and his peerless Maiden Queen.

Thou, then, take up the mighty epic strain,
Cowper, of England's Bards, the wisest and the best.
1796.

I have read your climax of praises in those three
Reviews.   These mighty spouters out of panegyric waters
have, two of 'em, scattered their spray even upon me, and
the waters are cooling and refreshing.   Prosaically, the
Monthly reviewers have made indeed a large article of it,
and done you justice.   The *Critical* have, in their wisdom,
selected not the very best specimens, and notice not,
except as one name on the muster-roll, the *Religious
Musings.* I suspect Master Dyer to have been the writer
of that article, as the substance of it was the very remarks
and the very language he used to me one day.   I fear
you will not accord entirely with my sentiments of Cowper,
as *expressed* above (perhaps scarcely just), but the poor
gentleman has just recovered from his lunacies, and that
begets pity, and pity love, and love admiration ; and then
it goes hard with people, but they lie ! Have you read
the Ballad called "Leonora," in the second Number of
the *Monthly Magazine ?* If you have ! ! ! ! There is
another fine song, from the same author (Burger), in the
third Number, of scarce inferior merit ; and (vastly below

these) there are some happy specimens of English hexa-
meters, in an imitation of Ossian, in the fifth Number.
For your Dactyls—I am sorry you are so sore about 'em
—a very Sir Fretful! In good troth, the Dactyls are
good Dactyls, but their measure is naught. Be not yourself " half anger, half agony," if I pronounce your darling
lines not to be the best you ever wrote—you have written
much.

Have a care, good Master poet, of the Statute *de
Contumeliâ.* What do you mean by calling Madame
Mara " harlot " and other naughty things ? The goodness of the verse would not save you in a Court of Justice.
But are you really coming to town ? Coleridge, a gentleman called in London lately from Bristol, and inquired
whether there were any of the family of a Mr. Chambers
living : this Mr. Chambers, he said, had been the making
of a friend's fortune, who wished to make some return
for it. He went away without seeing her. Now, a Mrs.
Reynolds, a very intimate friend of ours, whom you have
seen at our house, is the only daughter, and all that
survives, of Mr. Chambers ; and a very little supply
would be of service to her, for she married very unfortunately, and has parted with her husband. Pray find
out this Mr. Pember (for that was the gentleman's friend's
name) ; he is an attorney, and lives at Bristol. Find
him out, and acquaint him with the circumstances of the
case, and offer to be the medium of supply to Mrs. Reynolds, if he chooses to make her a present. She is in
very distressed circumstances. Mr. Pember, attorney,
Bristol. Mr. Chambers lived in the Temple ; Mrs.
Reynolds, his daughter, was my schoolmistress, and is in
the room at this present writing. This last circumstance
induced me to write so soon again. I have not further
to add. Our loves to Sara. C. LAMB.

Thursday.

LETTER VIII.]   *September* 27, 1796.

My dearest Friend—White, or some of my friends, or the public papers, by this time may have informed you of the terrible calamities that have fallen on our family. I will only give you the outlines :—My poor dear, dearest sister, in a fit of insanity, has been the death of her own mother. I was at hand only time enough to snatch the knife out of her grasp. She is at present in a madhouse, from whence I fear she must be moved to an hospital. God has preserved to me my senses : I eat, and drink, and sleep, and have my judgment, I believe, very sound. My poor father was slightly wounded, and I am left to take care of him and my aunt. Mr. Norris, of the Blue-coat School, has been very very kind to us, and we have no other friend ; but, thank God, I am very calm and composed, and able to do the best that remains to do. Write as religious a letter as possible, but no mention of what is gone and done with. With me " the former things are passed away," and I have something more to do than to feel.

God Almighty have us all in His keeping !

                                              C. LAMB.

Mention nothing of poetry. I have destroyed every vestige of past vanities of that kind. Do as you please, but if you publish, publish mine (I give free leave) without name or initial, and never send me a book, I charge you.

Your own judgment will convince you not to take any notice of this yet to your dear wife. You look after your family ; I have my reason and strength left to take care of mine. I charge you, don't think of coming to see me. Write. I will not see you if you come. God Almighty love you and all of us !

                                              C. LAMB.

exceedingly, and she loves dearly; and they, as the saying is, take to her very extraordinarily, if it is extraordinary that people who see my sister should love her. Of all the people I ever saw in the world, my poor sister was most and thoroughly devoid of the least tincture of selfishness. I will enlarge upon her qualities, poor dear, dearest soul, in a future letter, for my own comfort, for I understand her thoroughly; and, if I mistake not, in the most trying situation that a human being can be found in, she will be found—(I speak not with sufficient humility, I fear), but humanly and foolishly speaking, she will be found, I trust, uniformly great and amiable. God keep her in her present mind!—to whom be thanks and praise for all His dispensations to mankind.

C. LAMB.

These mentioned good fortunes and change of prospects had almost brought my mind over to the extreme, the very opposite to despair. I was in danger of making myself too happy. Your letter brought me back to a view of things which I had entertained from the beginning. I hope (for Mary I can answer)—but I hope that *I* shall through life never have less recollection nor a fainter impression of what has happened than I have now. 'Tis not a light thing, nor meant by the Almighty to be received lightly. I must be serious, circumspect, and deeply religious through life; and by such means may *both* of us escape madness in future, if it so please the Almighty.

Send me word how it fares with Sara. I repeat it, your letter was, and will be, an inestimable treasure to me. You have a view of what my situation demands of me, like my own view, and I trust a just one.

Coleridge, continue to write; but do not for ever offend me by talking of sending me cash. Sincerely, and on my soul, we do not want it. God love you both!

I will write again very soon. Do you write directly.

My dearest Friend——I grieve from my very soul to
observe you, in your plans of life, veering about from this
hope to the other, and settling nowhere. Is it an un-
toward fatality (speaking humanly) that does this for you
——a stubborn, irresistible concurrence of events ? or lies
the fault, as I fear it does, in your own mind ? You seem
to be taking up splendid schemes of fortune only to lay
them down again ; and your fortunes are an *ignis fatuus*
that has been conducting you, in thought, from Lancaster
Court, Strand, to somewhere near Matlock ; then jumping
across to Dr. Somebody's, whose son's tutor you were
likely to be ; and would to God the dancing demon *may*
conduct you at last, in peace and comfort, to the "life
and labours of a cottager." You see, from the above
awkward playfulness of fancy, that my spirits are not
quite depressed. I should ill deserve God's blessings,
which, since the late terrible event, have come down in
mercy upon us, if I indulged regret or querulousness.
Mary continues serene and cheerful. I have not by me
a little letter she wrote to me ; for, though I see her
almost every day, yet we delight to write to one another,
for we can scarce see each other but in company with
some of the people of the house.

I have not the letter by me, but will quote from
memory what she wrote in it : " I have no bad terrifying
dreams. At midnight, when I happen to awake, the
nurse sleeping by the side of me, with the noise of the
poor mad people around me, I have no fear. The spirit
of my mother seems to descend and smile upon me, and
bid me live to enjoy the life and reason which the Almighty has given me. I shall see her again in heaven :
she will then understand me better. My grandmother,
too, will understand me better, and will then say no more,
as she used to do, ' Polly, what are those poor crazy
moythered brains of yours thinking of always ?'" Poor
Mary ! my mother indeed *never understood* her right.

She loved her, as she loved us all, with a mother's love; but in opinion, in feeling, and sentiment, and disposition, bore so distant a resemblance to her daughter, that she never understood her right; never could believe how much *she* loved her; but met her caresses, her protestations of filial affection, too frequently with coldness and repulse. Still she was a good mother. God forbid I should think of her but *most* respectfully, *most* affectionately. Yet she would always love my brother above Mary, who was not worthy of one-tenth of that affection which Mary had a right to claim. But it is my sister's gratifying recollection that every act of duty and of love she could pay, every kindness (and I speak true, when I say to the hurting of her health, and, most probably, in great part to the derangement of her senses), through a long course of infirmities and sickness, she could show her, she ever did. I will, some day, as I promised, enlarge to you upon my sister's excellences: 'twill seem like exaggeration; but I will do it. At present, short letters suit my state of mind best. So take my kindest wishes for your comfort and establishment in life, and for Sara's welfare and comforts with you. God love you! God love us all!   C. LAMB.

LETTER XI.]   *October* 24, 1796.

Coleridge, I feel myself much your debtor for that spirit of confidence and friendship which dictated your last letter. May your soul find peace at last in your cottage life! I only wish you were but settled. Do continue to write to me. I read your letters with my sister, and they give us both abundance of delight. Especially they please us when you talk in a religious strain: not but we are offended occasionally with a certain freedom of expression, a certain air of mysticism, more consonant to the conceits of pagan philosophy than consistent with the humility of genuine piety. To instance now, in your last letter you say, "It is by the press that

God hath given finite spirits, both evil and good (I suppose
you mean *simply* bad men and good men), a portion as it
were of His Omnipresence !"   Now, high as the human
intellect comparatively will soar, and wide as its influence,
malign or salutary, can extend, is there not, Coleridge, a
distance between the Divine Mind and it, which makes
such language blasphemy ?   Again, in your first fine consolatory epistle, you say, "you are a temporary sharer in
human misery, that you may be an eternal partaker of
the Divine Nature."   What more than this do those men
say who are for exalting the man Christ Jesus into the
second person of an unknown Trinity ?—men whom you
or I scruple not to call idolaters.   Man, full of imperfections at best, and subject to wants which momentarily
remind him of dependence ; man, a weak and ignorant
being, " servile " from his birth " to all the skiey influences," with eyes sometimes open to discern the right
path, but a head generally too dizzy to pursue it ; man,
in the pride of speculation, forgetting his nature, and
hailing in himself the future God, must make the angels
laugh.   Be not angry with me Coleridge : I wish not to
cavil ; I know I cannot instruct you ; I only wish to
remind you of that humility which best becometh the
Christian character.   God, in the New Testament (*our
best guide*), is represented to us in the kind, condescend-
ing, amiable, familiar light of a *parent ;* and in my poor
mind 'tis best for us so to consider of him, as our *heavenly*
father, and our *best friend*, without indulging too bold
conceptions of his nature.   Let us learn to think humbly
of ourselves, and rejoice in the appellation of "dear
children," "brethren," and "co-heirs with Christ of the
promises," seeking to know no further.

I am not insensible, indeed I am not, of the value of
that first letter of yours, and I shall find reason to thank
you for it again and again, long after that blemish in it
is forgotten.   It will be a fine lesson of comfort to us,
whenever we read it ; and read it we often shall, Mary
and I.

Accept our loves and best kind wishes for the welfare of yourself and wife and little one.   Nor let me forget to wish you joy on your birthday, so lately past ; I thought you had been older.   My kind thanks and remembrances to Lloyd.

God love us all !—and may He continue to be the father and the friend of the whole human race !

Sunday Evening.   C. LAMB.

LETTER XII.]   *October* 28, 1796.

My dear Friend—I am not ignorant that to be "a partaker of the Divine Nature" is a phrase to be met with in Scripture : I am only apprehensive, lest we in these latter days, tinctured (some of us perhaps pretty deeply) with mystical notions and the pride of meta-physics, might be apt to affix to such phrases a meaning, which the primitive users of them, the simple fishermen of Galilee for instance, never intended to convey.   With that other part of your apology I am not quite so well satisfied.   You seem to me to have been straining your comparing faculties to bring together things infinitely distant and unlike,—the feeble narrow-sphered operations of the human intellect and the everywhere diffused mind of Deity, the peerless wisdom of Jehovah.   Even the expression appears to me inaccurate—"portion of Omni-presence."   Omnipresence is an attribute the very essence of which is unlimitedness.   How can Omnipresence be affirmed of anything in part ?   But enough of this spirit of disputatiousness.   Let us attend to the proper business of human life, and talk a little together respecting our domestic concerns.   Do you continue to make me ac-quainted with what you are doing, and how soon you are likely to be settled, once for all.

I have satisfaction in being able to bid you rejoice with me in my sister's continued reason, and composed-ness of mind.   Let us both be thankful for it.   I continue to visit her very frequently, and the people of the house are vastly indulgent to her. She is likely to be as comfortably situated in all respects as those who pay twice or thrice the sum. They love her, and she loves them, and makes herself very useful to them. Benevolence sets out on her journey with a good heart, and puts a good face on it, but is apt to limp and grow feeble, unless she calls in the aid of self-interest, by way of crutch. In Mary's case, as far as respects those she is with, 'tis well that these principles are so likely to co-operate. I am rather at a loss sometimes for books for her : our reading is somewhat confined, and we have nearly exhausted our London library. She has her hands too full of work to read much ; but a little she must read, for reading was her daily bread.

Have you seen Bowles's new poem on " Hope ?" What character does it bear ? Has he exhausted his stores of tender plaintiveness ? or is he the same in this last as in all his former pieces ? The duties of the day call me off from this pleasant intercourse with my friend : so for the present adieu.

Now for the truant borrowing of a few minutes from business. Have you met with a new poem called the *Pursuits of Literature?* From the extracts in the *British Review* I judge it to be a very humorous thing. In particular, I remember what I thought a very happy character of Dr. Darwin's poetry. Among all your quaint readings did your ever light upon Walton's *Complete Angler ?* I asked you the question once before : it breathes the very spirit of innocence, purity, and simplicity of heart. There are many choice old verses interspersed in it. It would sweeten a man's temper at any time to read it ; it would Christianise every discordant angry passion. Pray make yourself acquainted with it. Have you made it up with Southey yet ? Surely one of you two must have been a very silly fellow, and the other not much better, to fall out like boarding-school misses. Kiss, shake hands, and make it up.

When will he be delivered of his new epic ? *Madoc,*

I think, is to be the name of it; though that is a name not familiar to my ears. What progress do you make in your hymns? What Review are you connected with? If with any, why do you delay to notice White's book? You are justly offended at its profaneness; but surely you have undervalued its *wit*, or you would have been more loud in its praises. Do not you think that in *Slender's* death and madness there is most exquisite humour, mingled with tenderness, that is irresistible, truly Shakspearian? Be more full in your mention of it. Poor fellow, he has (very undeservedly) lost by it; nor do I see that it is likely ever to reimburse him the charge of printing, etc. Give it a lift, if you can. I suppose you know that Allen's wife is dead, and he, just situated as he was, never the better, as the worldly people say, for her death, her money with her children being taken off his hands. I am just now wondering whether you will ever come to town again, Coleridge; 'tis among the things I dare not hope, but can't help wishing. For myself, I can live in the midst of town luxury and super- fluity, and not long for them, and I can't see why your children might not hereafter do the same. Remember, you are not in Arcadia when you are in the west of England, and they may catch infection from the world without visiting the metropolis. But you seem to have set your heart upon this same cottage plan: and God prosper you in the experiment! I am at a loss for more to write about; so 'tis as well that I am arrived at the bottom of my paper.

God love you, Coleridge!—Our best loves and tenderest wishes await on you, your Sara, and your little one.

C. L.

LETTER XIII.]   *November* 8, 1796.

My brother, my friend,— I am distress'd for you, believe me I am; not so much for your painful, trouble- some complaint, which, I trust, is only for a time, as for those anxieties which brought it on, and perhaps even now may be nursing its malignity. Tell me, dearest of my friends, is your mind at peace? or has anything, yet unknown to me, happened to give you fresh disquiet, and steal from you all the pleasant dreams of future rest? Are you still (I fear you are) far from being comfortably settled? Would to God it were in my power to contribute towards the bringing of you into the haven where you would be! But you are too well skilled in the philosophy of consolation to need my humble tribute of advice. In pain, and in sickness, and in all manner of disappointments, I trust you have that within you which shall speak peace to your mind. Make it, I entreat you, one of your puny comforts, that I feel for you, and share all your griefs with you. I feel as if I were troubling you about *little* things, now I am going to resume the subject of our last two letters; but it may divert us both from unpleasanter feelings to make such matters, in a manner, of importance. Without further apology, then, it was not that I did not relish, that I did not in my heart thank you for those little pictures of your feelings which you lately sent me, if I neglected to mention them. You may remember you had said much the same things before to me on the same subject in a former letter, and I considered those last verses as only the identical thoughts better clothed; either way (in prose or verse) such poetry must be welcome to me. I love them as I love the Confessions of Rousseau, and for the same reason: the same frankness, the same openness of heart, the same disclosure of all the most hidden and delicate affections of the mind. They make me proud to be thus esteemed worthy of the place of friend-confessor, brother-confessor, to a man like Coleridge. This last is, I acknowledge, language too high for friendship; but it is also, I declare, too sincere for flattery. Now, to put on stilts, and talk magnificently about trifles,—I condescend, then, to your counsel, Coleridge, and allow my first Sonnet (sick to death am I to make mention of my Sonnets, and I blush to be so taken up with them, indeed I do) ; I allow it to run thus : *Fairy Land*, etc. etc., as I last wrote it.

The Fragments I now send you, I want printed to get rid of 'em ; for, while they stick burr-like to my memory, they tempt me to go on with the idle trade of versifying, which I long (most sincerely I speak it) I long to leave off, for it is unprofitable to my soul ; I feel it is ; and these questions about words, and debates about alterations, take me off, I am conscious, from the properer business of my life. Take my Sonnets, once for all ; and do not propose any reamendments, or mention them again in any shape to me, I charge you. I blush that my mind can consider them as things of any worth. And, pray, admit or reject these fragments as you like or dislike them, without ceremony. Call 'em Sketches, Fragments, or what you will ; but do not entitle any of my *things* Love Sonnets, as I told you to call 'em ; 'twill only make me look little in my own eyes ; for it is a passion of which I retain nothing. 'Twas a weakness, concerning which I may say, in the words of Petrarch (whose Life is now open before me), "if it drew me out of some vices, it also prevented the growth of many virtues, filling me with the love of the creature rather than the Creator, which is the death of the soul." Thank God, the folly has left me for ever. Not even a review of my love verses renews one wayward wish in me ; and if I am at all solicitous to trim 'em out in their best apparel, it is because they are to make their appearance in good company. Now to my fragments. Lest you have lost my " Grandame," she shall be one. 'Tis among the few verses I ever wrote, that to Mary is another, which profit me in the recollection. God love her !—and may we two never love each other less !

These, Coleridge, are the few sketches I have thought worth preserving. How will they relish thus detached ? Will you reject all or any of them ? They are thine : do whatsoever thou listest with them. My eyes ache with

writing long and late, and I wax wondrous sleepy. God
bless you and yours, me and mine ! Good-night.

C. LAMB.

I will keep my eyes open reluctantly a minute longer
to tell you that I love you for those simple, tender, heart-
flowing lines with which you conclude your last, and in
my eyes best, "Sonnet" (so you call 'em)—

> " So, for the mother's sake, the child was dear ;
>   And dearer was the mother for the child."

Cultivate simplicity, Coleridge; or rather, I should
say, banish elaborateness ; for simplicity springs spon-
taneous from the heart, and carries into daylight its own
modest buds, and genuine, sweet, and clear flowers of
expression. I allow no hot-beds in the gardens of
Parnassus. I am unwilling to go to bed and leave my
sheet unfilled (a good piece of night-work for an idle
body like me), so will finish with begging you to send
me the earliest account of your complaint, its progress,
or (as I hope to God you will be able to send me) the
tale of your recovery, or at least amendment. My
tenderest remembrances to your Sara——

Once more, Good-night.

LETTER XIV.]   *November* 14, 1796.

Coleridge, I love you for dedicating your poetry to
Bowles. Genius of the sacred fountain of tears, it was
he who led you gently by the hand through all this
valley of weeping ; showed you the dark green yew trees,
and the willow shades, where, by the fall of waters, you
might indulge an uncomplaining melancholy, a delicious
regret for the past, or weave fine visions of that awful
future,

> " When all the vanities of life's brief day
>   Oblivion's hurrying hand hath swept away,
>   And all its sorrows, at the awful blast
>   Of the archangel's trump, are but as shadows past."

I have another sort of dedication in my head for my

few things, which I want to know if you approve of, and can insert. I mean to inscribe them to my sister. It will be unexpected, and it will give her pleasure ; or do you think it will look whimsical at all ? As I have not spoke to her about it I can easily reject the idea. But there is a monotony in the affections, which people living together, or, as we do now, very frequently seeing each other, are apt to give in to ; a sort of indifference in the expression of kindness for each other, which demands that we should sometimes call to our aid the trickery of surprise. Do you publish with Lloyd, or without him ? In either case my little portion may come last ; and after the fashion of orders to a country correspondent, I will give directions how I should like to have 'em done. The title-page to stand thus :—

POEMS

BY

CHARLES LAMB, OF THE INDIA HOUSE.

Under this title the following motto, which, for want of room, I put over leaf, and desire you to insert, whether you like it or no. May not a gentleman choose what arms, mottoes, or armorial bearings the Herald will give him leave, without consulting his republican friend, who might advise none ? May not a publican put up the sign of the *Saracen's Head*, even though his undiscerning neighbour should prefer, as more genteel, the *Cat and Gridiron ?*

[MOTTO.]

" This beauty, in the blossom of my youth,
    When my first fire knew no adulterate incense,
    Nor I no way to flatter but my fondness,
    In the best language my true tongue could tell me,
    And all the broken sighs my sick heart lend me,
    I sued and served. Long did I love this lady."

MASSINGER.

THE DEDICATION.

THE FEW FOLLOWING POEMS,
CREATURES OF THE FANCY AND THE FEELING
IN LIFE'S MORE VACANT HOURS,
PRODUCED, FOR THE MOST PART, BY
LOVE IN IDLENESS,
ARE,
WITH ALL A BROTHER'S FONDNESS,
INSCRIBED TO
MARY ANNE LAMB,
THE AUTHOR'S BEST FRIEND AND SISTER.

This is the pomp and paraphernalia of parting, with which I take my leave of a passion which has reigned so royally (so long) within me; thus, with its trappings of laureatship, I fling it off, pleased and satisfied with myself that the weakness troubles me no longer. I am wedded, Coleridge, to the fortunes of my sister and my poor old father. Oh, my friend! I think sometimes, could I recall the days that are past, which among them should I choose? not those "merrier days," not the "pleasant days of hope," not "those wanderings with a fair-hair'd maid," which I have so often and so feelingly regretted, but the days, Coleridge, of a *mother's* fondness for her *school-boy.* What would I give to call her back to earth for *one* day!—on my knees to ask her pardon for all those little asperities of temper which, from time to time, have given her gentle spirit pain!—and the day, my friend, I trust, will come. There will be "time enough" for kind offices of love, if "Heaven's eternal year" be ours. Hereafter, her meek spirit shall not reproach me. Oh, my friend, cultivate the filial feelings! and let no man think himself released from the kind "charities" of relationship: these shall give him peace at the last; these are the best foundation for every species of benevolence. I rejoice to hear, by certain channels, that you, my friend, are reconciled with all your relations. 'Tis the most kindly and natural species of love, and we have all the associated train of early feelings to secure its strength and perpetuity. Send me an account of your health : *indeed* I am solicitous about you. God love you and yours.　　　　　　C. LAMB.

LETTER XV.]　　　　　　　　　　*December* 2, 1796.

I have delayed writing thus long, not having by me my copy of your poems, which I had lent. I am not satisfied with all your intended omissions. Why omit 40, 63, 84 ? Above all, let me protest strongly against your rejecting the "Complaint of Ninathoma," 86. The words, I acknowledge, are Ossian's, but you have added to them the "music of Caril." If a vicarious substitute be wanting, sacrifice (and 'twill be a piece of self-denial too), the "Epitaph on an Infant," of which its author seems so proud, so tenacious. Or, if your heart be set on *perpetuating* the four-line wonder, I'll tell you what to do ; sell the copyright of it at once to a country statuary. Commence in this manner Death's prime poet-laureate ; and let your verses be adopted in every village round, instead of those hitherto famous ones :—

> " Afflictions sore long time I bore ;
> Physicians were in vain."

I have seen your last very beautiful poem in the *Monthly Magazine :* write thus, and you most generally have written thus, and I shall never quarrel with you about simplicity. With regard to my lines—

> "Laugh all that weep," etc.,

I would willingly sacrifice them ; but my portion of the volume is so ridiculously little, that, in honest truth, I can't spare 'em. As things are, I have very slight pretensions to participate in the title-page. White's book is at length reviewed in the *Monthly ;* was it your doing, or Dyer's, to whom I sent him ?—or, rather, do you not write in the *Critical ?*—for I observed, in an article of

this month's, a line quoted out of that Sonnet on Mrs.
Siddons,

      " With eager wondering, and perturb'd delight."

And a line from *that* Sonnet would not readily have
occurred to a stranger. That sonnet, Coleridge, brings
afresh to my mind the time when you wrote those on
Bowles, Priestley, Burke ;—'twas two Christmases ago,
and in that nice little smoky room at the *Salutation*, which
is even now continually presenting itself to my recollection,
with all its associated train of pipes, tobacco, egg-hot,
welsh-rabbit, metaphysics, and poetry.—Are we *never* to
meet again? How differently I am circumstanced now!
I have never met with anyone—never shall meet with
anyone—who could or can compensate me for the loss
of your society. I have no one to talk all these matters
about to; I lack friends. I lack books to supply their
absence; but these complaints ill become me. Let me
compare my present situation, prospects, and state of
mind, with what they were but two months back—but
two months ! O my friend, I am in danger of forgetting
the awful lessons then presented to me ! Remind me of
them; remind me of my duty ! Talk seriously with me
when you do write ! I thank you, from my heart I
thank you, for your solicitude about my sister. She is
quite well, but must not, I fear, come to live with us yet
a good while. In the first place, because, at present, it
would hurt her, and hurt my father, for them to be
together; secondly, from a regard to the world's good
report; for, I fear, tongues will be busy whenever that
event takes place. Some have hinted, one man has
pressed it on me, that she should be in perpetual confinement : what she hath done to deserve, or the necessity
of such an hardship, I see not; do you? I am starving
at the India House,—near seven o'clock without my
dinner; and so it has been, and will be, almost all the
week. I get home at night o'erwearied, quite faint, and
then to cards with my father, who will not let me enjoy

a meal in peace; but I must conform to my situation; and I hope I am, for the most part, not unthankful.

I am got home at last, and, after repeated games at cribbage, have got my father's leave to write awhile; with difficulty got it, for when I expostulated about playing any more, he very aptly replied, "If you won't play with me, you might as well not come home at all." The argument was unanswerable, and I set to afresh. I told you I do not approve of your omissions; neither do I quite coincide with you in your arrangements. I have not time to point out a better, and I suppose some self-associations of your own have determined their place as they now stand. Your beginning, indeed, with the *Joan of Arc* lines, I coincide entirely with. I love a splendid outset—a magnificent portico; and the diapason is grand. When I read the *Religious Musings*, I think how poor, how unelevated, unoriginal, my blank verse is—"Laugh all that weep," especially, where the subject demanded a grandeur of conception; and I ask what business they have among yours? but friendship covereth a multitude of defects. I want some loppings made in the "Chatterton:" it wants but a little to make it rank among the finest irregular lyrics I ever read. Have you time and inclination to go to work upon it?—or is it too late?—or do you think it needs none? Don't reject those verses in your *Watchman*, "Dear native brook," etc.; nor I think those last lines you sent me, in which "all effortless" is without doubt to be preferred to "inactive." If I am writing more than ordinarily dully, 'tis that I am stupefied with a tooth-ache. Hang it! do not omit 48, 52, and 53: what you do retain, though, call Sonnets, for heaven's sake, and not Effusions. Spite of your ingenious anticipation of ridicule in your Preface, the last five lines of 50 are too good to be lost; the rest are not much worth. My tooth becomes importunate: I must finish. Pray, pray, write to me: if you knew with what an anxiety of joy I open such a long packet as you last sent me, you would not grudge giving a few minutes now and then to this intercourse (the only intercourse I fear we two shall ever have)—this conversation with your friend : such I boast to be called.   God love you and yours !   Write to me when you move, lest I should direct wrong.   Has Sara no poems to publish ?   Those lines, 129, are probably too light for the volume where the *Religious Musings* are ; but I remember some very beautiful lines, addressed by somebody at Bristol to somebody in London.   God bless you once more. *Thursday Night.*   C. LAMB.

LETTER XVI.]   [Fragment.]   *December* 5, 1796.

At length I have done with verse-making ; not that I relish other people's poetry less : theirs comes from 'em without effort ; mine is the difficult operation of a brain scanty of ideas, made more difficult by disuse.   I have been reading "The Task" with fresh delight.   I am glad you love Cowper.   I could forgive a man for not enjoying Milton ; but I would not call that man my friend who should be offended with the "divine chit-chat of Cowper." Write to me, God love you and yours !   C. L.

LETTER XVII.]   *December* 10, 1796.

I had put my letter into the post rather hastily, not expecting to have to acknowledge another from you so soon.   This morning's present has made me alive again. My last night's epistle was childishly querulous : but you have put a little life into me, and I will thank you for your remembrance of me, while my sense of it is yet warm ; for if I linger a day or two I may use the same phrase of acknowledgment, or similar, but the feeling that dictates it now will be gone.   I shall send you a *caput mortuum*, not a *cor vivens*.   Thy *Watchman's*, thy bellman's verses, I do retort upon thee, thou libellous varlet !   Why you cried the hours yourself, and who made you so proud !   But I submit, to show my humility most implicitly to your dogmas.   I reject entirely the copy of verses you reject. With regard to my leaving off versifying, you have said so many pretty things, so many fine compliments, ingeniously decked out in the garb of sincerity, and undoubtedly springing from a present feeling somewhat like sincerity, that you might melt the most un-muse-ical soul—did you not (now for a Rowland compliment for your profusion of Olivers!) did you not in your very epistle, by the many pretty fancies and profusion of heart displayed in it, dissuade and discourage me from attempting anything after you? At present I have not leisure to make verses, nor anything approaching to a fondness for the exercise. In the ignorant present time, who can answer for the future man? "At lovers' perjuries Jove laughs;" and poets have sometimes a disingenuous way of forswearing their occupation. This though is not my case. The tender cast of soul, sombred with melancholy and subsiding recollections, is favourable to the Sonnet or the Elegy; but from

> " The sainted growing woof
> The teasing troubles keep aloof."

The music of poesy may charm for a while the importunate teasing cares of life; but the teased and troubled man is not in a disposition to make that music.

You sent me some very sweet lines relative to Burns, but it was at a time when in my highly agitated and perhaps somewhat distorted state of mind I thought it a duty to read 'em hastily and burn 'em. I burned all my own verses; all my book of extracts from Beaumont and Fletcher and a thousand sources; I burned a little journal of my foolish passion which I had a long time kept—

> " Noting ere they past away
> The little lines of yesterday."

I almost burned all your letters,—I did as bad, I lent 'em to a friend to keep out of my brother's sight, should he come and make inquisition into our papers; for, much as he dwelt upon your conversation while you were among us, and delighted to be with you, it has been his fashion ever since to depreciate and cry you down : you were the cause of my madness—you and your "damned foolish sensibility and melancholy ;" and he lamented, with a true brotherly feeling, that we ever met ; even as the sober citizen, when his son went astray upon the mountains of Parnassus, is said to have "cursed Wit and Poetry and Pope." I quote wrong, but no matter. These letters I lent to a friend to be out of the way for a season ; but I have claimed 'em in vain, and shall not cease to regret their loss. Your packets, posterior to the date of my misfortunes, commencing with that valuable consolatory epistle, are every day accumulating : they are sacred things with me

Publish your Burns when and how you like, it will be new to me : my memory of it is very confused, and tainted with unpleasant associations. Burns was the god of my idolatry, as Bowles is of yours. I am jealous of your fraternising with Bowles, when I think you relish him more than Burns, or my old favourite, Cowper. But you conciliate matters when you talk of the "divine chit-chat" of the latter : by that expression I see you thoroughly relish him. I love Mrs. Coleridge for her excuses an hundredfold more dearly than if she heaped "line upon line," out-Hannah-ing Hannah More ; and would rather hear you sing "Did a very little baby," by your family fire-side, than listen to you when you were repeating one of Bowles's sweetest sonnets, in your sweet manner, while we two were indulging sympathy, a solitary luxury, by the fire-side at the *Salutation*. Yet have I no higher ideas of heaven. Your company was one "cordial in this melancholy vale :" the remembrance of it is a blessing partly, and partly a curse. When I can abstract myself from things present, I can enjoy it with a freshness of relish ; but it more constantly operates to an unfavourable comparison with the uninteresting converse I always and *only* can partake in. Not a soul loves Bowles here ; scarce one has heard of Burns ; few but laugh at me for reading my Testament. They talk a language I understand not. I conceal sentiments that would be a puzzle to them. I can only converse with you by letter, and with the dead in their books. My sister, indeed, is all I can wish in a companion; but our spirits are alike poorly, our reading and knowledge from the self-same sources; our communication with the scenes of the world alike narrow. Never having kept separate company, or any "company" "*together*"—never having read separate books, and few books *together*—what knowledge have we to convey to each other? In our little range of duties and connections, how few sentiments can take place, without friends, with few books, with a taste for religion, rather than a strong religious habit! We need some support, some leading-strings to cheer and direct us. You talk very wisely; and be not sparing of *your advice.* Continue to remember us, and to show us you do remember us: we will take as lively an interest in what concerns you and yours. All I can add to your happiness will be sympathy: you can add to mine *more ;* you can teach me wisdom. I am indeed an unreasonable correspondent; but I was unwilling to let my last night's letter go off without this qualifier: you will perceive by this my mind is easier, and you will rejoice. I do not expect or wish you to write till you are moved; and, of course, shall not, till you announce to me that event, think of writing myself. Love to Mrs. Coleridge and David Hartley, and my kind remembrance to Lloyd, if he is with you. C. LAMB.

I will get *Nature and Art:* have not seen it yet, nor any of Jeremy Taylor's works.

LETTER XVIII.] *December* 10, 1796.

I am sorry I cannot now relish your poetical present so thoroughly as I feel it deserves; but I do not the less thank Lloyd and you for it.

In truth, Coleridge, I am perplexed, and at times almost cast down. I am beset with perplexities. The old hag of a wealthy relation who took my aunt off our hands in the beginning of trouble, has found out that she is "indolent and mulish"—I quote her own words, and that her attachment to us is so strong that she can never be happy apart. The lady, with delicate irony, remarks, that if I am not an hypocrite I shall rejoice to receive her again; and that it will be a means of making me more fond of home to have so dear a friend to come home to! The fact is, she is jealous of my aunt's bestowing any kind recollections on us while she enjoys the patronage of her roof. She says she finds it inconsistent with her own "ease and tranquillity," to keep her any longer; and, in fine, summons me to fetch her home. Now, much as I should rejoice to transplant the poor old creature from the chilling air of such patronage, yet I know how straitened we are already, how unable already to answer any demand which sickness or any extraordinary expense may make. I know this; and all unused as I am to struggle with perplexities, I am somewhat nonplussed, to say no worse. This prevents me from a thorough relish of what Lloyd's kindness and yours have furnished me with. I thank you though from my heart, and feel myself not quite alone in the earth.

Before I offer, what alone I have to offer, a few obvious remarks on the poems you sent me, I can but notice the odd coincidence of two young men, in one age, carolling their grandmothers. Love, what L. calls the "feverish and romantic tie," hath too long domineered over all the charities of home : the dear domestic ties of father, brother, husband. The amiable and benevolent Cowper has a beautiful passage in his "Task,"—some natural and painful reflections on his deceased parents : and Hayley's sweet lines to his mother are notoriously the best things he ever wrote. Cowper's lines, some of them are—

" How gladly would the man recall to life
  The boy's neglected sire ! a Mother, too,
  That softer friend, perhaps more gladly still,
  Might he demand them at the gates of death."

I cannot but smile to see my granny so gaily decked forth : though, I think, whoever altered " thy " praises to " her " praises—" thy " honoured memory to " her " honoured memory, did wrong; they best expressed my feelings. There is a pensive state of recollection in which the mind is disposed to apostrophise the departed objects of its attachment ; and, breaking loose from grammatical precision, changes from the first to the third, and from the third to the first person, just as the random fancy or the feeling directs. Among Lloyd's sonnets, the 6th, 7th, 8th, 9th, and 11th are eminently beautiful. I think him too lavish of his expletives : the *do's* and *did's*, when they occur too often, bring a quaintness with them along with their simplicity, or rather air of antiquity, which the patrons of them seem desirous of conveying.

Another time, I may notice more particularly Lloyd's, Southey's, Dermody's Sonnets. I shrink from them now : my teasing lot makes me too confused for a clear judgment of things, too selfish for sympathy ; and these ill-digested, meaningless remarks, I have imposed on myself as a task, to lull reflection, as well as to show you I did not neglect reading your valuable present. Return my acknowledgments to Lloyd ; you two seem to be about realising an Elysium upon earth, and, no doubt, I shall be happier. Take my best wishes. Remember me most affectionately to Mrs. C.——, and give little David Hartley (God bless its little heart !) a kiss for me. Bring him up to know the meaning of his Christian name, and what that name (imposed upon him) will demand of him.

God love you ! C. LAMB.

I write, for one thing, to say that I shall write no

more till you send me word where you are, for you are
so soon to move.

My sister is pretty well, thank God. We think of
you very often. God bless you: continue to be my
correspondent, and I will strive to fancy that this world
is *not* "all barrenness."

LETTER XIX.]   *January* 2, 1797.

If the fraternal sentiment conveyed in the following
lines will atone for the total want of anything like merit
or genius in it, I desire you will print it next after my
other Sonnet to my Sister.

> Friend of my earliest years and childish days,
> My joys, my sorrows, thou with me hast shared,
> Companion dear ; etc.

This has been a sad long letter of business, with no
room in it for what honest Bunyan terms heart-work.
I have just room left to congratulate you on your removal
to Stowey; to wish success to all your projects; to "bid
fair peace" be to that house ; to send my love and best
wishes, breathed warmly, after your dear Sara, and her
little David Hartley. If Lloyd be with you, bid him
write to me : I feel to whom I am obliged primarily for
two very friendly letters I have received already from
him. A dainty sweet book that *Nature and Art* is. I
am at present re-re-reading Priestley's Examination of the
Scotch Doctors : how the rogue strings 'em up ! three
together ! You have no doubt read that clear, strong,
humorous, most entertaining piece of reasoning. If not,
procure it, and be exquisitely amused. I wish I could
get more of Priestley's works. Can you recommend me
to any more books, easy of access, such as circulating
shops afford ? God bless you and yours.

Monday Morning, at Office.

Poor Mary is very unwell with a sore throat and a slight species of scarlet fever. God bless her too.

Sunday Morning.—You cannot surely mean to degrade the Joan of Arc into a pot-girl. You are not going, I hope, to annex to that most splendid ornament of Southey's poem all this cock-and-a-bull story of Joan, the publican's daughter of Neufchatel, with the lamentable episode of a waggoner, his wife, and six children. The texture will be most lamentably disproportionate. The first forty or fifty lines of these addenda are, no doubt, in their way, admirable, too ; but many would prefer the Joan of Southey.

> " On mightiest deeds to brood
> Of shadowy vastness, such as made my heart
> Throb fast ; anon I paused, and in a state
> Of half expectance listen'd to the wind ; "

> "They wonder'd at me, who had known me once
> A cheerful careless damsel ; "

> " The eye,
> That of the circling throng and of the visible world
> Unseeing, saw the shapes of holy phantasy ; "

I see nothing in your description of the Maid equal to these. There is a fine originality certainly in those lines—

> " For she had lived in this bad world
> As in a place of tombs,
> And touch'd not the pollutions of the dead ; "

but your "fierce vivacity" is a faint copy of the "fierce and terrible benevolence" of Southey ; added to this, that it will look like rivalship in you, and extort a comparison with Southey,—I think to your disadvantage. And the lines, considered in themselves as an addition to what

you had before written (strains of a far higher mood), are
but such as Madame Fancy loves in some of her more
familiar moods, at such times as she has met Noll Goldsmith, and walked and talked with him, calling him
"old acquaintance." Southey certainly has no pretensions to vie with you in the sublime of poetry; but he
tells a plain tale better than you. I will enumerate
some woful blemishes, some of 'em sad deviations from
that simplicity which was your aim. "Hail'd who might
be near" (the "canvas-coverture moving," by the by, is
laughable); "a woman and six children" (by the way,—
why not nine children? It would have been just half as
pathetic again): "statues of sleep they seem'd:" "frost-
mangled wretch:" "green putridity:" "hail'd him immortal" (rather ludicrous again): "voic'd a sad and
simple tale" (abominable!): "unprovender'd:" "such
his tale:" "Ah! suffering to the height of what was
suffer'd" (a most *insufferable line*): "amazements of
affright:" "the hot sore brain attributes its own hues
of ghastliness and torture" (what shocking confusion of
ideas!).

In these delineations of common and natural feelings,
in the familiar walks of poetry, you seem to resemble
Montauban dancing with Roubigné's tenants, *"much of
his native loftiness remained in the execution."*

I was reading your *Religious Musings* the other
day, and sincerely I think it the noblest poem in the
language, next after the *Paradise Lost;* and even that
was not made the vehicle of such grand truths. "There
is one mind," etc., down to "Almighty's throne," are
without a rival in the whole compass of my poetical
reading.

> "Stands in the sun, and with no partial gaze
>   Views all creation."

I wish I could have written those lines. I rejoice that
I am able to relish them. The loftier walks of Pindus
are your proper region. There you have no compeer in

modern times. Leave the lowlands, unenvied, in possession of such men as Cowper and Southey. Thus am I
pouring balsam into the wounds I may have been inflicting
on my poor friend's vanity.

In your notice of Southey's new volume you omit to
mention the most pleasing of all, the "Miniature"—

> " There were
> Who form'd high hopes and flattering ones of thee,
> Young Robert,
> Spirit of Spenser !—was the wanderer wrong ? "

Fairfax I have been in quest of a long time. Johnson,
in his "Life of Waller," gives a most delicious specimen
of him, and adds, in the true manner of that delicate
critic, as well as amiable man, " It may be presumed that
this old version will not be much read after the elegant
translation of my friend, Mr. Hoole." I endeavoured—
I wished to gain some idea of Tasso from this Mr. Hoole,
the great boast and ornament of the India House, but
soon desisted. I found him more vapid than smallest
small beer "sun-vinegared." Your "Dream," down to
that exquisite line—

> " I can't tell half his adventures,"

is a most happy resemblance of Chaucer. The remainder
is so so. The best line, I think, is, " He belong'd, I
believe, to the witch Melancholy." By the way, when
will our volume come out ? Don't delay it till you have
written a new Joan of Arc. Send what letters you please
by me, and in any way you choose, single or double.
The India Company is better adapted to answer the cost
than the generality of my friend's correspondents,—such
poor and honest dogs as John Thelwall, particularly. I
cannot say I know Colson, at least intimately. I once
supped with him and Allen : I think his manners very
pleasing. I will not tell you what I think of Lloyd, for
he may by chance come to see this letter, and that thought
puts a restraint on me. I cannot think what subject

would suit your epic genius ; some philosophical subject,
I conjecture, in which shall be blended the sublime of
poetry and of science. Your proposed " Hymns" will
be a fit preparatory study wherewith " to discipline your
young noviciate soul." I grow dull ; I'll go walk myself
out of my dulness.

Sunday Night.—You and Sara are very good to think
so kindly and so favourably of poor Mary ; I would to
God all did so too. But I very much fear she must not
think of coming home in my father's lifetime. It is very
hard upon her ; but our circumstances are peculiar, and
we must submit to them. God be praised she is so well
as she is. She bears her situation as one who has no
right to complain. My poor old aunt, whom you have
seen, the kindest, goodest creature to me when I was at
school ; who used to toddle there to bring me good things,
when I, school-boy like, only despised her for it, and used
to be ashamed to see her come and sit herself down on
the old coal-hole steps as you went into the old grammar-
school, and open her apron, and bring out her bason, with
some nice thing she had caused to be saved for me ; the
good old creature is now lying on her death-bed. I cannot bear to think on her deplorable state. To the shock
she received on that our evil day, from which she never
completely recovered, I impute her illness. She says,
poor thing, she is glad she is come home to die with me.
I was always her favourite :

> " No after friendship e'er can raise
> The endearments of our early days,
> Nor e'er the heart such fondness prove,
> As when it first began to love."

Lloyd has kindly left me, for a keep-sake, *John
Woolman.* You have read it, he says, and like it. Will
you excuse one short extract ? I think it could not have
escaped you :—" Small treasure to a resigned mind is
sufficient. How happy is it to be content with a little,

to live in humility, and feel *that* in us, which breathes out this language—Abba! Father!"——I am almost ashamed to patch up a letter in this miscellaneous sort; but I please myself in the thought, that anything from me will be acceptable to you. I am rather impatient, childishly so, to see our names affixed to the same common volume. Send me two, when it does come out; two will be enough—or indeed one—but two better. I have a dim recollection that, when in town, you were talking of the Origin of Evil as a most prolific subject for a long poem. Why not adopt it, Coleridge?—there would be room for imagination. Or the description (from a Vision or Dream, suppose) of an Utopia in one of the planets (the Moon, for instance). Or a Five Days' Dream, which shall illustrate, in sensible imagery, Hartley's five Motives to Conduct:—1. Sensation; 2. Imagination; 3. Ambition; 4. Sympathy; 5. Theopathy:— *First*. Banquets, music, etc., effeminacy,—and their insufficiency. *Second*. "Beds of hyacinth and roses, where young Adonis oft reposes;" "Fortunate Isles;" "The pagan Elysium," etc.; poetical pictures; antiquity as pleasing to the fancy;—their emptiness, madness, etc. *Third*. Warriors, Poets; some famous yet more forgotten; their fame or oblivion now alike indifferent; pride, vanity, etc. *Fourth*. All manner of pitiable stories, in Spenser-like verse; love; friendship, relationship, etc. *Fifth*. Hermits; Christ and his apostles; martyrs; heaven, etc. An imagination like yours, from these scanty hints, may expand into a thousand great ideas, if indeed you at all comprehend my scheme, which I scarce do myself.

Monday Morn.—"A London letter—Ninepence halfpenny!" Look you, master poet, I have remorse as well as another man, and my bowels can sound upon occasion. But I must put you to this charge, for I cannot keep back my protest, however ineffectual, against the annexing your latter lines to those former—this putting of new wine into old bottles. This my duty done, I will cease

from writing till you invent some more reasonable mode
of conveyance. Well may the " ragged followers of the
Nine" set up for flocci-nauci-what-do-you-call-'em-ists !
and I do not wonder that in their splendid visions of
Utopias in America they protest against the admission of
those *yellow*-complexioned, *copper*-coloured, *white*-livered
gentlemen, who never proved themselves their friends.
Don't you think your verses on a "Young Ass" too
trivial a companion for the "Religious Musings"?—
" Scoundrel monarch," alter that; and the " Man of
Ross " is scarce admissible, as it now stands, curtailed of
its fairer half: reclaim its property from the " Chatterton," which it does but encumber, and it will be a
rich little poem. I hope you expunge great part of
the old notes in the new edition : that, in particular,
most barefaced, unfounded, impudent assertion, that Mr.
Rogers is indebted for his story to *Loch Lomond,* a poem
by Bruce ! I have read the latter. I scarce think you
have. Scarce anything is common to them both. The
poor author of the *Pleasures of Memory* was sorely hurt,
Dyer says, by the accusation of unoriginality. He never
saw the poem. I long to read your poem on Burns ; I
retain so indistinct a memory of it. In what shape and
how does it come into public ? As you leave off writing
poetry till you finish your Hymns, I suppose you print,
now, all you have got by you. You have scarce enough
unprinted to make a second volume with Lloyd. Tell
me all about it. What is become of Cowper ? Lloyd
told me of some verses on his mother. If you have them
by you, pray send 'em me. I do so love him ! Never mind
their merit. May be *I* may like 'em, as your taste and
mine do not always exactly *identify*. Yours,

C. LAMB.

January 10, 1797.

I need not repeat my wishes to have my little sonnets printed *verbatim* my last way. In particular, I fear lest you should prefer printing my first sonnet, as you have done more than once, " Did the wand of Merlin wave?" It looks so like *Mr.* Merlin, the ingenious successor of the immortal Merlin, now living in good health and spirits, and flourishing in magical reputation in Oxford Street; and, on my life, one half who read it would understand it so. Do put 'em forth, finally, as I have in various letters settled it; for first a man's self is to be pleased, and then his friends; and, of course, the greater number of his friends, if they differ *inter se.* Thus taste may safely be put to the vote. I do long to see our names together; not for vanity's sake, and naughty pride of heart altogether, for not a living soul I know, or am intimate with, will scarce read the book : so I shall gain nothing, *quoad famam ;* and yet there is a little vanity mixes in it, I cannot help denying. I am aware of the unpoetical cast of the six last lines of my last sonnet, and think myself unwarranted in smuggling so tame a thing into the book; only the sentiments of those six lines are thoroughly congenial to me in my state of mind, and I wish to accumulate perpetuating tokens of my affection to poor Mary. That it has no originality in its cast, nor anything in the feelings but what is common and natural to thousands, nor ought properly to be called poetry, I see; still it will tend to keep present to my mind a view of things which I ought to indulge. These six lines, too, have not, to a reader, a connectedness with the foregoing.—Omit it, if you like.— What a treasure it is to my poor, indolent, and unemployed mind, thus to lay hold on a subject to talk about, though 'tis but a sonnet, and that of the lowest order ! How mournfully inactive I am !—'Tis night : Good-night.

My sister, I thank God, is nigh recovered : she was seriously ill. Do, in your next letter, and that right soon, give me some satisfaction respecting your present situation at Stowey. Is it a farm you have got? And what does your worship know about farming?

Coleridge, I want you to write an epic poem. Nothing short of it can satisfy the vast capacity of true poetic genius. Having one great end to direct all your poetical faculties to, and on which to lay out your hopes, your ambition will show you to what you are equal. By the sacred energies of Milton! by the dainty, sweet, and soothing phantasies of honey-tongued Spenser! I adjure you to attempt the epic, or do something more ample than writing an occasional brief ode or sonnet; something, "to make yourself for ever known,—to make the age to come your own." But I prate; doubtless you meditate something. When you are exalted among the lords of epic fame, I shall recall with pleasure, and exultingly, the days of your humility, when you disdained not to put forth, in the same volume with mine, your *Religious Musings* and that other poem from the *Joan of Arc*, those promising first-fruits of high renown to come. You have learning, you have fancy, you have enthusiasm, you have strength, and amplitude of wing enow for flights like those I recommend. In the vast and unexplored regions of fairy-land there is ground enough unfound and unculti-vated: search there, and realise your favourite Susque-hannah scheme. In all our comparisons of taste, I do not know whether I have ever heard your opinion of a poet, very dear to me,—the now-out-of-fashion Cowley. Favour me with your judgment of him, and tell me if his prose essays, in particular, as well as no inconsiderable part of his verse, be not delicious. I prefer the graceful rambling of his essays, even to the courtly elegance and ease of Addison; abstracting from this the latter's exquisite humour.

When the little volume is printed, send me three or four, at all events not more than six copies, and tell me if I put you to any additional expense, by printing with you. I have no thought of the kind, and in that case must reimburse you.

Priestley, whom I sin in almost adoring, speaks of "such a choice of company as tends to keep up that right bent and firmness of mind which a necessary intercourse with the world would otherwise warp and relax." "Such fellowship is the true balsam of life ; its cement is infinitely more durable than that of the friendships of the world ; and it looks for its proper fruit and complete gratification to the life beyond the grave." Is there a possible chance for such an one as I to realise in this world such friendships ? Where am I to look for 'em ? What testimonials shall I bring of my being worthy of such friendship ? Alas ! the great and good go together in separate herds, and leave such as I to lag far, far behind in all intellectual, and, far more grievous to say, in all moral accomplishments. Coleridge, I have not one truly elevated character among my acquaintance : not one Christian : not one but undervalues Christianity. Singly, what am I to do ? Wesley (have you read his life ?) was *he* not an elevated character ? Wesley has said, "Religion is not a solitary thing." Alas ! it necessarily is so with me, or next to solitary. 'Tis true you write to me ; but correspondence by letter, and personal intimacy, are very widely different. Do, do write to me, and do some good to my mind, already how much "warped and relaxed " by the world ! 'Tis the conclusion of another evening. Good night. God have us all in his keeping !

If you are sufficiently at leisure, oblige me with an account of your plan of life at Stowey—your literary occupations and prospects ; in short, make me acquainted with every circumstance which, as relating to you, can be interesting to me. Are you yet a Berkleyan ? Make me one. I rejoice in being, speculatively, a Necessarian. Would to God, I were habitually a practical one ! Confirm me in the faith of that great and glorious doctrine, and keep me steady in the contemplation of it. You some time since expressed an intention you had of finishing some extensive work on the Evidences of Natural and Revealed Religion. Have you let that intention go ?

Or are you doing anything towards it? Make to yourself other ten talents. My letter is full of nothingness. I talk of nothing. But I must talk. I love to write to you. I take a pride in it. It makes me think less meanly of myself. It makes me think myself not totally disconnected from the better part of mankind. I know I am too dissatisfied with the beings around me; but I cannot help occasionally exclaiming, "Woe is me, that I am constrained to dwell with Meshech, and to have my habitation among the tents of Kedar!" I know I am noways better in practice than my neighbours, but I have a taste for religion, an occasional earnest aspiration after perfection, which they have not. I gain nothing by being with such as myself: we encourage one another in mediocrity. I am always longing to be with men more excellent than myself. All this must sound odd to you; but these are my predominant feelings when I sit down to write to you, and I should put force upon my mind were I to reject them. Yet I rejoice, and feel my privilege with gratitude, when I have been reading some wise book, such as I have just been reading, *Priestley on Philosophical Necessity*, in the thought that I enjoy a kind of communion, a kind of friendship even, with the great and good. Books are to me instead of friends. I wish they did not resemble the latter in their scarceness.

And how does little David Hartley? "*Ecquid in antiquam virtutem?*" Does his mighty name work wonders yet upon his little frame and opening mind? I did not distinctly understand you: you don't mean to make an actual ploughman of him! Is Lloyd with you yet? Are you intimate with Southey? What poems is he about to publish? He hath a most prolific brain, and is indeed a most sweet poet. But how can you answer all the various mass of interrogation I have put to you in the course of this sheet? Write back just what you like, only write something, however brief. I have now nigh finished my page, and got to the end of another evening (Monday evening), and my eyes are heavy and sleepy, and my brain unsuggestive. I have just heart enough awake to say good-night once more, and God love you, my dear friend; God love us all! Mary bears an affectionate remembrance of you. CHARLES LAMB.

LETTER XXII.] *January* 16, 1797.

Dear C——,—You have learned by this time, with surprise, no doubt, that Lloyd is with me in town. The emotions I felt on his coming so unlooked for, are not ill expressed in what follows, and what (if you do not object to them as too personal, and to the world obscure, or otherwise wanting in worth) I should wish to make a part of our little volume. I shall be sorry if that volume comes out, as it necessarily must do, unless you print those very schoolboy-ish verses I sent you on not getting leave to come down to Bristol last Summer. I say I shall be sorry that I have addressed you in nothing which can appear in our joint volume; so frequently, so habitually, as you dwell in my thoughts, 'tis some wonder those thoughts came never yet in contact with a poetical mood. But you dwell in my heart of hearts, and I love you in all the naked honesty of prose. God bless you, and all your little domestic circle! My tenderest remembrances to your beloved Sara, and a smile and a kiss from me to your dear dear little David Hartley. The verses I refer to above, slightly amended, I have sent (forgetting to ask your leave, tho' indeed I gave them only your initials) to the *Monthly Magazine*, where they may possibly appear next month, and where I hope to recognise your poem on Burns.

TO CHARLES LLOYD, AN UNEXPECTED VISITOR.

Alone, obscure, without a friend,
  A cheerless, solitary thing,
Why seeks my Lloyd the stranger out !
  What offering can the stranger bring

Of social scenes, home-bred delights,
    That him in aught compensate may
For Stowey's pleasant winter nights,
    For loves and friendships far away,

In brief oblivion to forego
    Friends, such as thine, so justly dear,
And be awhile with me content
    To stay, a kindly loiterer, here?

For this a gleam of random joy
    Hath flush'd my unaccustomed cheek;
And, with an o'er-charged bursting heart,
    I feel the thanks I cannot speak.

O! sweet are all the Muse's lays,
    And sweet the charm of matin bird—
'Twas long, since these estranged ears
    The sweeter voice of friend had heard.

The voice hath spoke: the pleasant sounds,
    In memory's ear, in after time
Shall live, to sometimes rouse a tear,
    And sometimes prompt an honest rhyme.

For when the transient charm is fled,
    And when the little week is o'er,
To cheerless, friendless solitude
    When I return, as heretofore—

Long, long, within my aching heart
    The grateful sense shall cherished be;
I'll think less meanly of myself,
    That Lloyd will sometimes think on me.

O Coleridge, would to God you were in London with
us, or we two at Stowey with you all! Lloyd takes up
his abode at the *Bull and Mouth;* the *Cat and Salutation* would have had a charm more forcible for me.   *O
noctes cœnœque Deûm!*   Anglice—Welsh rabbit, punch,
and poesy.   Should you be induced to publish those very
schoolboy-ish verses, print 'em as they will occur, if at
all, in the *Monthly Magazine;* yet I should feel ashamed
that to you I wrote nothing better: but they are too
personal, and almost trifling and obscure withal.   Some

lines of mine to Cowper were in the last *Monthly Magazine :* they have not body of thought enough to plead for the retaining of 'em. My sister's kind love to you all.

C. LAMB.

LETTER XXIII.]   *February* 13, 1797.

Your poem is altogether admirable : parts of it are even exquisite ; in particular, your personal account of the Maid far surpasses anything of the sort in Southey. I perceived all its excellences, on a first reading, as readily as now you have been removing a supposed film from my eyes. I was only struck with a certain faulty disproportion in the matter and the *style*, which I still think I perceive, between these lines and the former ones. I had an end in view : I wished to make you reject the poem only as being discordant with the other ; and, in subservience to that end, it was politically done in me to overpass and make no mention of merit, which, could you think me capable of *overlooking*, might reasonably damn for ever in your judgment all pretensions, in me, to be critical. There—I will be judged by Lloyd, whether I have not made a very handsome recantation. I was in the case of a man whose friend has asked him his opinion of a certain young lady. The deluded wight gives judgment against her *in toto*—doesn't like her face, her walk, her manners ; finds fault with her eyebrows ; can see no wit in her. His friend looks blank ; he begins to smell a rat ; wind veers about ; he acknowledges her good sense, her judgment in dress, a certain simplicity of manners and honesty of heart, something too in her manners which gains upon you after a short acquaintance ; and then her accurate pronunciation of the French language, and a pretty uncultivated taste in drawing. The reconciled gentleman smiles applause, squeezes him by the hand, and hopes he will do him the honour of taking a bit of dinner with Mrs. —— and him,—a plain family dinner,—some day next week ; "for, I suppose, you never heard we were married. I'm glad to see you like my wife, however; you'll come and see her, ha?" Now am I too proud to retract entirely? Yet I do perceive I am in some sort straitened. You are manifestly wedded to this poem; and what fancy has joined let no man separate. I turn me to the *Joan of Arc*, second book.

The solemn openings of it are with sounds which, Lloyd would say, "are silence to the mind." The deep preluding strains are fitted to initiate the mind, with a pleasing awe, into the sublimest mysteries of theory concerning man's nature, and his noblest destination—the philosophy of a first cause — of subordinate agents in creation superior to man—the subserviency of pagan worship and pagan faith to the introduction of a purer and more perfect religion, which you so elegantly describe as winning, with gradual steps, her difficult way northward from Bethabara. After all this cometh Joan, a *publican's* daughter, sitting on an ale-house *bench*, and marking the *swingings* of the *signboard*, finding a poor man, his wife, and six children, starved to death with cold, and thence roused into a state of mind proper to receive visions, emblematical of equality; which, what the devil Joan had to do with, I don't know, or indeed with the French and American revolutions; though that needs no pardon, it is executed so nobly. After all, if you perceive no disproportion, all argument is vain : I do not so much object to parts. Again, when you talk of building your fame on these lines in preference to the *Religious Musings*, I cannot help conceiving of you, and of the author of that, as two different persons, and I think you a very vain man.

I have been re-reading your letter. Much of it I *could* dispute ; but with the latter part of it, in which you compare the two Joans with respect to their predispositions for fanaticism, I, *toto corde*, coincide ; only I think that Southey's strength rather lies in the description of the emotions of the Maid under the weight of inspiration. These (I see no mighty difference between *her* describing them or *your* describing them), these if you only equal, the previous admirers of his poem, as is natural, will prefer his. If you surpass, prejudice will scarcely allow it, and I scarce think you will surpass, though your specimen at the conclusion (I am in earnest) I think very nigh equals them. And in an account of a fanatic or of a prophet, the description of her *emotions* is expected to be most highly finished. By the way, I spoke far too disparagingly of your lines, and I am ashamed to say, purposely. I should like you to specify or particularise. The story of the " Tottering Eld," of " his eventful years all come and gone," is too general. Why not make him a soldier, or some character, however, in which he has been witness to frequency of " cruel wrong and strange distress !" I think I should. When I laughed at the " miserable man crawling from beneath the coverture," I wonder I did not perceive that it was a laugh of horror—such as I have laughed at Dante's picture of the famished Ugolino. Without falsehood, I perceive an hundred beauties in your narrative. Yet I wonder you do not perceive something out-of-the-way, something unsimple and artificial in the expression, "voiced a sad tale." I hate made-dishes at the muses' banquet. I believe I was wrong in most of my other objections. But surely " hailed him immortal," adds nothing to the terror of the man's death, which it was your business to heighten, not diminish by a phrase which takes away all terror from it. I like that line, " They closed their eyes in sleep, nor knew 'twas death." Indeed there is scarce a line I do not like. " *Turbid* ecstacy," is surely not so good as what you *had* written, " troublous." Turbid rather suits the muddy kind of inspiration which London porter confers. The versification is, throughout, to my ears unexceptionable, with no disparagement to the measure of the *Religious Musings*, which is exactly fitted to the thoughts.

You were building your house on a rock when you rested your fame on that poem. I can scarce bring my-

self to believe that I am admitted to a familiar correspondence, and all the licence of friendship, with a man
who writes blank verse like Milton. Now, this is delicate
flattery, *indirect* flattery. Go on with your *Maid of
Orleans*, and be content to be second to yourself. I shall
become a convert to it when 'tis finished.

This afternoon I attend the funeral of my poor old
aunt, who died on Thursday. I own I am thankful that
the good creature has ended all her days of suffering and
infirmity. She was to me the "cherisher of infancy,"
and one must fall on those occasions into reflections,
which it would be commonplace to enumerate, concerning
death, "of chance and change, and fate in human life."
Good God, who could have foreseen all this but four
months back ! I had reckoned, in particular, on my
aunt's living many years ; she was a very hearty old
woman. But she was a mere skeleton before she died,
looked more like a corpse that had lain weeks in the
grave, than one fresh dead. "Truly the light is sweet,
and a pleasant thing it is for the eyes to behold the sun;
but if a man live many years and rejoice in them all, yet
let him remember the days of darkness, for they shall be
many." Coleridge, why are we to live on after all the
strength and beauty of existence is gone, when all the
life of life is fled, as poor Burns expresses it ? Tell Lloyd
I have had thoughts of turning Quaker, and have been
reading, or am rather just beginning to read, a most
capital book, good thoughts in good language, William
Penn's *No Cross, no Crown.* I like it immensely. Unluckily I went to one of his meetings, tell him, in St.
John Street, yesterday, and saw a man under all the
agitations and workings of a fanatic, who believed himself under the influence of some "inevitable presence."
This cured me of Quakerism. I love it in the books of
Penn and Woolman ; but I detest the vanity of a man
thinking he speaks by the Spirit, when what he says an
ordinary man might say without all that quaking and
trembling. In the midst of his inspiration (and the

effects of it were most noisy) was handed into the midst of the meeting a most terrible blackguard Wapping sailor. The poor man, I believe, had rather have been in the hottest part of an engagement, for the congregation of broad-brims, together with the ravings of the prophet, were too much for his gravity, though I saw even he had delicacy enough not to laugh out. And the inspired gentleman, though his manner was so supernatural, yet neither talked nor professed to talk anything more than good sober sense, common morality, with now and then a declaration of not speaking from himself. Among other things, looking back to his childhood and early youth, he told the meeting what a graceless young dog he had been; that in his youth he had a good share of wit. Reader, if thou hadst seen the gentleman, thou wouldst have sworn that it must indeed have been many years ago, for his rueful physiognomy would have scared away the playful goddess from the meeting, where he presided, for ever. A wit! a wit! what could he mean? Lloyd, it minded me of *Falkland* in the *Rivals*, "Am I full of wit and humour? No, indeed you are not. Am I the life and soul of every company I come into? No, it cannot be said you are." That hard-faced gentleman, a wit! Why, Nature wrote on his fanatic forehead fifty years ago, " Wit never comes, that comes to all." I should be as scandalised at a *bon mot* issuing from his oracle-looking mouth, as to see Cato go down a country dance. God love you all! You are very good to submit to be pleased with reading my nothings. 'Tis the privilege of friendship to talk nonsense, and to have her nonsense respected.—Yours ever,

C. LAMB.

LETTER XXIV.]   *April* 7, 1797.

Your last letter was dated the 10th of February; in it you promised to write again the next day. At least, I did not expect so long, so unfriend-like a silence. There was a time, Col., when a remissness of this sort in a dear friend would have lain very heavy on my mind; but latterly I have been too familiar with neglect to feel much from the semblance of it. Yet, to suspect one's self overlooked, and in the way to oblivion, is a feeling rather humbling ; perhaps, as tending to self-mortification, not unfavourable to the spiritual state. Still, as you meant to confer no benefit on the soul of your friend, you do not stand quite clear from the imputation of unkindliness (a word, by which I mean the diminutive of unkindness).

Lloyd tells me he has been very ill, and was on the point of leaving you. I addressed a letter to him at Birmingham : perhaps he got it not, and is still with you. I hope his ill-health has not prevented his attending to a request I made in it, that he would write again very soon to let me know how he was. I hope to God poor Lloyd is not very bad, or in a very bad way. Pray satisfy me about these things.

And then David Hartley was unwell ; and how is the small philosopher, the minute philosopher ? and David's mother ? Coleridge, I am not trifling ; nor are these matter-of-fact questions only. You are all very dear and precious to me. Do what you will, Coleridge, you may hurt me and vex me by your silence, but you cannot estrange my heart from you all. I cannot scatter friendships like chuck-farthings, nor let them drop from mine hand like hour-glass sand. I have but two or three people in the world to whom I am more than indifferent, and I can't afford to whistle them off to the winds.

By the way, Lloyd may have told you about my sister. I told him. If not, I have taken her out of her confinement, and taken a room for her at Hackney, and spend my Sundays, holidays, etc., with her. She boards herself. In a little half-year's illness, and in such an illness, of such a nature, and of such consequences, to get her out into the world again, with a prospect of her never being so ill again,—this is to be ranked not among the common blessings of Providence. May that merciful God make tender my heart, and make me as thankful, as in my distress I was earnest, in my prayers. Congratulate me

on an ever-present and never-alienable friend like her.
And do, do insert, if you have not *lost*, my Dedication.
It will have lost half its value by coming so late.   If you
really are going on with that volume, I shall be enabled
in a day or two to send you a short poem to insert.   Now,
do answer this.   Friendship, and acts of friendship, should
be reciprocal, and free as the air.   A friend should never
be reduced to beg an alms of his fellow; yet I will beg
an alms : I entreat you to write, and tell me all about
poor Lloyd, and all of you.   God love and preserve you
all !   C. LAMB.

LETTER XXV.]   *April* 15, 1797.

The above you will please to print immediately before
the blank verse fragments.   Tell me if you like it.   I
fear the latter half is unequal to the former, in parts of
which I think you will discover a delicacy of pencilling
not quite un-Spenser-like.   The latter half aims at the
measure, but has failed to attain the *poetry* of Milton in
his *Comus*, and Fletcher in that exquisite thing ycleped
the *Faithful Shepherdess*, where they both use eight-
syllable lines.   But this latter half was finished in great
haste, and as a task, not from that impulse which affects
the name of inspiration.

By the way, I have lit upon Fairfax's *Godfrey of
Bullen*, for half-a-crown.   Rejoice with me.

Poor dear Lloyd !   I had a letter from him yesterday ;
his state of mind is truly alarming.   He has, by his own
confession, kept a letter of mine unopened three weeks ;
afraid, he says, to open it, lest I should speak upbraidingly
to him ; and yet this very letter of mine was in answer
to one, wherein he informed me that an alarming illness
had alone prevented him from writing.   You will pray
with me, I know, for his recovery ; for surely, Coleridge,
an exquisiteness of feeling like this must border on derangement.   But I love him more and more, and will not give
up the hope of his speedy recovery, as he tells me he is
under Dr. Darwin's regimen.

God bless us all, and shield us from insanity, which is
" the sorest malady of all."

My kind love to your wife and child.

C. LAMB.

Pray write now.

LETTER XXVI.]   *June* 13, 1797.

I stared with wild wonderment to see thy well-known
hand again. It revived many a pleasing recollection of
an epistolary intercourse, of late strangely suspended,
once the pride of my life. Before I even opened thy
letter I figured to myself a sort of complacency which my
little hoard at home would feel at receiving the new-
comer into the little drawer where I keep my treasures
of this kind. You have done well in writing to me.
The little room (was it not a little one?) at the *Salutation* was already in the way of becoming a fading idea !
It had begun to be classed in my memory with those
"wanderings with a fair-hair'd maid," in the recollection
of which I feel I have no property. You press me, very
kindly do you press me, to come to Stowey. Obstacles,
strong as death, prevent me at present ; maybe I may be
able to come before the year is out. Believe me, I will
come as soon as I can ; but I dread naming a probable
time. It depends on fifty things, besides the expense,
which is not nothing. Lloyd wants me to come to see
him ; but, besides that you have a prior claim on me, I
should not feel myself so much at home with him, till he
gets a house of his own. As to Richardson, caprice may
grant what caprice only refused ; and it is no more hardship, rightly considered, to be dependent on him for
pleasure, than to lie at the mercy of the rain and sunshine for the enjoyment of a holiday : in either case we
are not to look for a suspension of the laws of Nature.
"Gryll will be Gryll." Vide Spenser.

I could not but smile at the compromise you make
with me for printing Lloyd's poems first ; but there is in

nature, I fear, too many tendencies to envy and jealousy not to justify you in your apology. Yet, if any one is welcome to pre-eminence from me, it is Lloyd, for he would be the last to desire it. So pray, let his name *uniformly* precede mine, for it would be treating me like a child to suppose it could give me pain. Yet, alas! I am not insusceptible of the bad passions. Thank God, I have the ingenuousness to be ashamed of them. I am dearly fond of Charles Lloyd; he is all goodness; and I have too much of the world in my composition to feel myself thoroughly deserving of his friendship.

Lloyd tells me that Sheridan put you upon writing your tragedy. I hope you are only Coleridgeising when you talk of finishing it in a few days. Shakspeare was a more modest man; but you best know your own power.

Of my last poem you speak slightingly. Surely the longer stanzas were pretty tolerable: at least there was one good line in it,

"Thick-shaded trees, with dark green leaf rich clad."

To adopt your own expression, I call this a "rich" line, a fine full line. And some others I thought even beautiful. Believe me, my little gentleman will feel some repugnance at riding behind in the basket; though, I confess, in pretty good company. Your picture of idiocy, with the sugar-loaf head, is exquisite; but are you not too severe upon our more favoured brethren in fatuity? Lloyd tells me how ill your wife and child have been. I rejoice that they are better. My kindest remembrances, and those of my sister. I send you a trifling letter; but you have only to think that I have been skimming the superficies of my mind, and found it only froth. Now, do write again! You cannot believe how I long and love always to hear about you. Yours most affectionately, CHARLES LAMB.

Monday Night.

LETTER XXVII.]   *June* 24, 1797.

Did you seize the grand opportunity of seeing Kosciusko while he was at Bristol? I never saw a hero; I
wonder how they look. I have been reading a most
curious romance-like work, called the *Life of John
Buncle, Esq.* 'Tis very interesting, and an extraordinary
compound of all manner of subjects, from the depth of
the ludicrous to the heights of sublime religious truth.
There is much abstruse science in it above my cut, and
an infinite fund of pleasantry. John Buncle is a famous
fine man, formed in Nature's most eccentric hour. I am
ashamed of what I write; but I have no topic to talk of.
I see nobody. I sit and read, or walk alone, and hear
nothing. I am quite lost to conversation from disuse;
and out of the sphere of my little family (who, I am
thankful, are dearer and dearer to me every day) I see
no face that brightens up at my approach. My friends
are at a distance. Worldly hopes are at a low ebb with
me, and unworldly thoughts are familiarised to me,
though I occasionally indulge in them. Still I feel a
calm not unlike content. I fear it is sometimes more
akin to physical stupidity than to a heaven-flowing
serenity and peace. What right have I to obtrude all
this upon you? and what is such a letter to you? and if
I come to Stowey, what conversation can I furnish to
compensate my friend for those stores of knowledge and of
fancy; those delightful treasures of wisdom which I know
he will open to me? But it is better to give than to
receive; and I was a very patient hearer and docile
scholar, in our winter evening meetings at Mr. May's;
was I not, Col.? What I have owed to thee, my heart
can ne'er forget.

God love you and yours!   C. L.

Saturday.

LETTER XXVIII.]   *July* 1797.

I discern a possibility of my paying you a visit next

week. May I, can I, shall I come so soon? Have you *room* for me, *leisure* for me? and are you pretty well? Tell me all this honestly—immediately. And by what *day* coach could I come soonest and nearest to Stowey? A few months hence may suit you better; certainly me, as well. If so, say so. I long, I yearn, with all the longings of a child do I desire to see you, to come among you—to see the young philosopher, to thank Sara for her last year's invitation in person—to read your tragedy— to read over together our little book—to breathe fresh air—to revive in me vivid images of " *Salutation* scenery." There is a sort of sacrilege in my letting such ideas slip out of my mind and memory. Still that Richardson remaineth—a thorn in the side of Hope, when she would lean towards Stowey. Here I will leave off, for I dislike to fill up this paper (which involves a question so connected with my heart and soul) with meaner matter, or subjects to me less interesting. I can talk, as I can think, nothing else.

Thursday. C. LAMB.

LETTER XXIX.] *(Late in) July* 1797.

I am scarcely yet so reconciled to the loss of you, or so subsided into my wonted uniformity of feeling, as to sit calmly down to think of you and write to you. But I reason myself into the belief that those few and pleasant holidays shall not have been spent in vain. I feel improvement in the recollection of many a casual conversation. The names of Tom Poole, of Wordsworth and his good sister, with thine and Sara's, are become "familiar in my mouth as household words." You would make me very happy if you think W. has no objection, by transcribing for me that Inscription of his. I have some scattered sentences ever floating on my memory, teasing me that I cannot remember more of it. You may believe I will make no improper use of it. Believe me I can think now of many subjects on which I had planned gaining information from you; but I forgot my "treasure's worth" while I possessed it. Your leg is now become to me a matter of much more importance; and many a little thing, which when I was present with you seemed scarce to *indent* my notice, now presses painfully on my remembrance. Is the Patriot come? Are Wordsworth and his sister gone yet? I was looking out for John Thelwall all the way from Bridgewater; and had I met him, I think it would have moved almost me to tears. You will oblige me, too, by sending me my great-coat, which I left behind in the oblivious state the mind is thrown into at parting. Is it not ridiculous that I sometimes envy that great-coat lingering so cunningly behind! At present I have none: so send it to me by a Stowey waggon, if there be such a thing, directing for C. L., No. 45, Chapel Street, Pentonville, near London. But above all, *that Inscription!* It will recall to me the tones of all your voices, and with them many a remembered kindness to one who could and can repay you all only by the silence of a grateful heart. I could not talk much while I was with you; but my silence was not sullenness, nor I hope from any bad motive; but, in truth, disuse has made me awkward at it. I know I behaved myself, particularly at Tom Poole's, and at Cruikshank's, most like a sulky child; but company and converse are strange to me. It was kind in you all to endure me as you did.

Are you and your dear Sara—to me also very dear, because very kind—agreed yet about the management of little Hartley? And how go on the little rogue's teeth! I will see White to-morrow and he shall send you information on that matter; but as perhaps I can do it as well, after talking with him, I will keep this letter open.

My love and thanks to you and all of you.

C. L.

Wednesday Evening.

celerity t'other morning at office. I expect you to like it better than anything of mine; Lloyd does, and I do myself.

You use Lloyd very ill, never writing to him. I tell you again that his is not a mind with which you should play tricks. He deserves more tenderness from you.

For myself, I must spoil a little passage of Beaumont and Fletcher's to adapt it to my feelings :—

> "I am prouder
> That I was once your friend, tho' now forgot,
> Than to have had another true to me."

If you don't write to me now, as I told Lloyd, I shall get angry, and call you hard names—Manchineel, and I don't know what else. I wish you would send me my great-coat. The snow and the rain season is at hand, and I have but a wretched old coat, once my father's, to keep 'em off, and that is transitory.

> "When time drives flocks from field to fold,
> When ways grow foul and blood gets cold,"

I shall remember where I left my coat. Meet emblem wilt thou be, old Winter, of a friend's neglect—cold, cold, cold! C. LAMB.

LETTER XXXI.] *January* 28, 1798.

You have writ me many kind letters, and I have answered none of them. I don't deserve your attentions. An unnatural indifference has been creeping on me since my last misfortunes, or I should have seized the first opening of a correspondence with *you*. To you I owe much, under God. In my brief acquaintance with you in London, your conversations won me to the better cause, and rescued me from the polluting spirit of the world. I might have been a worthless character without you; as it is, I do possess a certain improvable portion of devotional feelings, tho' when I view myself in the light of divine truth, and not according to the common measures of human judgment, I am altogether corrupt and sinful. This is no cant. I am very sincere.

These last afflictions, Coleridge, have failed to soften and bend my will. They found me unprepared. My former calamities produced in me a spirit of humility and a spirit of prayer. I thought they had sufficiently disciplined me ; but the event ought to humble me. If God's judgment now fail to take away from me the heart of stone, what more grievous trials ought I not to expect ? I have been very querulous, impatient under the rod—full of little jealousies and heart-burnings. I had well-nigh quarrelled with Charles Lloyd ; and for no other reason, I believe, than that the good creature did all he could to make me happy. The truth is, I thought he tried to force my mind from its natural and proper bent. He continually wished me to be from home ; he was drawing me *from* the consideration of my poor dear Mary's situation, rather than assisting me to gain a proper view of it with religious consolations. I wanted to be left to the tendency of my own mind, in a solitary state, which, in times past, I knew had led to quietness and a patient bearing of the yoke. He was hurt that I was not more constantly with him ; but he was living with White, a man to whom I had never been accustomed to impart my *dearest feelings*, tho' from long habits of friendliness, and many a social and good quality, I loved him very much. I met company there sometimes—indiscriminate company. Any society almost, when I am in affliction, is sorely painful to me. I seem to breathe more freely, to think more collectedly, to feel more properly and calmly, when alone. All these things the good creature did with the kindest intentions in the world, but they produced in me nothing but soreness and discontent. I became, as he complained, "jaundiced" towards him . . . but he has forgiven me ; and his smile, I hope, will draw all such humours from me. I am recovering, God be praised for it, a healthiness of mind, something like calmness ; but I want more religion. I am jealous of human helps and leaning-places. I rejoice in your good fortunes. May God at the last settle you !—You have had many and painful trials ; humanly speaking they are going to end ; but we should rather pray that discipline may attend us thro' the whole of our lives. . . . A careless and a dissolute spirit has advanced upon *me* with large strides. Pray God that my present afflictions may be sanctified to me ! Mary is recovering ; but I see no opening yet of a situation for her. Your invitation went to my very heart ; but you have a power of exciting interest, of leading all hearts captive, too forcible to admit of Mary's being with you. I consider her as perpetually on the brink of madness. I think you would almost make her dance within an inch of the precipice ; she must be with duller fancies, and cooler intellects. I know a young man of this description, who has suited her these twenty years, and may live to do so still, if we are one day restored to each other. In answer to your suggestions of occupation for me, I must say that I do not think my capacity altogether suited for disquisitions of that kind. . . . I have read little, I have a very weak memory, and retain little of what I read ; am unused to compositions in which any methodising is required ; but I thank you sincerely for the hint, and shall receive it as far as I am able ; that is, endeavour to engage my mind in some constant and innocent pursuit. I know my capacities better than you do.

Accept my kindest love, and believe me yours, as ever.   C. L.

S. T. Coleridge,
at the Reverend A. Rowe's,
    Shrewsbury.

To ROBERT SOUTHEY.

LETTER XXXII.]   *July* 28, 1798.

Dear Southey—I am ashamed that I have not thanked you before this for the *Joan of Arc*, but I did not know your address, and it did not occur to me to write through Cottle. The poem delighted me, and the notes amused me; but methinks she of Neufchatel, in the print, holds her sword too "like a dancer." I sent your *notice* to Phillips, particularly requesting an immediate insertion, but I suppose it came too late. I am sometimes curious to know what progress you make in that same "Calendar": whether you insert the nine worthies and Whittington? what you do or how you can manage when two Saints meet and quarrel for precedency? Martlemas, and Candlemas, and Christmas, are glorious themes for a writer like you, antiquity-bitten, smit with the love of boars' heads and rosemary; but how you can ennoble the 1st of April I know not. By the way, I had a thing to say, but a certain false modesty has hitherto prevented me: perhaps I can best communicate my wish by a hint. My birthday is on the 10th of February, New Style; but if it interferes with any remarkable event, why rather than my country should lose her fame, I care not if I put my nativity back eleven days. Fine family patronage for your "Calendar," if that old lady of prolific memory were living, who lies (or lyes) in some church in London (saints forgive me, but I have forgot *what* church), attesting that enormous legend of as many children as days in the year. I marvel her impudence did not grasp at a leap-year. Three hundred and sixty-five dedications, and all in a family! You might spit, in spirit, on the oneness of Mæcenas's patronage!

Samuel Taylor Coleridge, to the eternal regret of his native Devonshire, emigrates to Westphalia: "Poor Lamb" (these were his last words), "if he wants any *knowledge*, he may apply to me." In ordinary cases I thanked him. I have an "Encyclopædia" at hand; but on such an occasion as going over to a German university, I could not refrain from sending him the following propositions, to be by him defended or oppugned (or both) at Leipsic or Göttingen.

THESES QUÆDAM THEOLOGICÆ.

I.

" Whether God loves a lying angel better than a true man ? "

II.

" Whether the archangel Uriel *could* knowingly affirm an untruth, and whether, if he *could*, he *would ?* "

III.

" Whether honesty be an angelic virtue, or not rather belonging to that class of qualities which the schoolmen term ' virtutes minus splendidæ, et hominis et terræ nimis participes ' ? "

IV.

" Whether the seraphim ardentes do not manifest their goodness by the way of vision and theory ? and whether practice be not a sub-celestial, and merely human virtue ? "

V.

" Whether the higher order of seraphim illuminati ever *sneer ?* "

VI.

" Whether pure intelligences can *love*, or whether they can love anything besides pure intellect ? "

VII.

" Whether the beatific vision be anything more or less than a perpetual representment to each individual angel of his own present attainments, and future capabilities, something in the manner of mortal looking-glasses ? "

VIII.

" Whether an ' immortal and amenable soul ' may not come *to be damned at last, and the man never suspect it beforehand ?* "

Samuel Taylor Coleridge hath not deigned an answer. Was it impertinent of me to avail myself of that offered source of knowledge ?

Wishing *Madoc* may be born into the world with as splendid promise as the second birth, or purification, of the Maid of Neufchatel,—I remain yours sincerely,

C. LAMB.

I hope Edith is better ; my kindest remembrances to her. You have a good deal of trifling to forgive in this letter.

"Love and remembrances to Cottle."

LETTER XXXIII.]   *October* 18, 1798.

Dear Southey—I have at last been so fortunate as to pick up Wither's Emblems for you, that "old book and quaint," as the brief author of *Rosamund Gray* hath it ; it is in a most detestable state of preservation, and the cuts are of a fainter impression than I have seen. Some child, the curse of antiquaries and bane of bibliopical rarities, hath been dabbling in some of them with its paint and dirty fingers ; and, in particular, hath a little sullied the author's own portraiture, which I think valuable, as the poem that accompanies it is no common one ; this last excepted, the Emblems are far inferior to old Quarles. I once told you otherwise, but I had not then read old Quarles with attention. I have picked up, too, another copy of Quarles for ninepence ! ! ! O tempora ! O lectores ! so that if you have lost or parted with your own copy, say so, and I can furnish you, for you prize these things more than I do. You will be amused, I think, with honest Wither's "Supersedeas to all them whose custom it is, without any deserving, to importune authors to give unto them their books." I am sorry 'tis imperfect, as the lottery board annexed to it also is. Methinks you might modernise and elegantise this Supersedeas, and place it in front of your *Joan of Arc*, as a *friend* to talk to—but wait in patience, and you will in good time make friends. The having a friend is not indispensably necessary to virtue or happiness. Religion removes those barriers of sentiment which partition us from the disinterested love of our brethren—we are commanded to love our enemies, to do good to those that hate us; how much more is it our duty then to cultivate a forbearance and complacence towards those who only differ from us in dispositions and ways of thinking? There is always, without very unusual care there must always be, something of Self in friendship; we love our friend because he is like ourselves; can consequences altogether unmix'd and pure be reasonably expected from such a source—do not even the publicans and sinners the same? Say, that you love a friend for his moral qualities, is it not rather because those qualities resemble what you fancy your own? This, then, is not without danger. The only true cement of a valuable friendship, the only thing that even makes it not sinful, is when two friends propose to become mutually of benefit to each other in a moral or religious way. But even this friendship is perpetually liable to the mixture of something not pure; we love our friend, because he is *ours*—so we do our money, our wit, our knowledge, our virtue; and wherever this sense of APPROPRIATION and PROPERTY enters, so much is to be subtracted from the value of that friendship or that virtue. Our duties are to do good, expecting nothing again; to bear with contrary dispositions; to be candid and forgiving, not to crave and long after a communication of sentiment and feeling, but rather to avoid dwelling upon those feelings, however good, because they are our own. A man may be intemperate and selfish who indulges in *good feelings* for the mere pleasure they give him. I do not wish to deter you from making a friend, a true friend, and such a friendship, where the parties are not blind to each other's faults, is very useful and valuable. I perceive a tendency in you to this error, Robert. I know you have chosen to take up an high opinion of my moral worth, but I say it before God, and I do not lie, you are mistaken in me. I could not bear to lay open all my failings to you, for the sentiment of shame would be too pungent. Let this be as an example to you. Robert, friends fall off, friends mistake us, they change, they grow unlike us, they go away, they die; but God is everlasting and incapable of change, and to Him we may look with cheerful, unpresumptuous hope, while we discharge the duties of life in situations more untowardly than yours. You complain of the impossibility of improving yourself, but be assured that the opportunity of improvement lies more in the mind than the situation. Humble yourself before God, cast out the selfish principle, wait in patience, do good in every way you can to all sorts of people, never be easy to neglect a duty tho' a small one, praise God for all, and see His hand in all things, and He will in time raise you up *many friends*—or be Himself instead an unchanging friend. God bless you.   C. LAMB.

LETTER XXXVII.]   *October (later)* 1798.

My dear Robert—I acknowledge I have been sadly remiss of late. If I descend to any excuse (and all excuses that come short of a direct denial of a charge are poor creatures at best), it must be taken from my state of mind for some time past, which has been stupid rather, and unfilled with any object, than occupied, as you may imagine, with any favourite idea to the exclusion of friend Robert. You, who are subject to all the varieties of the mind, will give me credit in this.

I am sadly sorry that you are relapsing into your old complaining strain. I wish I could adapt my consolations to your disease, but, alas! I have none to offer which your own mind, and the suggestions of books, cannot better supply. Are you the first whose situation hath not been exactly squar'd to his ideas? or rather, will you find me that man who does not complain of the one with the mind than that last poem, which is yet one of the finest written. But I am getting too dogmatical; and before I degenerate into abuse, I will conclude with assuring you that I am

Sincerely yours,

C. LAMB.

I am going to meet Lloyd at Ware on Saturday, to return on Sunday. Have you any commands or commendations to the metaphysician? I shall be very happy if you will dine or spend any time with me in your way through the great ugly city; but I know you have other ties upon you in these parts.

Love and respects to Edith, and friendly remembrances to Cottle.

To ROBERT LLOYD.

LETTER XL.]   *November* 13, 1798.

Now 'tis Robert's turn.

My dear Robert—One passage in your Letter a little displeas'd me. The rest was nothing but kindness, which Robert's letters are ever brimful of. You say that " this World to you seems drain'd of all its sweets ! " At first I had hoped you only meant to insinuate the high price of Sugar ! but I am afraid you meant more. O Robert, I don't know what you call sweet. Honey and the honey-comb, roses and violets, are yet in the earth. The sun and moon yet reign in Heaven, and the lesser lights keep up their pretty twinklings. Meats and drinks, sweet sights and sweet smells, a country walk, spring and autumn, follies and repentance, quarrels and reconcile-ments, have all a sweetness by turns. Good humour and good nature, friends at home that love you, and friends abroad that miss you, you possess all these things, and more innumerable, and these are all sweet things. . . . You may extract honey from everything; do not go a gathering after gall. The Bees are wiser in their genera-

tion than the race of sonnet writers and complainers,
Bowles's and Charlotte Smiths, and all that tribe, who
can see no joys but what are past, and fill people's heads
with notions of the unsatisfying nature of Earthly
comforts.   I assure you I find this world a very pretty
place.   My kind love to all your Sisters and to Thomas
—he never writes to me—and tell Susanna I forgive her.
                                              C. LAMB.

London, the 13th November 1798.

LETTER XLI.]   *November 20, 1798.*

As the little copy of verses I sent gave Priscilla and
Robert some pleasure, I now send them another little
tale, which is all I can send, for my stock will be
exhausted. . . . 'Tis a tale of witchcraft, told by an old
Steward in the family to Margaret, the ward of Sir
Walter Woodvil.   *Who* Sir Walter is you may come to
know bye and bye, when I have finish'd a Poem, from
which this and the other are extracts, and all the
extracts I can make without mutilating :

> OLD STEWARD. One summer night Sir Walter, as it chanc'd,
> Was pacing to and fro in the avenue
> That westward fronts our house,
> Among those aged oaks said to have been planted
> Three hundred years ago
> By a neighb'ring Prior of the Woodvil name ;
> But so it was,
> Being o'er task'd in thought he heeded not
> The importune suit of one who stood by the gate,
> And begg'd an alms.
> Some say, he shov'd her rudely from the gate
> With angry chiding ; but I can never think,
> (Sir Walter's nature hath a sweetness in it,)
> That he could treat a woman, an old woman
> With such discourtesy,
> For old she was who begg'd an alms of him.
> Well, he refus'd her.
> (Whether for importunity I know not,
> Or that she came between his meditations,)

But better had he met a Lion in the Streets,
Than this old woman that night,
For she was one who practis'd the black arts,
And serv'd the Devil, being since burnt for witchcraft.
She look'd at him like one that meant to blast him,
And with a frightful noise,
('Twas partly like a woman's voice,
And partly like the hissing of a snake,)
She nothing spake but this : Sir Walter told the words.

      " A mischief, mischief, mischief,
        And a nine times killing curse,
    By day and by night, to the caitive wight,
  Who shakes the poor, like snakes, from his door,
        And shuts up the womb of his purse :
        And a mischief, mischief, mischief,
        And a ninefold with'ring curse—
  For that shall come to thee, that will undo thee,
        Both all that thou fear'st and worst."

These words four times repeated, she departed
Leaving Sir Walter like a man, beneath
Whose feet a scaffolding had suddenly fall'n.
  MARGARET. A terrible curse !
    OLD STEWARD. O Lady ! such bad things are said of that
      old woman,
You would be loth to hear them !
As, namely, that the milk she gave was sour,
And the babe, who suck'd her, shrivell'd like a mandrake*
And things besides, with a bigger horror in them
Almost, I think, unlawful to be told !
  MARGARET. Then I must never hear them.   But proceed
And say what follow'd on the witch's curse.
    OLD STEWARD. Nothing immediate ; but some nine months
      after
Young Stephen Woodvil suddenly fell sick,
And none could tell what ail'd him ; for he lay,
And pin'd, and pin'd, till all his hair came off,
And he, that was full flesh'd, became as thin
As a two months' babe that has been starv'd in the nursing.
And sure, I think,
He bore his illness like a little child ;
With such rare sweetness, and dumb melancholy,
He strove to clothe his agony in smiles,
Which he would force up in his poor pale cheeks,
Like ill-tim'd guests that had no proper dwelling there.
And, when they ask'd him his complaint, he laid
His hand upon his heart to show the place

Where Susan came to him a nights, he said,
And prick'd him with a pin.
And thereupon Sir Walter call'd to mind
The beggar witch who stood in the gateway,
And begg'd an alms.
   MARGARET. And so he died ?
   OLD STEWARD. 'Tis thought so.
   MARGARET. But did the witch confess ?
   OLD STEWARD. All this and more at her death.
   MARGARET. I do not love to credit tales of magic.
Heav'n's music, which is order, seems unstrung,
And this brave world,
Creation's beauteous workmanship, unbeautify'd,
Disorder'd, marr'd, where such strange things are acted.

   * A *mandrake* is a root resembling the human form, as sometimes a carrot does, and the old superstition is, that when the mandrake is torn out of the earth a dreadful shriek is heard, which makes all who hear it go mad. 'Tis a fatal poison besides.

   I will here conclude my tiny portion of Prose with hoping you may like the story, and my kind remembrances to all.   C. LAMB.

Write soon, Robert.

To ROBERT SOUTHEY.

LETTER XLII.]   *November* 28, 1798.

   I can have no objection to your printing "Mystery of God" with my name, and all due acknowledgments for the honour and favour of the communication; indeed, 'tis a poem that can dishonour no name. Now, that is in the true strain of modern modestovanitas. . . . But for the sonnet, I heartily wish it, as I thought it was, dead and forgotten. If the exact circumstances under which I wrote could be known or told, it would be an interesting sonnet; but to an indifferent and stranger reader it must appear a very bald thing, certainly inadmissible in a compilation. I wish you could affix a different name to the volume. There is a contemptible book, a wretched assortment of vapid feelings, entitled *Pratt's Gleanings*, which hath damned and impropriated the title for ever. Pray think of some other. The gentleman is better known (better had he remained unknown) by an Ode to Benevolence, written and spoken for and at the annual dinner of the Humane Society, who walk in procession once a year, with all the objects of their charity before them, to return God thanks for giving them such benevolent hearts.

I like " Bishop Bruno," but not so abundantly as your " Witch Ballad," which is an exquisite thing of its kind.

I showed my " Witch " and " Dying Lover " to Dyer last night; but George could not comprehend how *that* could be poetry which did not go upon ten feet, as George and his predecessor had taught it to do; so George read me some lectures on the distinguishing qualities of the Ode, the Epigram, and the Epic, and went home to illustrate his doctrine, by correcting a proof sheet of his own Lyrics. George writes odes where the rhymes, like fashionable man and wife, keep a comfortable distance of six or eight lines apart, and calls that " observing the laws of verse !" George tells you, before he recites, that you must listen with great attention, or you'll miss the rhymes. I did so, and found them pretty exact. George, speaking of the dead Ossian, exclaimeth, " Dark are the poet's eyes !" I humbly represented to him that his own eyes were dark, and many a living bard's besides, and recommended " Closed are the poet's eyes." But that would not do. I found there was an antithesis between the darkness of his eyes and the splendour of his genius ; and I acquiesced.

Your recipe for a Turk's poison is invaluable, and truly Marlowish. . . . Lloyd objects to " shutting up the womb of his purse " in my curse (which, for a Christian witch in a Christian country, is not too mild, I hope). Do you object ? I think there is a strangeness in the idea, as well as " shaking the poor like snakes from his door," which suits the speaker. Witches illustrate, as

fine ladies do, from their own familiar objects, and snakes
and the shutting up of wombs are in their way.   I don't
know that this last charge has been before brought
against 'em nor either the sour milk or the mandrake
babe; but I affirm these be things a witch would do if
she could.

My Tragedy will be a medley (as I intend it to be a
medley) of laughter and tears, prose and verse, and in
some places rhyme, songs, wit, pathos, humour, and, if
possible, sublimity; at least it is not a fault in my intention if it does not comprehend most of these discordant
atoms.   Heaven send they dance not the "Dance of
Death!"   I hear that the Two Noble Englishmen have
parted no sooner than they set foot on German earth; but
I have not heard the reason.   Possibly to give moralists
an handle to exclaim, "Ah me! what things are perfect?"
I think I shall adopt your emendation in the "Dying
Lover," though I do not myself feel the objection against
"Silent Prayer."

My tailor has brought me home a new coat lapelled,
with a velvet collar.   He assures me everybody wears
velvet collars now.   Some are born fashionable, some
achieve fashion, and others, like your humble servant,
have fashion thrust upon them.   The rogue has been
making inroads hitherto by modest degrees, foisting upon
me an additional button, recommending gaiters; but to
come upon me thus, in a full tide of luxury, neither
becomes him as a tailor nor the ninth of a man.   My
meek gentleman was robbed the other day, coming with
his wife and family in a one-horse shay from Hampstead.
The villains rifled him of four guineas, some shillings and
half-pence, and a bundle of customers' measures, which
they swore were bank notes.   They did not shoot him,
and when they rode off he addrest them with profound
gratitude, making a congee: "Gentlemen, I wish you
good-night, and we are very much obliged to you that
you have not used us ill!"   And this is the cuckoo that
has had the audacity to foist upon me ten buttons on a

side, and a black velvet collar ! A cursed ninth of a scoundrel !

When you write to Lloyd, he wishes his Jacobin correspondents to address him as *Mr.* C. L. Love and respects to Edith. I hope she is well.

Yours sincerely, C. LAMB.

LETTER XLIII.] *December* 27, 1798.

Dear Southey—Your friend John May has formerly made kind offers to Lloyd of serving me in the India House, by the interest of his friend Sir Francis Baring. It is not likely that I shall ever put his goodness to the test on my own account, for my prospects are very comfortable ; but I know a man, a young man, whom he could serve through the same channel, and, I think, would be disposed to serve if he were acquainted with his case. This poor fellow (whom I know just enough of to vouch for his strict integrity and worth) has lost two or three employments from illness, which he cannot regain ; he was once insane, and, from the distressful uncertainty of his livelihood, has reason to apprehend a return of that malady. He has been for some time dependent on a woman whose lodger he formerly was, but who can ill afford to maintain him ; and I know that on Christmas night last he actually walked about the streets all night, rather than accept of her bed, which she offered him, and offered herself to sleep in the kitchen; and that, in consequence of that severe cold, he is labouring under a bilious disorder, besides a depression of spirits, which incapacitates him from exertion when he most needs it. For God's sake, Southey, if it does not go against you to ask favours, do it now ; ask it as for me : but do not do a violence to your feelings, because he does not know of this application, and will suffer no disappointment. What I meant to say was this,—there are in the India House, what are called *extra clerks*, not on the establishment, like me, but employed in extra business, by-jobs; these get about £50 a year, or rather more, but never rise. A director can put in at any time a young man in this office, and it is by no means considered so great a favour as making an established clerk. He would think himself as rich as an emperor if he could get such a certain situation, and be relieved from those disquietudes which, I do fear, may one day bring back his distemper.

You know John May better than I do, but I know enough to believe that he is a good man. He did make me that offer I have mentioned, but you will perceive that such an offer cannot authorise me in applying for another person.

But I cannot help writing to you on the subject, for the young man is perpetually before my eyes, and I shall feel it a crime not to strain all my petty interest to do him service, though I put my own delicacy to the question by so doing. I have made one other unsuccessful attempt already. At all events I will thank you to write, for I am tormented with anxiety.   C. LAMB.

LETTER XLIV.]   *January* 21, 1799.

I am requested by Lloyd to excuse his not replying to a kind letter received from you. He is at present situated in most distressful family perplexities, which I am not at liberty to explain, but they are such as to demand all the strength of his mind, and quite exclude any attention to foreign objects. His brother Robert (the flower of his family) hath eloped from the persecutions of his father, and has taken shelter with me. What the issue of his adventure will be, I know not. He hath the sweetness of an angel in his heart, combined with admirable firmness of purpose; an uncultivated, but very original, and I think superior, genius. But this step of his is but a small part of their family troubles.

I am to blame for not writing to you before on *my own account;* but I know you can dispense with the expressions of gratitude, or I should have thanked you before for all May's kindness. He has liberally supplied the person I spoke to you of with money, and had procured him a situation just after himself had lighted upon a similar one, and engaged too far to recede. But May's kindness was the same, and my thanks to you and him are the same. May went about on this business as if it had been his own. But you knew John May before this, so I will be silent.

I shall be very glad to hear from you when convenient. I do not know how your Calendar and other affairs thrive; but above all, I have not heard a great while of your "Madoc"—the *opus magnum*. I would willingly send you something to give a value to this letter; but I have only one slight passage to send you, scarce worth the sending, which I want to edge in somewhere into my play, which, by the way, hath not received the addition of ten lines, besides, since I saw you. A father, old Walter Woodvil (the witch's *protégé*), relates this of his son John, who "fought in adverse armies," being a royalist, and his father a parliamentary man :—

" I saw him in the day of Worcester fight,
  Whither he came at twice seven years,
  Under the discipline of the Lord Falkland
  (His uncle by the mother's side,
  Who gave his youthful politics a bent
  Quite *from* the principles of his father's house);
  There laid I see this valiant Lamb of Mars,
  This sprig of honour, this unbearded John,
  This veteran in green years, this sprout, this Woodvil
  (With dreadless ease guiding a fire-hot steed,
  Which seem'd to scorn the manage of a boy),
  Prick forth with such a *mirth* into the field,
  To mingle rivalship and acts of war
  Even with the sinewy masters of the art.
  You would have thought the work of blood had been
  A play-game merely, and the rabid Mars
  Had put his harmful hostile nature off
  To instruct raw youth in images of war,
  And practice of the unedged players' foils.
  The rough fanatic and blood-practised soldiery
  Seeing such hope and virtue in the boy,

> Disclosed their ranks to let him pass unhurt,
> Checking their swords' uncivil injuries,
> As loth to mar that curious workmanship
> Of Valour's beauty portray'd in his face."

Lloyd objects to "portray'd in his face," do you? I like the line.

I shall clap this in somewhere. I think there is a spirit through the lines; perhaps the 7th, 8th, and 9th owe their origin to Shakspeare, though no image is borrowed.

He says in *Henry the Fourth*—

> "This infant Hotspur,
> Mars in swathing clothes."

But pray did Lord Falkland die before Worcester fight? In that case I must make bold to unclify some other nobleman.

Kind love and respects to Edith.   C. LAMB.

LETTER XLV.]   *March* 15, 1799.

Dear Southey—I have received your little volume, for which I thank you, though I do not entirely approve of this sort of intercourse, where the presents are all one side. I have read the last Eclogue again with great pleasure. It hath gained considerably by abridgment, and now I think it wants nothing but enlargement. You will call this one of tyrant Procrustes's criticisms, to cut and pull so to his own standard; but the old lady is so great a favourite with me, I want to hear more of her; and of "Joanna" you have given us still less. But the picture of the rustics leaning over the bridge, and the old lady travelling abroad on summer evening to see her garden watered, are images so new and true, that I decidedly prefer this "Ruin'd Cottage" to any poem in the book. Indeed I think it the only one that will bear comparison with your "Hymn to the Penates," in a former volume.

I compare dissimilar things, as one would a rose and a

house with a tapestry bedroom, the "Judgment of Solomon" composing one panel, and "Actæon spying Diana naked" the other. I could tell of an old marble hall, with Hogarth's prints, and the Roman Cæsars in marble hung round. I could tell of a *wilderness*, and of a village church, and where the bones of my honoured grandam lie ; but there are feelings which refuse to be translated, sulky aborigines, which will not be naturalised in another soil. Of this nature are old family faces, and scenes of infancy.

I have given your address, and the books you want, to the Arches ; they will send them as soon as they can get them, but they do not seem quite familiar to their names. I have seen Gebor ! Gebor aptly so denominated from Geborish, *quasi* Gibberish. But Gebor hath some lucid intervals. I remember darkly one beautiful simile veiled in uncouth phrases about the youngest daughter of the Ark. I shall have nothing to communicate, I fear, to the Anthology. You shall have some fragments of my play, if you desire them ; but I think I would rather print it whole. Have you seen it, or shall I lend you a copy ? I want your opinion of it.

I must get to business ; so farewell. My kind remembrances to Edith. C. LAMB.

To THOMAS MANNING.

LETTER LI.] *December* 28, 1799.

Dear Manning—Having suspended my correspondence a decent interval, as knowing that even good things may be taken to satiety, a wish cannot but recur to learn whether you be still well and happy. Do all things continue in the state I left them in Cambridge ?

Do your night parties still flourish ? and do you continue to bewilder your company with your thousand faces, running down through all the keys of idiotism (like Lloyd over his perpetual harpsichord), from the smile and the glimmer of half-sense and quarter-sense, to the grin and hanging lip of Betty Foy's own Johnny? And does the face-dissolving curfew sound at twelve? How unlike the great originals were your petty terrors in the postscript! not fearful enough to make a fairy shudder, or a Lilliputian fine lady, eight months full of child, miscarry. Yet one of them, which had more beast than the rest, I thought faintly resembled *one* of your brutifications. But, seriously, I long to see your own honest Manning-face again. I did not mean a pun,—your *man's* face, you will be apt to say, I know your wicked will to pun. I cannot now write to Lloyd and you too; so you must convey as much interesting intelligence as this may contain, or be thought to contain, to him and Sophia, with my dearest love and remembrances.

By the by, I think you and Sophia both incorrect with regard to the *title* of the *play*. Allowing your objection (which is not necessary, as pride may be, and is in real life often, cured by misfortunes not directly originating from its own acts, as Jeremy Taylor will tell you a naughty desire is sometimes sent to cure it; I know you read these *practical divines*)—but allowing your objection, does not the betraying of his father's secret directly spring from pride?—from the pride of wine, and a full heart, and a proud over-stepping of the ordinary rules of morality, and contempt of the prejudices of mankind, which are not to bind superior souls—" as *trust* in *the matter* of *secrets* all *ties* of *blood*, etc. etc., keeping of *promises*, the feeble mind's religion, binding our *morning knowledge* to the performance of what *last night's ignorance* spake "—does he not prate, that "*Great Spirits*" must do more than die for their friend? Does not the pride of wine incite him to display some evidence of friendship, which its own irregularity shall make great? This I know, that I meant his punishment not alone to be a cure for his daily and habitual *pride*, but the direct consequence and appropriate punishment of a particular act of pride.

Public affairs—except as they touch upon me, and so turn into private,—I cannot whip up my mind to feel any interest in. I grieve, indeed, that War, and Nature, and Mr. Pitt, that hangs up in Lloyd's best parlour, should have conspired to call up three necessaries, simple commoners as our fathers knew them, into the upper house of luxuries; bread, and beer, and coals, Manning. But as to France and Frenchmen, and the Abbé Sièyes and his constitutions, I cannot make these present times present to me. I read histories of the past, and I live in them ; although, to abstract senses, they are far less momentous than the noises which keep Europe awake. I am reading *Burnet's History of his own Times*. Did you ever read that garrulous, pleasant history? He tells his story like an old man past political service, bragging to his sons on winter evenings of the part he took in public transactions, when his " old cap was new." Full of scandal, which all true history is. No palliatives ; but all the stark wickedness, that actually gives the *momentum* to national actors. Quite the prattle of age, and out-lived importance. Truth and sincerity staring out upon you perpetually in *alto relievo*. Himself a party man—he makes you a party man. None of the cursed philosophical Humeian indifference, so cold, and unnatural, and inhuman ! None of the cursed Gibbonian fine writing, so fine and composite ! None of Dr. Robertson's periods with three members. None of Mr. Roscoe's sage remarks, all so apposite, and coming in so clever, lest the reader should have had the trouble of drawing an inference. Burnet's good old prattle I can bring present to my mind : I can make the revolution present to me : the French revolution, by a converse perversity in my nature, I fling as far *from* me. To quit this tiresome subject, and to relieve you from two or three dismal yawns, which I hear in spirit, I here conclude my more than commonly obtuse letter , dull, up to the dulness of a Dutch commentator on Shakspeare.

My love to Lloyd and to Sophia. C. L.

Dear Manning—I am living in a continuous feast. Coleridge has been with me now for nigh three weeks, and the more I see of him in the quotidian undress and relaxation of his mind, the more cause I see to love him, and believe him a *very good man,* and all those foolish impressions to the contrary fly off like morning slumbers. He is engaged in translations, which I hope will keep him this month to come. He is uncommonly kind and friendly to me. He ferrets me day and night to *do something.* He tends me, amidst all his own worrying and heart-oppressing occupations, as a gardener tends his young *tulip.* Marry come up; what a pretty similitude, and how like your humble servant! He has lugged me to the brink of engaging to a newspaper, and has suggested to me, for a first plan, the forgery of a supposed manuscript of Burton, the anatomist of melancholy. I have even written the introductory letter; and if I can pick up a few guineas this way, I feel they will be most *refreshing,* bread being so dear. If I go on with it, I will apprise you of it, as you may like to see my things! and the *tulip,* of all flowers, loves to be admired most.

Pray pardon me, if my letters do not come very thick. I am so taken up with one thing or other, that I cannot pick out (I will not say time, but) fitting times to write to you. My dear love to Lloyd and Sophia, and pray split this thin letter into three parts, and present them with the *two biggest* in my name.

They are my oldest friends; but, ever the new friend driveth out the old, as the ballad sings! God bless you all three! I would hear from Lloyd if I could.

Flour has just fallen nine shillings a sack: we shall be all too rich.

Tell Charles I have seen his mamma, and have almost fallen in love with *her,* since I mayn't with Olivia. She is so fine and graceful, a complete matron-lady-quaker. She has given me two little books. Olivia grows a charming girl—full of feeling, and thinner than she was; but I have not time to fall in love.

Mary presents her *general compliments*. She keeps in fine health.

Huzza boys! and down with the Atheists!

To SAMUEL TAYLOR COLERIDGE.

LETTER LVII.]   *May* 12, 1800.

My dear Coleridge—I don't know why I write, except from the propensity which misery has to tell her griefs. Hetty died on Friday night, about eleven o'clock, after eight days' illness. Mary, in consequence of fatigue and anxiety, is fallen ill again, and I was obliged to remove her yesterday. I am left alone in a house with nothing but Hetty's dead body to keep me company. To-morrow I bury her, and then I shall be quite alone, with nothing but a cat, to remind me that the house has been full of living beings like myself. My heart is quite sunk, and I don't know where to look for relief. Mary will get better again, but her constantly being liable to such relapses is dreadful; nor is it the least of our evils that her case and all our story is so well known around us. We are in a manner *marked*. Excuse my troubling you, but I have nobody by me to speak to me. I slept out last night, not being able to endure the change and the stillness; but I did not sleep well, and I must come back to my own bed. I am going to try and get a friend to come and be with me to-morrow. I am completely shipwrecked. My head is quite bad. I almost wish that Mary were dead. God bless you! Love to Sara and Hartley.   C. LAMB.

Monday.

To THOMAS MANNING.

Dear Manning—I am quite out of spirits, and feel as if I should never recover them. But why should not this pass away? I am foolish, but judge of me by my situation. Our servant is dead, and my sister is ill— so ill as to make a removal to a place of confinement absolutely necessary. I have been left *alone* in a house where but ten days since living beings were, and noises of life were heard. I have made the experiment and find I cannot bear it any longer. Last night I went to sleep at White's, with whom I am to be until I can find a settlement. I have given up my house, and must look out for lodgings. I expect Mary will get better before many weeks are gone,—but at present I feel my daily and hourly prop has fallen from me. I totter and stagger with weakness, for nobody can supply her place to me. White has *all kindness,* but not *sympathy.* R. Lloyd, my only correspondent, you except, is a good Being, but a weak one. I know not where to look but to you. If you will suffer me to weary your shoulders with part of my Burthen, I shall write again to let you know how I go on. Meantime a letter from you would be a considerable relief to me.—Believe me, yours most sincerely,

                                        C. L.

Dear Manning—I feel myself unable to thank you sufficiently for your kind letter. It was doubly acceptable to me, both for the choice poetry and the kind honest prose which it contained. It was just such a letter as I should have expected from Manning.

I am in much better spirits than when I wrote last. I have had a very eligible offer to lodge with a friend in town. He will have rooms to let at Midsummer; by which time I hope my sister will be well enough to join

print, or do it in better verses. It did well enough five years ago when I came to see you, and was moral coxcomb enough at the time you wrote the lines, to feed upon such epithets; but, besides that, the meaning of "gentle" is equivocal at best, and almost always means poor-spirited; the very quality of gentleness is abhorrent to such vile trumpetings. My *sentiment* is long since vanished. I hope my *virtues* have done *sucking*. I can scarce think but you meant it in joke. I hope you did, for I should be ashamed to believe that you could think to gratify me by such praise, fit only to be a cordial to some green-sick sonneteer.

I have hit off the following in imitation of old English poetry, which, I imagine, I am a dab at. The measure is unmeasurable; but it most resembles that beautiful ballad, the " Old and Young Courtier ;" and in its feature of taking the extremes of two situations for just parallel, it resembles the old poetry certainly. If I could but stretch out the circumstances to twelve more verses, *i.e.*, if I had as much genius as the writer of that old song, I think it would be excellent. It was to follow an imitation of Burton in prose, which you have not seen. But fate "and wisest Stewart" say No.

I can send you 200 pens and six quires of paper *immediately*, if they will answer the carriage by coach. It would be foolish to pack 'em up *cum multis libris et cæteris;* they would all spoil. I only wait your commands to coach them. I would pay five-and-forty thousand carriages to read W.'s tragedy, of which I have heard so much and seen so little—only what I saw at Stowey. Pray give me an order in writing on Longman for *Lyrical Ballads.* I have the first volume, and, truth to tell, six shillings is a broad shot. I cram all I can in, to save a multiplying of letters,—those pretty comets with swinging tails.

I'll just crowd in, God bless you ! C. Lamb.

Wednesday night.

To THOMAS MANNING.

Dear Manning—I am going to ask a favour of you, and am at a loss how to do it in the most delicate manner. For this purpose I have been looking into Pliny's Letters, who is noted to have had the best grace in begging of all the ancients (I read him in the elegant translation of Mr. Melmoth), but not finding any case there exactly similar with mine, I am constrained to beg in my own barbarian way. To come to the point then, and hasten into the middle of things : have you a copy of your Algebra to give away? I do not ask it for myself; I have too much reverence for the Black Arts ever to approach thy circle, illustrious Trismegist! But that worthy man, and excellent poet, George Dyer, made me a visit yesternight, on purpose to borrow one ; supposing, rationally enough, I must say, that you had made me a present of one before this ; the omission of which I take to have proceeded only from negligence ; but it is a fault. I could lend him no assistance. You must know he is just now diverted from the pursuit of the BELL LETTERS by a paradox, which he has heard his friend Frend (that learned mathematician) maintain, that the negative quantities of mathematicians were *meræ nugæ*, things scarcely *in rerum naturâ*, and smacking too much of mystery for gentlemen of Mr. Frend's clear Unitarian capacity. However, the dispute once set a-going, has seized violently on George's pericranick ; and it is necessary for his health that he should speedily come to a resolution of his doubts. He goes about teasing his friends with his new mathematics : he even frantically talks of purchasing Manning's Algebra, which shows him far gone ; for, to my knowledge, he has not been master of seven shillings a good time. George's pockets and ——'s brain are two things in nature which do not abhor a vacuum. . . . Now, if you could step in, in this trembling suspense of his reason, and he should find on Saturday morning, lying for him at the Porter's Lodge, Clifford's Inn (his safest address), Manning's Algebra, with a neat manuscript in the blank leaf, running thus " FROM THE AUTHOR," it might save his wits, and restore the unhappy author to those studies of poetry and criticism which are at present suspended, to the infinite regret of the whole literary world. *N.B.*— Dirty backs, smeared leaves, and dogs' ears, will be rather a recommendation than otherwise. *N.B.*—He must have the book as soon as possible, or nothing can withhold him from madly purchasing the book on tick. . . . Then shall we see him sweetly restored to the chair of Longinus—to dictate in smooth and modest phrase the laws of verse; to prove that Theocritus first introduced the Pastoral, and Virgil and Pope brought it to its perfection; that Gray and Mason (who always hunt in couples in George's brain) have shown a great deal of poetical fire in their lyric poetry; that Aristotle's rules are not to be servilely followed, which George has shown to have imposed great shackles upon modern genius. His poems, I find, are to consist of two vols.— reasonable octavo; and a third book will exclusively contain criticisms, in which he asserts he has gone *pretty deeply* into the laws of blank verse and rhyme—epic poetry, dramatic and pastoral ditto—all which is to come out before Christmas. But, above all, he has *touched* most *deeply* upon the Drama, comparing the English with the modern German stage, their merits and defects. Apprehending that his *studies* (not to mention his *turn*, which I take to be chiefly towards the lyrical poetry) hardly qualified him for these disquisitions, I modestly inquired what plays he had read? I found by George's reply that he *had* read Shakspeare, but that was a good while since : he calls him a great but irregular genius, which I think to be an original and just remark.

Beaumont and Fletcher, Massinger, Ben Jonson, Shirley, Marlowe, Ford, and the worthies of Dodsley's Collection —he confessed he had read none of them, but professed his *intention* of looking through them all, so as to be able to *touch* upon them in his book.   So Shakspeare, Otway, and I believe Rowe, to whom he was naturally directed by Johnson's Lives, and these not read lately, are to stand him in stead of a general knowledge of the subject.   God bless his dear absurd head!

By the by, did I not write you a letter with something about an invitation in it?   But let that pass; I suppose it is not agreeable.

N.B.—It would not be amiss if you were to accompany your *present* with a dissertation on negative quantities.   C. L.

LETTER LXIV.]   1800.

George Dyer is an Archimedes, and an Archimagus, and a Tycho Brahe, and a Copernicus; and thou art the darling of the Nine, and midwife to their wandering babe also!   We take tea with that learned poet and critic on Tuesday night, at half-past five, in his neat library.   The repast will be light and Attic, with criticism.   If thou couldst contrive to wheel up thy dear carcass on the Monday, and after dining with us on tripe, calves' kidneys, or whatever else the Cornucopia of St. Clare may be willing to pour out on the occasion, might we not adjourn together to the Heathen's—thou with thy Black Back, and I with some innocent volume of the Bell Letters, Shenstone, or the like: it would make him wash his old flannel gown (that has not been washed to my knowledge since it has been *his*—Oh the long time!) with tears of joy.   Thou shouldst settle his scruples and unravel his cobwebs, and sponge off the sad stuff that weighs upon his dear wounded pia mater.   Thou shouldst restore light to his eyes, and him to his friends and the public.   Parnassus should shower her civic crowns upon thee for saving the wits of a citizen ! I thought I saw a lucid interval in George the other night; he broke in upon my studies just at tea-time, and brought with him Dr. Anderson, an old gentleman who ties his breeches' knees with packthread, and boasts that he has been disappointed by ministers. The Doctor wanted to see *me ;* for I being a Poet, he thought I might furnish him with a copy of verses to suit his *Agricultural Magazine*. The Doctor, in the course of the conversation, mentioned a poem called the "Epigoniad," by one Wilkie, an epic poem, in which there is not one tolerable good line all through, but every incident and speech borrowed from Homer. George had been sitting inattentive, seemingly, to what was going on—hatching of negative quantities—when, suddenly, the name of his old friend Homer stung his pericranicks, and, jumping up, he begged to know where he could meet with Wilkie's works. It was a curious fact, he said, that there should be such an epic poem and he not know of it; and he *must* get a copy of it, as he was going to touch pretty deeply upon the subject of the Epic—and he was sure there must be some things good in a poem of 8000 lines ! I was pleased with this transient return of his reason and recurrence to his old ways of thinking: it gave me great hopes of a recovery, which nothing but your book can completely insure. Pray come on Monday, if you *can*, and stay your own time. I have a good large room with two beds in it, in the handsomest of which thou shalt repose a-nights, and dream of Spheroides. I hope you will understand by the nonsense of this letter that I am *not* melancholy at the thoughts of thy coming: I thought it necessary to add this, because you love *precision*. Take notice that our stay at Dyer's will not exceed eight o'clock; after which our pursuits will be our own. But indeed I think a little recreation among the Bell Letters and poetry will do you some service in the interval of severer studies. I hope we shall fully discuss with George Dyer what I have never yet heard done to my

satisfaction, the reason of Dr. Johnson's malevolent stric-
tures on the higher species of the Ode.

LETTER LXV.] [*August* 9, 1800.]

Dear Manning—I suppose you have heard of Sophia
Lloyd's good fortune, and paid the customary compliments to the parents. Heaven keep the new-born infant
from star blasting and moon blasting, from epilepsy,
marasmus, and the devil! May he live to see many
days, and they good ones; some friends, and they *pretty
regular correspondents!* with as much wit and wisdom
as will eat their bread and cheese together under a poor
roof without quarrelling! as much goodness as will earn
heaven. Here I must leave off, my benedictory powers
failing me.

And now, when shall I catch a glimpse of your honest
face-to-face countenance again?—your fine *dogmatical
sceptical* face by punch-light? Oh! one glimpse of the
human face, and shake of the human hand, is better than
whole reams of this cold, thin correspondence; yea, of
more worth than all the letters that have sweated the
fingers of sensibility, from Madame Sévigné and Balzac
to Sterne and Shenstone.

Coleridge is settled with his wife and the young
philosopher at Keswick, with the Wordsworths. They
have contrived to spawn a new volume of lyrical ballads,
which is to see the light in about a month, and causes
no little excitement in the *literary world*. George Dyer
too, that good-natured heathen, is more than nine months
gone with his twin volumes of ode, pastoral, sonnet, elegy,
Spenserian, Horatian, Akensidish, and Masonic verse.
Clio prosper the birth! it will be twelve shillings out of
somebody's pocket. I find he means to exclude " personal satire," so it appears by his truly original advertisement. Well, God put it into the hearts of the English
gentry to come in shoals and subscribe to his poems, for

He never put a kinder heart into flesh of man than
George Dyer's !

Now farewell, for dinner is at hand.   C. L.

LETTER LXVI.]   *August* 11, 1800.

My dear fellow (*N.B.* mighty familiar of late !) for
me to come to Cambridge now is one of heaven's impossibilities. Metaphysicians tell us, even it can work
nothing which implies a contradiction. I can explain
this by telling you that I am engaged to do double duty
(this hot weather !) for a man who has taken advantage
of this very weather to go and cool himself in " green
retreats " all the month of August.

But for you to come to London instead !—muse upon
it, revolve it, cast it about in your mind. I have a bed
at your command. You shall drink rum, brandy, gin,
aqua-vitæ, usquebaugh, or whiskey a' nights ; and for the
after-dinner trick, I have eight bottles of genuine port,
which, mathematically divided, gives $1\frac{1}{7}$ for every day
you stay, provided you stay a week. Hear John
Milton sing,

> " Let Euclid rest and Archimedes pause."
> *Twenty-first Sonnet.*

And elsewhere,—

> " What neat repast shall feast us, light [1] and choice,
> Of Attic taste, with wine,[2] whence we may rise
> To hear the lute well touch'd, or artful voice
> Warble immortal notes and Tuscan air ? "

Indeed the poets are full of this pleasing morality,—

> " Veni cito, Domine Manning ! "

Think upon it. Excuse the paper ; it is all I have.

                    C. LAMB.

[1] We poets generally give *light* dinners.
[2] No doubt the poet here alludes to port wine at 38s. the
dozen.

To SAMUEL TAYLOR COLERIDGE.

LETTER LXVII.]   *August* 14, 1800.

My head is playing all the tunes in the world, ringing such peals! It has just finished the "Merry Christ Church Bells," and absolutely is beginning "Turn again, Whittington," Buz, buz, buz, bum, bum, bum, wheeze, wheeze, wheeze, fen, fen, fen, tinky, tinky, tinky, *cr'annch.* I shall certainly come to be condemned at last. I have been drinking too much for two days running. I find my moral sense in the last stage of a consumption, and my religion getting faint. This is disheartening; but I trust the devil will not overpower me. In the midst of this infernal larum, Conscience is barking and yelping as loud as any of them. I have sat down to read over again your satire upon me in the *Anthology*, and I think I do begin to spy out something like beauty and design in it. I perfectly accede to all your alterations, and only desire that you had cut deeper, when your hand was in.

In sober truth, I cannot see any great truth in the little dialogue called "Blenheim." It is rather novel and pretty, but the thought is very obvious and is but poor prattle, a thing of easy imitation. *Pauper vult videri et est.*

In the next edition of the *Anthology* (which Phœbus avert, and those nine other wandering maids also!) please to blot out "gentle-hearted," and substitute drunken dog, ragged head, seld-shaven, odd-eyed, stuttering, or any other epithet which truly and properly belongs to the gentleman in question. And for Charles read Tom, or Bob, or Richard for mere delicacy. Hang you, I was beginning to forgive you, and believe in earnest that the lugging in of my proper name was purely unintentional on your part, when looking back for further conviction, stares me in the face, "Charles Lamb of the *India House.*" *Now* I am convinced it was all done in malice,

heaped sack-upon-sack, congregated, studied malice.   You
dog! your 141st page shall not save you.   I own I was
just ready to acknowledge that there is a something not
unlike good poetry in that page, if you had not run into
the unintelligible abstraction-fit about the manner of the
Deity's making spirits perceive his presence.   God, nor
created thing alive can receive any honour from such thin
show-box attributes.   By the by, where did you pick up
that scandalous piece of private history about the angel
and the Duchess of Devonshire?   If it is a fiction of your
own, why truly it was a very modest one *for you*.   Now
I do affirm, that "Lewti" is a very beautiful poem.   I
was in earnest when I praised it.   It describes a silly
species of one not the wisest of passions.   *Therefore* it
cannot deeply affect a disenthralled mind.   But such
imagery, such novelty, such delicacy, and such versification never got into an *Anthology* before.   I am only
sorry that the cause of all the passionate complaint is
not greater than the trifling circumstance of Lewti being
out of temper one day.   "Gaulberto" certainly has considerable originality, but sadly wants finishing.   It is,
as it is, one of the very best in the book.   Next to
"Lewti" I like the "Raven," which has a good deal of
humour.   I was pleased to see it again, for you once
sent it me, and I have lost the letter which contained it.
Now I am on the subject of Anthologies, I must say I
am sorry the old pastoral way has fallen into disrepute.
The gentry which now indite sonnets are certainly the
legitimate descendants of the ancient shepherds.   The
same simpering face of description, the old family face, is
visibly continued in the line.   Some of their ancestors'
labours are yet to be found in Allan Ramsay's and Jacob
Tonson's Miscellanies.   But miscellanies decaying, and
the old pastoral way dying of mere want, their successors
(driven from their paternal acres) now-a-days settle and
lie upon Magazines and Anthologies.   This race of men
are uncommonly addicted to superstition.   Some of them
are idolaters, and worship the moon.   Others deify

qualities, as Love, Friendship, Sensibility; or bare accidents, as Solitude. Grief and Melancholy have their respective altars and temples among them, as the heathens builded theirs to Mors, Febris, Pallor, etc. They all agree in ascribing a peculiar sanctity to the number 14. One of their own legislators affirmeth, that whatever exceeds that number "encroacheth upon the province of the elegy"—*vice versa*, whatever "cometh short of that number abutteth upon the premises of the epigram." I have been able to discover but few *images* in their temples, which, like the caves of Delphos of old, are famous for giving *echoes*. They impute a religious importance to the letter O, whether because by its round-ness it is thought to typify the moon, their principal goddess, or for its analogies to their own labours, all ending where they began, or for whatever other high and mystical reference, I have never been able to discover, but I observe they never begin their invocations to their gods without it, except indeed one insignificant sect among them, who use the Doric A, pronounced like Ah ! broad, instead. These boast to have restored the old Dorian mood.

Now I am on the subject of poetry, I must announce to you, who doubtless in your remote part of the island have not heard tidings of so great a blessing, that George Dyer hath prepared two ponderous volumes full of poetry and criticism. They impend over the town, and are threatened to fall in the Winter. The first volume con-tains every sort of poetry, except personal satire, which George, in his truly original prospectus, renounceth for ever, whimsically foisting the intention in between the price of his book and the proposed number of subscribers. (If I can, I will get you a copy of his *handbill*.) He has tried his *vein* in every species besides—the Spenserian, Thomsonian, Masonic, and Akensidish more especially. The second volume is all criticism; wherein he demon-strates to the entire satisfaction of the literary world, in a way that must silence all reply for ever, that the

Pastoral was introduced by Theocritus, and polished by Virgil and Pope; that Gray and Mason (who always hunt in couples in George's brain) have a good deal of poetical fire and true lyric genius; that Cowley was ruined by excess of wit (a warning to all moderns); that Charles Lloyd, Charles Lamb, and William Wordsworth, in later days, have struck the true chords of poesy. O George, George! with a head uniformly wrong, and a heart uniformly right, that I had power and might equal to my wishes: then I would call the gentry of thy native island, and they should come in troops, flocking at the sound of thy prospectus trumpet, and crowding who shall be first to stand in thy list of subscribers! I can only put twelve shillings into thy pocket (which, I will answer for them, will not stick there long), out of a pocket almost as bare as thine. Is it not a pity so much fine writing should be erased? But, to tell the truth, I began to scent that I was getting into that sort of style which Longinus and Dionysius Halicarnassus aptly call "the affected."   C. L.

To THOMAS MANNING.

LETTER LXVIII.]   *August* 22, 1800.

Dear Manning—You needed not imagine any apology necessary. Your fine hare and fine birds (which are just now dangling by our kitchen blaze) discourse most eloquent music in your justification. You just nicked my palate. For with all due decorum and leave may it be spoken, my worship hath taken physic to-day, and being low and puling, requireth to be pampered. Foh! how beautiful and strong those buttered onions come to my nose! For you know we extract a divine spirit of gravy from those materials, which, duly compounded with a consistence of bread and cream (y'clept bread-sauce), each to each giving double grace, do mutually illustrate and set off (as skilful gold foils to rare jewels)

your partridge, pheasant, woodcock, snipe, teal, widgeon
and the other lesser daughters of the ark. My friendship, struggling with my carnal and fleshly prudence
(which suggests that a bird a man is the proper allotment
in such cases), yearneth sometimes to have thee here to
pick a wing or so. I question if your Norfolk sauces
match our London culinaric.

George Dyer has introduced me to the table of an
agreeable old gentleman, Dr. Anderson, who gives hot
legs of mutton and grape pies at his sylvan lodge at
Isleworth ; where, in the middle of a street, he has shot
up a wall most preposterously before his small dwelling,
which, with the circumstance of his taking several panes
of glass out of bed-room windows (for air), causeth his
neighbours to speculate strangely on the state of the
good man's pericranicks. Plainly, he lives under the
reputation of being deranged. George does not mind
this circumstance ; he rather likes him the better for it.
The Doctor, in his pursuits, joins agricultural to poetical
science, and has set George's brains mad about the old
Scotch writers, Barbour, Douglas's Æneid, Blind Harry,
etc. We returned home in a return postchaise (having
dined with the Doctor), and George kept wondering and
wondering, for eight or nine turnpike miles, what was
the name, and striving to recollect the name, of a poet
anterior to Barbour. I begged to know what was
remaining of his works. "There is nothing *extant* of
his works, Sir ; but by all accounts he seems to have
been a fine genius !" This fine genius, without anything
to show for it, or any title beyond George's courtesy,
without even a name ; and Barbour, and Douglas, and
Blind Harry now are the predominant sounds in George's
pia mater, and their buzzings exclude politics, criticism,
and algebra—the late lords of that illustrious lumber-
room. Mark, he has never read any of these books, but
is impatient till he reads them *all* at the Doctor's suggestion. Poor Dyer ! his friends should be careful what
sparks they let fall into such inflammable matter.

Lloyd, and all Lloyd's family; but I could not get him to betray his trust by giving *me* a sight of it. Lloyd is sadly deficient in some of those virtuous vices. I have just lit upon a most beautiful fiction of Hell punishments by the author of *Hurlothrumbo*, a mad farce. The inventor imagines that in Hell there is a great caldron of hot water, in which a man can scarce hold his finger, and an immense sieve over it, into which the probationary souls are put—

> " And all the little souls
> Pop thro' the riddle holes ! "

George Dyer is the only literary character I am happily acquainted with. The oftener I see him, the more deeply I admire him. He is goodness itself. If I could but calculate the precise date of his death, I would write a novel on purpose to make George the hero. I could hit him off to a hair.

George brought a Dr. Anderson to see me. The doctor is a very pleasant old man, a great genius for agriculture, one that ties his breeches-knees with pack-thread, and boasts of having had disappointments from ministers. The doctor happened to mention an epic poem by one Wilkie, called the *Epigoniad*, in which he assured us there is not one tolerable line from beginning to end, but that all the characters, incidents, etc., are verbally copied from *Homer*. George, who had been sitting quite inattentive to the Doctor's criticism, no sooner heard the sound of *Homer* strike his pericranicks, than up he gets, and declares he must see that poem immediately : where was it to be had ? An epic poem of 8000 lines, and *he* not hear of it ! There must be some good things in it, and it was necessary he should see it, for he had touched pretty deeply upon that subject in his criticisms on the Epic. George has touched pretty deeply upon the Lyric, I find ; he has also prepared a dissertation on the Drama and the comparison of the English and German theatres. As I rather doubted his competency to do the latter, knowing that his peculiar *turn* lies in the lyric species of composition, I questioned George what English plays he had read. I found that he *had* read Shakspeare (whom he calls an original, but irregular, genius); but it was a good while ago; and he has dipped into Rowe and Otway, I suppose having found their names in *Johnson's Lives* at full length; and upon this slender ground he has undertaken the task. He never seemed even to have heard of Fletcher, Ford, Marlowe, Massinger, and the worthies of Dodsley's collection; but he is to read all these, to prepare him for bringing out his "Parallel" in the Winter. I find he is also determined to vindicate poetry from the shackles which Aristotle and some others have imposed upon it, which is very good-natured of him, and very necessary just now. Now I am *touching* so *deeply* upon poetry, can I forget that I have just received from Cottle a magnificent copy of his Guinea *Alfred*. Four-and-twenty books to read in the dog-days! I got as far as the Mad Monk the first day, and fainted. Mr. Cottle's genius strongly points him to the *Pastoral*, but his inclinations divert him perpetually from his calling. He imitates Southey, as Rowe did Shakspeare, with his "Good morrow to ye; good master Lieutenant." Instead of *a* man, *a* woman, *a* daughter, he constantly writes, one a man, one a woman, one his daughter. Instead of *the* king, *the* hero, he constantly writes, he the king, he the hero; two flowers of rhetoric, palpably from the "Joan." But Mr. Cottle soars a higher pitch: and when he *is* original, it is in a most original way indeed. His terrific scenes are indefatigable. Serpents, asps, spiders, ghosts, dead bodies, staircases made of nothing, with adders' tongues for bannisters. What a brain he must have! He puts as many plums in his pudding as my grandmother used to do;—and then his emerging from Hell's horrors into light, and treading on pure flats of this earth—for twenty-three books together !   C. L.

To THOMAS MANNING.

C. L.'s moral sense presents her compliments to Doctor Manning, is very thankful for his medical advice, but is happy to add that her disorder has died of itself.

Dr. Manning, Coleridge has left us, to go into the North, on a visit to Wordsworth. With him have flown all my splendid prospects of engagement with the *Morning Post*, all my visionary guineas, the deceitful wages of unborn scandal. In truth, I wonder you took it up so seriously. All my intention was but to make a little sport with such public and fair game as Mr. Pitt, Mr. Wilberforce, Mrs. Fitzherbert, the Devil, etc.— gentry dipped in Styx all over, whom no paper-javelin-lings can touch. To have made free with these cattle, where was the harm? 'twould have been but giving a polish to lamp-black, not nigrifying a negro primarily. After all, I cannot but regret my involuntary virtue. Damn virtue that's thrust upon us; it behaves itself with such constraint, till conscience opens the window and lets out the goose. I had struck off two imitations of Burton, quite abstracted from any modern allusions, which it was my intent only to lug in from time to time to make 'em popular.

Stuart has got these, with an introductory letter; but, not hearing from him, I have ceased from my labours, but I write to him to-day to get a final answer. I am afraid they won't do for a paper. Burton is a scarce gentleman, not much known, else I had done 'em pretty well.

I have also hit off a few lines in the name of Burton, being a " Conceit of Diabolic Possession." Burton was a man often assailed by deepest melancholy, and at other times much given to laughing and jesting, as is the way with melancholy men. I will send them to you: they were almost extempore, and no great things; but you will indulge them. Robert Lloyd is come to town. Priscilla meditates going to see *Pizarro* at Drury Lane to-night (from her uncle's), under cover of coming to dine with me . . . *heu tempora ! heu mores !*—I have barely time to finish, as I expect her and Robin every minute. —Yours as usual.   C. L.

To SAMUEL TAYLOR COLERIDGE.

LETTER LXXIII.]   *October* 9, 1800.

I suppose you have heard of the death of Amos Cottle. I paid a solemn visit of condolence to his brother, accompanied by George Dyer, of burlesque memory. I went, trembling to see poor Cottle so immediately upon the event. He was in black; and his younger brother was also in black. Everything wore an aspect suitable to the respect due to the freshly dead. For some time after our entrance, nobody spake till George modestly put in a question, whether *Alfred* was likely to sell. This was Lethe to Cottle, and his poor face, wet with tears, and his kind eye brightened up in a moment. Now I felt it was my cue to speak. I had to thank him for a present of a magnificent copy, and had promised to send him my remarks,—the least thing I could do; so I ventured to suggest, that I perceived a considerable improvement he had made in his first book since the state in which he first read it to me. Joseph, who till now had sat with his knees cowering in by the fireplace, wheeled about, and with great difficulty of body shifted the same round to the corner of a table where I was sitting, and first stationing one thigh over the other, which is his sedentary mood, and placidly fixing his benevolent face right against mine, waited my observations. At that moment it came strongly into my mind, that I had got Uncle Toby before me, he looked so kind and so good. I could not say an

this monster, like Aaron's serpent, swallowed up the impression of the rest. He opened his cursed mouth, when he made at me, as wide as his head was broad. I hallooed out quite loud, and felt pains all over my body with the fright.

I have had the felicity of hearing George Dyer read out one book of the *Farmer's Boy*. I thought it rather childish. No doubt, there is originality in it (which, in your self-taught geniuses, is a most rare quality, they generally getting hold of some bad models, in a scarcity of books, and forming their taste on them), but no *selection*. *All* is described.

Mind, I have only heard read one book.—Yours sincerely, Philo-Snake,   C. L.

LETTER LXXVI.]   *November* 3, 1800.

Ecquid meditatur Archimedes ? What is Euclid doing? What hath happened to learned Trismegist? Doth he take it in ill part, that his humble friend did not comply with his courteous invitation? Let it suffice, I could not come. Are impossibilities nothing ?—be they abstractions of the intellect ?—or not (rather) most sharp and mortifying realities? nuts in the Will's mouth too hard for her to crack? brick and stone walls in her way, which she can by no means eat through? sore lets, *impedimenta viarum* no thoroughfares? *racemi nimium alte pendentes ?* Is the phrase classic? I allude to the grapes in Æsop, which cost the fox a strain, and gained the world an aphorism. Observe the superscription of this letter. In adapting the size of the letters, which constitute *your* name and Mr. *Crisp's* name respectively, I had an eye to your different stations in life. 'Tis truly curious, and must be soothing to an *aristocrat*. I wonder it has never been hit on before my time. I have made an acquisition latterly of a *pleasant hand*, one Rickman, to whom I was introduced by George Dyer, not the most flattering auspices under which one man can be introduced to another. George brings all sorts of people together, setting up a sort of agrarian law, or common property, in matter of society; but for once he has done me a great pleasure, while he was only pursuing a principle, as *ignes fatui may* light you home. This Rickman lives in our Buildings, immediately opposite our house; the finest fellow to drop in a' nights, about nine or ten o'clock— cold bread and cheese time—just in the *wishing* time of the night, when you *wish* for somebody to come in, without a distinct idea of a probable anybody. Just in the nick, neither too early to be tedious, nor too late to sit a reasonable time. He is a most pleasant hand; a fine rattling fellow, has gone through life laughing at solemn apes;—himself hugely literate, oppressively full of information in all stuff of conversation, from matter of fact to Xenophon and Plato—can talk Greek with Porson, politics with Thelwall, conjecture with George Dyer, nonsense with me, and anything with anybody; a great farmer, somewhat concerned in an agricultural magazine; reads no poetry but Shakspeare; very intimate with Southey, but never reads his poetry; relishes George Dyer; thoroughly penetrates into the ridiculous wherever found; understands the *first time* (a great desideratum in common minds)—you need never twice speak to him; does not want explanations, translations, limitations, as Professor Godwin does when you make an assertion; *up* to anything; *down* to everything; whatever *sapit hominem*. A perfect *man*. All this farrago, which must perplex you to read, and has put me to a little trouble to *select*, only proves how impossible it is to describe a *pleasant hand*. You must see Rickman to know him, for he is a species in one; a new class; an exotic; any slip of which I am proud to put in my garden-pot; the clearest headed fellow; fullest of matter, with least verbosity. If there be any alloy in my fortune to have met with such a man, it is that he commonly divides his time between town and country, having some foolish family ties at Christchurch, by which means he can only gladden our London hemisphere with returns of light.   He is now going for six weeks.

At last I have written to Kemble, to know the event of my play, which was presented last Christmas.   As I suspected, came an answer back that the copy was lost, and could not be found—no hint that anybody had to this day ever looked into it—with a courteous (reasonable!) request of another copy (if I had one by me), and a promise of a definite answer in a week.   I could not resist so facile and moderate a demand ; so scribbled out another, omitting sundry things, such as the witch story, about half of the forest scene (which is too leisurely for story), and transposing that soliloquy about England getting drunk, which, like its reciter, stupidly stood alone, nothing prevenient or antevenient ; and cleared away a good deal besides ; and sent this copy, written *all out* (with alterations, etc., *requiring judgment*) in one day and a half! I sent it last night, and am in weekly expectation of the tolling bell and death-warrant.

This is all my London news.   Send me some from the *banks of Cam*, as the poets delight to speak, especially George Dyer, who has no other name nor idea nor definition of Cambridge.   Its being a market town, sending members to Parliament, never entered into his definition. It was and is simply the banks of the Cam, or the fair Cam, as Oxford is the banks of the Isis, or the fair Isis. Yours in all humility, most illustrious Trismegist,

C. LAMB.

(Read on ; there's more at the bottom.)

You ask me about the *Farmer's Boy.*   Don't you think the fellow who wrote it (who is a shoemaker) has a poor mind?   Don't you find he is always silly about *poor Giles,* and those abject kind of phrases, which mark a man that looks up to wealth?   None of Burns's poet dignity.   What do you think?   I have just opened him; but he makes me sick.

Dyer knows the shoemaker, a damn'd stupid hound in company; but George promises to introduce him indiscriminately to all friends.

LETTER LXXVII.]   *November* 28, 1800.

Dear Manning—I have received a very kind invitation from Lloyd and Sophia, to go and spend a month with them at the Lakes. Now it fortunately happens (which is so seldom the case) that I have spare cash by me, enough to answer the expenses of so long a journey; and I am determined to get away from the office by some means. The purpose of this letter is to request of you (my dear friend), that you will not take it unkind if I decline my proposed visit to Cambridge *for the present.* Perhaps I shall be able to take Cambridge *in my way,* going or coming. I need not describe to you the expectations which such an one as myself, pent up all my life in a dirty city, have formed of a tour to the Lakes. Consider Grasmere! Ambleside! Wordsworth! Coleridge! I hope you will. Hills, woods, lakes, and mountains, to the devil. I will eat snipes with thee, Thomas Manning. Only confess, confess, a *bite.*

P.S.—I think you named the 16th; but was it not modest of Lloyd to send such an invitation! It shows his knowledge of *money* and *time.* I should be loth to think he meant

> " Ironic satire sidelong sklented
> On my poor pursie."—BURNS.

For my part, with reference to my friends northward, I must confess that I am not romance-bit about *Nature.* The earth, and sea, and sky (when all is said), is but as a house to dwell in. If the inmates be courteous, and good liquors flow like the conduits at an old coronation, if they can talk sensibly, and feel properly, I have no need to stand staring upon the gilded looking-glass (that strained my friend's purse-strings in the purchase) nor his five-shilling print, over the mantelpiece, of old Nabbs the carrier (which only betrays his false taste). Just as important to me (in a sense) is all the furniture of my world; eye-pampering, but satisfies no heart. Streets, streets, streets, markets, theatres, churches, Covent Gardens, shops sparkling with pretty faces of industrious milliners, neat sempstresses, ladies cheapening, gentlemen behind counters lying, authors in the street with spectacles, George Dyers (you may know them by their gait), lamps lit at night, pastrycooks' and silversmiths' shops, beautiful Quakers of Pentonville, noise of coaches, drowsy cry of mechanic watchmen at night, with bucks reeling home drunk; if you happen to wake at midnight, cries of "Fire!" and "Stop thief!"; inns of court, with their learned air, and halls, and butteries, just like Cambridge colleges; old book-stalls, "Jeremy Taylors," "Burtons on Melancholy," and "Religio Medicis," on every stall. These are thy pleasures, O London! with thy many sins. O City, abounding in w . . ., for these may Keswick and her giant brood go hang! C. L.

To WILLIAM GODWIN.

LETTER LXXVIII.]

Thursday Morning,
December 4, 1800.

Dear Sir—I send this speedily after the heels of Cooper (O! the dainty expression) to say that Mary is obliged to stay at home on Sunday to receive a female friend, from whom I am equally glad to escape. So that we shall be by ourselves. I write, because it may make *some* difference in your marketing, etc. C. L.

I am sorry to put you to the expense of twopence postage. But I calculate thus: if Mary comes she will——

eat Beef 2 plates,	.	4d.
Batter Pudding 1 do. .	.	2d.
Beer, a pint, . . .	.	2d.
Wine, 3 glasses,	.	11d. I drink no wine !
Chesnuts, after dinner,	.	2d.
Tea and supper at moderate calculation, . .	.	9d.

$$\text{2s. 6d.}$$

From which deduct   2d. postage.

$$\text{2s. 4d.}$$

You are a clear gainer by her not coming.

LETTER LXXIX.]

Wednesday Morning,
December 11, 1800.

Dear Sir—I expected a good deal of pleasure from your company to-morrow, but I am sorry I must beg of you to excuse me. I have been confined ever since I saw you with one of the severest colds I ever experienced, occasioned by being in the night air on Sunday and on the following day very foolishly. I am neither in health nor spirits to meet company. I hope and trust I shall get out on Saturday night. You will add to your many favours by transmitting to me as early as possible as many tickets as conveniently you can spare,—Yours truly,   C. L.

I have been plotting how to abridge the Epilogue. But I cannot see that any lines can be spared, retaining the connection, except these two, which are better out.

" Why should I instance, etc.,
  The sick man's purpose, etc.,"

and then the following line must run thus,

" The truth by an example best is shown."

Excuse this *important* postscript.

A *breach of promise* was a sort of crime—
Which of you handsome English ladies here,
But deems the penance bloody and severe?
A whimsical old Saragossa fashion,
That a dead father's dying inclination,
Should *live* to thwart a living daughter's passion :
Unjustly on the sex *we* men exclaim,
Rail at *your* vices,—and commit the same ;—
Man is a promise-breaker from the womb,
And goes a promise-breaker to the tomb—
What need we instance here the lover's vow,
The sick man's purpose, or the great man's bow ?
The truth by few examples best is shown—
Instead of many which are better known,
Take poor Jack Incident, that's dead and gone.
Jack," etc. etc. etc.

Now you have it all—how do you like it ? I am
going to hear it recited ! ! !   C. L.

To WILLIAM GODWIN.

LETTER LXXXI.]   *Late o' Sunday, December* 14, 1800.

Dear Sir—I have performed my office in a slovenly
way, but judge for me. I sat down at six o'clock, and
never left reading (and I read out to Mary) your play till
10. In this sitting I noted down lines as they occurred,
exactly as you will read my rough paper. Do not be
frightened at the bulk of my remarks, for they are almost
all upon single lines, which, put together, do not amount
to a hundred, and many of them merely verbal. I had
but one object in view, abridgment for compression sake.
I have used a dogmatical language (which is truly ludicrous when the trivial nature of my remarks is considered);
and, remember, my office was to hunt out faults. You
may fairly abridge one half of them, as a fair deduction
for the infirmities of Error and a single reading, which
leaves only fifty objections, most of them merely against
words, on no short play. Remember, you constituted me

Executioner, and a hangman has been seldom seen to be ashamed of his profession before Master Sheriff. We'll talk of the Beauties (of which I am more than ever sure) when we meet.—Yours truly,   C. L.

I will barely add, as you are on the very point of printing, that in my opinion neither prologue nor epilogue should accompany the play. It can only serve to remind your readers of its fate. *Both* suppose an audience, and, that jest being gone, must convert into burlesque. Nor would I (but therein custom and decorum must be a law) print the actors' names. Some things must be kept out of sight.

I have done, and I have but a few square inches of paper to fill up. I am emboldened by a little jorum of punch (vastly good) to say that next to *one man*, I am the most hurt at our ill success. The breast of Hecuba, where she did suckle Hector, looked not to be more lovely than Marshal's forehead when it spit forth sweat, at Critic-swords contending. I remember two honest lines by Marvel (whose poems by the way I am just going to possess).

> " Where every Mower's wholesome heat
>   Smells like an Alexander's sweat."

To THOMAS MANNING.

LETTER LXXXII.]   *December* 16, 1800.

We are damn'd !—Not the facetious epilogue itself could save us ; for, as the editor of the *Morning Post* (quick-sighted gentleman !) hath this morning truly observed (I beg pardon if I falsify his *words ;* their profound *sense* I am sure I retain ;) both prologue and epilogue were worthy of accompanying such a piece ; and indeed (mark the profundity, Mr. Manning !) were received with proper indignation by such of the audience only as thought

either worth attending to. Professor, thy glories wax
dim ! Again, the incomparable author of the *True Briton*
declareth in *his* paper (bearing same date) that the epilogue
was an indifferent attempt at humour and character, and
failed in both. I forbear to mention the other papers,
because I have not read them. O Professor, how different
thy feelings now (*quantum mutatus ab illo professore,
qui in agris philosophiæ tantas victorias acquisivisti*),—
how different thy proud feelings but one little week ago
—thy anticipations of thy nine nights—those visionary
claps, which have soothed thy soul by day and thy dreams
by night ! Calling in accidentally on the Professor while
he was out, I was ushered into the study ; and my nose
quickly (most sagacious always) pointed me to four tokens
lying loose upon thy table, Professor, which indicated thy
violent and satanical pride of heart. *Imprimis*, there
caught mine eye a list of six persons, thy friends, whom
thou didst meditate inviting to a sumptuous dinner on
the Thursday, anticipating the profits of thy Saturday's
play to answer charges : I was in the honoured file !
Next (a stronger evidence of thy violent and almost
satanical pride) lay a list of all the morning papers (from
the *Morning Chronicle* downwards to the *Porcupine*),
with the places of their respective offices, where thou
wast meditating to insert, and didst insert, an elaborate
sketch of the story of thy play ; stones in thy enemy's
hand to bruise thee with, and severely wast thou bruised,
O Professor ! nor do I know what oil to pour into thy
wounds. Next (which convinced me to a dead conviction
of thy pride, violent and almost satanical pride !) lay a list
of books which thy un-tragedy-favoured pocket could
never answer ; Dodsley's Old Plays, Malone's Shakspeare
(still harping upon thy play, thy philosophy abandoned
meanwhile to Christians and superstitious minds) ; nay,
I believe (if I can believe my memory) that the ambitious
Encyclopædia itself was part of thy meditated acquisitions;
but many a playbook was there. All these visions are
damned ; and thou, Professor, must read Shakspeare in

future out of a common edition ; and, hark ye ! pray read
him to a little better purpose.   Last and strongest against
thee (in colours manifest as the hand upon Belshazzar's
wall) lay a volume of poems by C. Lloyd and C. Lamb.
Thy heart misgave thee, that thy assistant might possibly
not have talent enough to furnish thee an epilogue !
Manning, all these things came over my mind ; all the
gratulations that would have thickened upon him, and
even some have glanced aside upon his humble friend ;
the vanity, and the fame, and the profits (the Professor
is £500 ideal money out of pocket by this failure, besides
£200 he would have got for the copyright, and the Professor is never much beforehand with the world ; what
he gets is all by the sweat of his brow and dint of brain,
for the Professor, though a sure man, is also a slow) ;
and now to muse upon thy altered physiognomy, thy pale
and squalid appearance (a kind of *blue sickness* about the
eyelids), and thy crest fallen, and thy proud demand of
£200 from thy bookseller changed to an uncertainty of
his taking it at all, or giving the full £50.   The Professor
has won my heart by this *his* mournful catastrophe.   You
remember Marshall, who dined with him at my house ; I
met him in the lobby immediately after the damnation of
the Professor's play, and he looked to me like an angel ; his
face was lengthened, and all over perspiration.   I never
saw such a care-fraught visage ; I could have hugged him,
I loved him so intensely.   " From every pore of him a
perfume fell."   I have seen that man in many situations,
and, from my soul, I think that a more god-like honest
soul exists not in this world.   The Professor's poor nerves
trembling with the recent shock, he hurried him away to
my house to supper, and there we comforted him as well
as we could.   He came to consult me about a change of
catastrophe ; but alas ! the piece was condemned long
before that crisis.   I at first humoured him with a
specious proposition, but have since joined his true friends
in advising him to give it up.   He did it with a pang,
and is to print it as *his*.   L.

December 27, 1800.

At length George Dyer's phrenitis has come to a crisis ; he is raging and furiously mad. I waited upon the heathen, Thursday was a se'nnight. The first symptom which struck my eye, and gave me incontrovertible proof of the fatal truth, was a pair of nankeen pantaloons four times too big for him, which the said Heathen did pertinaciously affirm to be new.

They were absolutely ingrained with the accumulated dirt of ages ; but he affirmed them to be clean. He was going to visit a lady that was nice about those things, and that's the reason he wore nankeen that day. And then he danced, and capered, and fidgeted, and pulled up his pantaloons, and hugged his intolerable flannel vestment closer about his poetic loins. Anon he gave it loose to the zephyrs which plentifully insinuate their tiny bodies through every crevice, door, window, or wainscot, expressly formed for the exclusion of such impertinents. Then he caught at a proof sheet, and catched up a laundress's bill instead—made a dart at Bloomfield's Poems, and threw them in agony aside. I could not bring him to one direct reply ; he could not maintain his jumping mind in a right line for the tithe of a moment by Clifford's Inn clock. He must go to the printer's immediately : (the most unlucky accident !) he had struck off five hundred impressions of his Poems, which were ready for delivery to subscribers, and the Preface must all be expunged. There were eighty pages of Preface, and not till that morning had he discovered that in the very first page of said Preface he had set out with a principle of Criticism fundamentally wrong, which vitiated all his following reasoning. The Preface must be expunged, although it cost him £30, the lowest calculation, taking in paper and printing ! In vain have his real friends remonstrated against this Midsummer madness. George is as obstinate as a Primitive Christian, and wards and parries off all our thrusts with one unanswerable fence :—" Sir, 'tis of great consequence that the *world* is not *misled !*"

As for the other Professor, he has actually begun to dive into Tavernier and Chardin's *Persian* Travels for a story, to form a new drama for the sweet tooth of this fastidious age. Hath not Bethlehem College a fair action for non-residence against such professors ? Are poets so *few* in *this age*, that He must write poetry ? *Is morals* a subject so exhausted, that he must quit that line ? Is the metaphysic well (without a bottom) drained dry ?

If I can guess at the wicked pride of the Professor's heart, I would take a shrewd wager that he disdains ever again to dip his pen in *Prose.* Adieu, ye splendid theories ! Farewell, dreams of political justice ! Law-suits, where I was council for Archbishop Fenelon *versus* my own mother, in the famous fire cause !

Vanish from my mind, professors, one and all ! I have metal more attractive on foot.

Man of many snipes,—I will sup with thee (Deo volente, et diabolo nolente,) on Monday night, the 5th of January, in the new year, and crush a cup to the infant century.

A word or two of my progress : Embark at six o'clock in the morning, with a fresh gale, on a Cambridge one-decker ; very cold till eight at night ; land at St. Mary's lighthouse, muffins and coffee upon table (or any other curious production of Turkey, or both Indies), snipes exactly at nine, punch to commence at ten, with *argu-ment ;* difference of opinion is expected to take place about eleven ; perfect unanimity, with some haziness and dimness, before twelve. *N.B.*—My single affection is not so singly wedded to snipes ; but the curious and epicurean eye would also take a pleasure in beholding a delicate and well-chosen assortment of teals, ortolans, the unctuous and palate-soothing flesh of geese, wild and tame, night-ingales' brains, the sensorium of a young sucking pig, or any other Christmas dish, which I leave to the judgment of you and the cook of Gonville.   C. LAMB.

himself. We next discussed the question, whether Pope was a poet? I find Dr. Gregory is of opinion he was not, though Miss Seward does not at all concur with him in this. We then sat upon the comparative merits of the ten translations of *Pizarro*, and Miss Benjay or Benje advised Mary to take two of them home (she thought it might afford her some pleasure to compare them *verbatim*); which we declined. It being now nine o'clock, wine and macaroons were again served round, and we parted, with a promise to go again next week, and meet the Miss Porters, who, it seems, have heard much of Mr. Coleridge, and wish to meet *us*, because we are *his* friends. I have been preparing for the occasion. I crowd cotton in my ears. I read all the reviews and magazines of the past month against the dreadful meeting, and I hope by these means to cut a tolerable second-rate figure.

Pray let us have no more complaints about shadows. We are in a fair way, *through you*, to surfeit sick upon them.

Our loves and respects to your host and hostess. Our dearest love to Coleridge.

Take no thought about your proof sheets; they shall be done as if Woodfall himself did them. Pray send us word of Mrs. Coleridge and little David Hartley, your little reality.

Farewell, dear Substance. Take no umbrage at anything I have written. C. LAMB, *Umbra.*

Land of Shadows,
Shadow Month the 16th or 17th, 1800.

Coleridge, I find loose among your papers a copy of *Christabel*. It wants about thirty lines; you will very much oblige me by sending me the beginning as far as that line,—

"And the spring comes slowly up this way;"

and the intermediate lines between—

> "The lady leaps up suddenly,
>   The lovely Lady Christabel ; "

and the lines,—

> "She folded her arms beneath her cloak,
>   And stole to the other side of the oak."

The trouble to you *will be small,* and the benefit to us *very great.* A pretty antithesis ! A figure in speech I much applaud.

Godwin has called upon us. He spent one evening here : was very friendly : kept us up till midnight, drank punch, and talked about you. He seems above all men mortified at your going away. Suppose you were to write to that good-natured heathen : " Or is he a *shadow ?* "

If I do not *write,* impute it to the long postage, of which you have so much cause to complain. I have scribbled over a *queer letter,* as I find by perusal, but it means no mischief.

I am, and will be, yours ever, in sober sadness,

C. L.

Write your *German* as plain as sunshine, for that must correct itself. You know I am *homo unius linguæ :* in English—illiterate, a dunce, a ninny.

To WILLIAM WORDSWORTH.

LETTER LXXXV.]   *January* 30, 1801.

I ought before this to have replied to your very kind invitation into Cumberland. With you and your sister I could gang anywhere ; but I am afraid whether I shall ever be able to afford so desperate a journey. Separate from the pleasure of your company, I don't much care if I never see a mountain in my life. I have passed all my days in London, until I have formed as many and intense local attachments as any of you mountaineers can have done with dead Nature. The lighted shops of the Strand

and Fleet Street; the innumerable trades, tradesmen, and customers, coaches, waggons, playhouses; all the bustle and wickedness round about Covent Garden; the very women of the Town; the watchmen, drunken scenes, rattles; life awake, if you awake, at all hours of the night; the impossibility of being dull in Fleet Street; the crowds, the very dirt and mud, the sun shining upon houses and pavements, the print shops, the old bookstalls, parsons cheapening books, coffee-houses, steams of soups from kitchens, the pantomimes—London itself a pantomime and a masquerade—all these things work themselves into my mind, and feed me, without a power of satiating me. The wonder of these sights impels me into night-walks about her crowded streets, and I often shed tears in the motley Strand from fulness of joy at so much life. All these emotions must be strange to you; so are your rural emotions to me. But consider, what must I have been doing all my life, not to have lent great portions of my heart with usury to such scenes?

My attachments are all local, purely local. I have no passion (or have had none since I was in love, and then it was the spurious engendering of poetry and books) for groves and valleys. The rooms where I was born, the furniture which has been before my eyes all my life, a book-case which has followed me about like a faithful dog (only exceeding him in knowledge), wherever I have moved, old chairs, old tables, streets, squares, where I have sunned myself, my old school,—these are my mistresses. Have I not enough, without your mountains? I do not envy you. I should pity you, did I not know that the mind will make friends of anything. Your sun, and moon, and skies, and hills, and lakes, affect me no more, or scarcely come to me in more venerable characters, than as a gilded room with tapestry and tapers, where I might live with handsome visible objects. I consider the clouds above me but as a roof beautifully painted, but unable to satisfy the mind: and at last, like the pictures of the apartment of a connoisseur, unable to afford him any longer a pleasure. So fading upon me, from disuse, have been the beauties of Nature, as they have been confinedly called; so ever fresh, and green, and warm are all the inventions of men, and assemblies of men in this great city. I should certainly have laughed with dear Joanna.

Give my kindest love, and my sister's, to D. and yourself; and a kiss from me to little Barbara Lewthwaite. Thank you for liking my play.   C. L.

LETTER LXXXVI.]   *January* 1801.

Thanks for your letter and present. I had already borrowed your second volume. What most pleases me is, "The Song of Lucy." *Simon's sickly daughter*, in "The Sexton," made me *cry*. Next to these are the description of these continuous echoes in the story of "Joanna's Laugh," where the mountains and all the scenery absolutely seem alive; and that fine Shakspearian character of the "happy man," in the "Brothers,"

> ———"that creeps about the fields,
> Following his fancies by the hour, to bring
> Tears down his cheek, or solitary smiles
> Into his face, until the setting sun
> Write Fool upon his forehead!"

I will mention one more—the delicate and curious feeling in the wish for the "Cumberland Beggar," that he may have about him the melody of birds, although he hear them not. Here the mind knowingly passes a fiction upon herself, first substituting her own feeling for the Beggar's, and in the same breath detecting the fallacy, will not part with the wish. The "Poet's Epitaph" is disfigured, to my taste, by the common satire upon parsons and lawyers in the beginning, and the coarse epithet of "pin-point," in the sixth stanza. All the rest is eminently good, and your own. I will just add that it appears to me a fault in the "Beggar," that the instructions conveyed in it are too direct, and like a lecture: they don't

the "Queene-like-Closet or rare boke of Recipes in medicine and cookery, fitted to all capacities."

Accordingly in these *the fancy* is perpetually applied to ; any slight conceit, allusion, or analogy, any " prettiness," a story true or false, serves for an argument adapted to women and young persons, and "incompetent judgments ;" whereas the *Liberty of Prophecy* (a book in your father's bookcase) is a series of severe and masterly reasoning, fitted to great Clerks and learned Fathers, with no more of Fancy than is subordinate and ornamental. —Such various powers had the Bishop of Down and Connor, Administrator of the See of Dromore !

My theme and my story !—Farewell.

C. LAMB.

To THOMAS MANNING.

LETTER XCI.] *April* 1801.

I was not aware that you owed me anything beside that guinea ; but I daresay you are right. I live at No. 16 Mitre Court Buildings, a pistol-shot off Baron Maseres'. You must introduce me to the Baron. I think we should suit one another mainly. He lives on the ground floor, for convenience of the gout; I prefer the attic story, for the air. He keeps three footmen and two maids ; I have neither maid nor laundress, not caring to be troubled with them. His forte, I understand, is the higher mathematics ; my turn, I confess, is more to poetry and the belles lettres. The very antithesis of our characters would make up a harmony. You must bring the Baron and me together. *N.B.*—When you come to see me, mount up to the top of the stairs—I hope you are not asthmatical— and come in flannel, for 'tis pure airy up there. And bring your glass, and I will show you the Surrey Hills. My bed faces the river, so as by perking up upon my haunches, and supporting my carcass with my elbows, without much wrying my neck, I can see the white sails glide by the bottom of the King's Bench Walks as I lie in my bed. An excellent tiptoe prospect in the best room :—casement windows, with small panes, to look more like a cottage. Mind, I have got no bed for you, that's flat ; sold it to pay expenses of moving,—the very bed on which Manning lay ; the friendly, the mathematical Manning ! How forcibly does it remind me of the interesting Otway ! "The very bed which on thy marriage night gave thee into the arms of Belvidera, by the coarse hands of ruffians—" (upholsterers' men), etc. My tears will not give me leave to go on. But a bed I will get you, Manning, on condition you will be my day-guest.

I have been ill more than a month, with a bad cold, which comes upon me (like a murderer's conscience) about midnight, and vexes me for many hours. I have successively been drugged with Spanish licorice, opium, ipecacuanha, paregoric, and tincture of foxglove (tinctura purpuræ digitalis of the ancients). I am afraid I must leave off drinking.

To ROBERT LLOYD.

LETTER XCII.]   *April* 1801.

I am not dead nor asleep. But Manning is in town, and Coleridge is in town, and I am making a thorough alteration in the structure of my play for Publication. My brain is overwrought with variety of worldly-intercourse. I have neither time nor mind for scribbling. Who shall deliver me from the body of this Death ?

Only continue to write and to believe that when the Hour comes I shall strike like Jack of the Clock, *id est*, I shall once more become a regular correspondent of Robert and Plumstead. How is the benevolent, loud-talking, Shakspeare-loving Brewer ?

To your inquiry respecting a selection from Bp. Taylor I answer—it cannot be done, and if it could, it would not *take* with John Bull. It cannot be done, for who can disentangle and unthread the rich texture of Nature and Poetry, sewn so thick into a stout coat of theology, without spoiling both *lace* and *coat ?* How beggarly and how bald do even Shakspeare's Princely Pieces look when thus violently divorced from *connection* and *circumstance !* When we meet with "To be or not to be," or Jacques' moralisings upon the Deer, or Brutus and Cassius' quarrel and reconciliation—in an Enfield Speaker, or in Elegant Extracts,—how we stare, and will scarcely acknowledge to ourselves (what we are conscious we feel) that they are flat and have no power. Something exactly like this have I experienced when I have picked out similes and stars from "Holy Dying" and shown them *per se,* as you'd show specimens of minerals or pieces of rock. Compare the grand effect of the star-paved firmament, and imagine a boy capable of picking out those pretty twinklers one by one and playing at chuck-farthing with them. Everything in heaven and earth, in man and in story, in books and in fancy, acts by Confederacy, by juxtaposition, by circumstance and place. Consider a fine family (if I were not writing to you I might instance your own) of sons and daughters, with a respectable father and a handsome mother at their heads, all met in one house, and happy round one table. Earth cannot show a more lovely and venerable sight, such as the Angels in heaven might lament that in their country there is no marrying or giving in marriage. Take and split this Body into individuals—show the separate caprices, vagaries, etc., of Charles, Rob, or Plum, one a Quaker, another a Churchman. The eldest daughter seeking a husband out of the pale of parental faith—another warping, perhaps—the father a prudent, circumspective, do-me-good sort of a man *blest* with children whom no ordinary rules can circumscribe. I have not room for all particulars—but just as this happy and venerable Body of a family loses by splitting and considering individuals too nicely, so it is when we pick out Best Bits out of a great writer. 'Tis the *sum* total of his mind which affects us.

                                                                    C. L.

To WILLIAM GODWIN.

LETTER XCIII.]   *June* 29, 1801.

Dear Sir—Dr. Christy's Brother and Sister are come
to town and have shown me great civilities.   I in return
wish to requite them, having, *by God's grace*, principles
of generosity *implanted* (as the moralists say) in my
nature, which have been duly cultivated and watered by
good and religious friends, and a pious education.   They
have picked up in the northern parts of the island an
astonishing admiration of the great author of the New
Philosophy in England, and I have ventured to promise
their taste an evening's gratification by seeing Mr. Godwin
face to *face ! ! ! ! !*   Will you do them, and me *in* them,
the pleasure of drinking tea and supping with me at the
old number 16 on Friday or Saturday next ?   An early
nomination of the day will very much oblige yours
sincerely,   CH. LAMB.

To ROBERT LLOYD.

LETTER XCIV.]   *July* 26, 1801.

Cooke in " Richard the Third " is a perfect caricature.
He gives you the *monster* Richard, but not the *man*
Richard.   Shakspeare's bloody character impresses you
with awe and deep admiration of his witty parts, his
consummate hypocrisy, and indefatigable prosecution of
purpose.   You despise, detest, and loathe the cunning,
vulgar, low and fierce Richard, which Cooke substitutes
in his place.   He gives you no other idea than of a
vulgar villain, rejoicing in his being able to overreach,
and not possessing that joy in *silent* consciousness, but
betraying it, like a *poor* villain, in sneers and distortions
of the face, like a droll at a country fair : not to add that
cunning so self-betraying and manner so vulgar could
never have deceived the politic Buckingham nor the soft
Lady Anne : *both* bred in courts, would have turned with

Imperial Majesty. It was written originally in English for the use of the *two* and *twenty* readers of the *Albion* (this *calculation* includes a printer, four pressmen, and a devil); but becoming of no use when the *Albion* stopped, I got it translated into Usbeck Tartar by my good friend Tibet Kulm, who is to come to London with a *civil* invitation from the Cham to the English nation to go over to the worship of the Lama.

The *Albion* is dead—dead as nail in door—and my revenues have died with it; but I am not as a man without hope. I have got a sort of opening to the *Morning Chronicle*, by means of that common dispenser of benevolence, Mister Dyer. I have not seen Perry, the editor, yet: but I am preparing a specimen. I shall have a difficult job to manage, for you must know that Mr. Perry, in common with the great body of the Whigs, thinks the *Albion* very low. I find I must rise a peg or so, be a little more decent, and less abusive; for, to confess the truth, I had arrived to an abominable pitch; I spared neither age nor sex when my cue was given me. *N'importe* (as they say in French), any climate will suit me. So you are about to bring your old face-making face to London. You could not come in a better time for my purposes; for I have just lost Rickman, a faint idea of whose character I sent you. He has gone to Ireland for a year or two to make his fortune; and I have lost by his going what seems to me I can never recover—*a finished man.* His memory will be to me as the brazen serpent to the Israelites,—I shall look up to it, to keep me upright and honest. But he may yet bring back his honest face to England one day. I wish your affairs with the Emperor of China had not been *so urgent*, that you might have stayed in Great Britain a year or two longer, to have seen him; for, judging from *my own* experience, I almost dare pronounce you never saw his equal. I never saw a man that could be at all a second or substitute for him in any sort.

Imagine that what is here erased was an apology and

explanation, perfectly satisfactory you may be sure for rating this man so highly at the expense of ——, and ——, and ——, and M——, and ——, and ——, and ——. But Mr. Burke has explained this phenomenon of our nature very prettily in his letter to a Member of the National Assembly, or else in Appeal to the old Whigs, I forget which. Do you remember an instance from Homer (who understood these matters tolerably well), of Priam driving away his other sons with expressions of wrath and bitter reproach, when Hector was just dead?

I live where I did, in a *private* manner, because I don't like *state*. Nothing is so disagreeable to me as the clamours and applauses of the mob. For this reason I live in an *obscure* situation in one of the courts of the Temple.   C. L.

I send you all of Coleridge's letters to me, which I have preserved : some of them are upon the subject of my play. I also send you Kemble's two letters, and the prompter's courteous epistle, with a curious critique on "Pride's Cure," by a young physician from EDINBRO', who modestly suggests quite another kind of a plot. These are monuments of my disappointment which I like to preserve.

In Coleridge's letters you will find a good deal of amusement, to see genuine talent struggling against a pompous display of it. I also send you the Professor's letter to me (careful Professor ! to conceal his *name* even from his correspondent), ere yet the Professor's pride was cured. Oh monstrous and almost satanical pride !

You will carefully keep all (except the Scotch Doctor's, *which burn*) *in statu quo*, till I come to claim mine own.   C. LAMB.

To WILLIAM GODWIN.

LETTER XCVIII.]   [*Margate ?*] *September* **9,** 1801.

Dear Sir—Nothing runs in my head when I think of your story, but that you should make it as like the life of Savage as possible. That is a known and familiar tale, and its effect on the public mind has been very great. Many of the incidents in the true history are readily made dramatical. For instance, Savage used to walk backwards and forwards o' nights to his mother's window, to catch a glimpse of her, as she passed with a candle. With some such situation the play might happily open. I would plunge my Hero, exactly like Savage, into difficulties and embarrassments, the consequences of an unsettled mind : out of which he may be extricated by the unknown interference of his mother. He should be attended from the beginning by a Friend, who should stand in much the same relation towards him as Horatio to Altamont in the play of the " Fair Penitent." A character of this sort seems indispensable. This Friend might gain interviews with the mother, when the son was refused sight of her. Like Horatio with Calista, he might wring her soul. Like Horatio, he might learn the secret *first.* He might be exactly in the same perplexing situation, when he had learned it, whether to tell it or conceal it from the Son (I have still Savage in my head), who might *kill* a man (as he did) in an affray—he should receive a pardon, as Savage did—and the mother might interfere to have him *banished.* This should provoke the friend to demand an interview with her husband, and disclose the whole secret. The husband, refusing to believe anything to her dishonour, should fight with him. The husband repents before he dies. The mother explains and confesses everything in his presence. The son is admitted to an interview with his now acknowledged mother. Instead of embraces, she

resolves to abstract herself from all pleasure, even from
his sight, in voluntary penance all her days after.   This
is crude indeed ! ! but I am totally unable to suggest a
better.   I am the worst hand in the world at a plot.
But I understand enough of passion to predict that your
story, with some of Savage's, which has no repugnance,
but a natural alliance with it, cannot fail.   The mystery
of the suspected relationship—the suspicion, generated
from slight and forgotten circumstances, coming at last to
act as Instinct, and so to be mistaken for Instinct—the
son's unceasing pursuit and throwing of himself in his
mother's way, something like Falkland's eternal persecu-
tion of Williams—the high and intricate passion in the
mother, the being obliged to shun and keep at a distance
the thing nearest to her heart—to be cruel, where her
heart yearns to be kind, without a possibility of explanation.   You have the power of life and death and the
hearts of your auditors in your hands—still Harris will
want a skeleton, and he must have it.   I can only put in
some sorry hints.   The discovery to the son's friend may
take place not before the third act—in some such way as
this.   The mother may cross the street—he may point
her out to some gay companion of his as the Beauty of
Leghorn—the pattern for wives, etc. etc.   His companion,
who is an Englishman, laughs at his mistake, and knows
her to have been the famous Nancy Dawson, or any one
else, who captivated the English king.   Some such way
seems dramatic, and speaks to the Eye.   The audience
will enter into the Friend's surprise and into the perplexity
of his situation.   These Ocular Scenes are so many great
landmarks, rememberable headlands and lighthouses in
the voyage.   Macbeth's witch has a good advice to a
tragic writer, what to do with his spectator.

" *Show* his *eyes*, and grieve his heart."

The most difficult thing seems to be, What to do with
the husband ?   You will not make him jealous of his own
son ?   that is a stale and an unpleasant trick in Douglas,

etc. Can't you keep him out of the way till you want him, as the husband of Isabella is conveniently sent off till his cue comes? There will be story enough without him, and he will only puzzle all. Catastrophes are worst of all. Mine is most stupid. I only propose it to fulfil my engagement, not in hopes to convert you.

It is always difficult to get rid of a woman at the end of a tragedy. *Men* may fight and die. A woman must either take poison, *which is a nasty trick*, or go mad, which is not fit to be shown—or retire, which is poor : only retiring is most reputable.

I am sorry I can furnish you no better : but I find it extremely difficult to settle my thoughts upon anything but the scene before me, when I am from home : I am from home so seldom. If any the least hint crosses me, I will write again, and I very much wish to read your plan, if you could abridge and send it. In this little scrawl you must take the will for the deed, for I most sincerely wish success to your play.—Farewell,

C. L.

To JOHN RICKMAN, Esq.

Dear Rickman—Your Letter has found me at Margate, where I am come with Mary to drink sea water and pick up shells. I am glad to hear that your new dignities sit so easy upon you. No doubt you are one of those easy " well dressed " gentlemen, that we may know at first sight to belong to the " Castle," when we meet them in the Park. Your Letter contains a very fair offer about my Play, which I must first dispatch. I seriously feel very much obliged to you *and all that*, but I have a scheme in my head to print it about Xmas time, when the Town is fuller !! about that time I expect the repayment of a Loan, which was bigger than I ought to

have trusted, but I hope not bigger than my borrowing
friend will then be able to repay.   If he should disappoint
me, I may throw myself upon you: meantime I am too
proud ever to etc. . . .   I do not write in *any* paper.
George Dyer, that common Lyar of Benevolence, has
taken some pains to introduce me to the *Morning
Chronicle*, and I did something for them, but I soon
found that it was a different thing writing for the Lordly
Editor of the great Whig Paper to what it was scribbling
for the poor *Albion*.   More than three-fourths of what I
did was superciliously rejected; whereas in the old
Albion the seal of my well-known handwriting was
enough to drive any nonsense current.   I believe I shall
give up this way of writing, and turn honest, scramble
on as well as I can for a year, and make a Book, for why
should every creature make books but I?

G. Burnett had just finished his Essay when I came
away.   Mushrooms scramble up in a night; but diamonds,
you know, lie a long while ripening in the bed.   The
purport of it is to persuade the world that opinions
tending to the subversion of Established Religion and
Governments, systems of medicine, etc., should not be
rashly vented in every company: a good orthodox doctrine
which has been preached up with the "holy text of Pike
and Gun" with you in Ireland, and is pretty familiar in
England, but it is novel to George; at least he never
wrote an Essay upon the subject before.   Critics should
think of this, before they loosely cry out, This is
commonplace, what is there new in it? it may be all
new to the Author, *he* may never have thought of it
before, and it may have cost him as much brain-sweat
as a piece of the most inveterate originality.   However
George is in pretty good keeping, while the merits of
his essay lie under consideration.   He has got into joint
rooms with a young Surgeon, whose Uncle is an eminent
wine merchant, and gives his nephew long tick, so they
drink two sorts of wine, and live happy.   George was
turned out of his White Friars Lodging because he wanted

too much attendance. He used to call up the girl, and send her down again, because he had forgot what he wanted ; and then call her again, when his thought came back, to ask what a Clock it was. Fenwick has been urgent with me to write to you about his plan, and I gave him a drunken promise that I would, but you have saved me a disagreeable topic, for I know you have enough to do, and must serve him at your leisure. The Welfare of Ireland, perhaps of the whole world, must not stand still, while the interests of a newspaper are debating !! He is very sanguine, and if he tells true, he has had very important encouragement; but he always said and thought, that the *Albion* had very sufficient patronage. Some people can *see anything* but their own interest, and they chuse to look at that through glasses. Dr. Christie has transported his solemn physiognomy to Portsmouth in his way to India. He departed without calling upon me, tho' he never could have called upon a more welcome occasion ; consequently he did not get your letter, but I imparted its contents to his brother. I know no more news from here, except that the Professor (Godwin) is COURTING. The Lady is a Widow [1] with green spectacles and one child, and the Professor is grown quite juvenile. He bows when he is spoke to, and smiles without occasion, and wriggles as fantastically as Malvolio, and has more affectation than a canary bird pluming his feathers when he thinks somebody looks at him. He lays down his spectacles, as if in scorn, and takes 'em up again from necessity, and winks that she mayn't see he gets sleepy about eleven o'Clock. You never saw such a philosophic coxcomb, nor any one play the Romeo so unnaturally. His second play, my god-son, is flatly rejected by Harris, because it is a Persian story about Shaw Abbas and the valiant Sefi his son : but Harris has offered to pay him at all events, if he will take a domestic plain story, not heroic nor foreign ; so, after many indignant declarations that he could not bear such a *creeping way* (his expression)

[1] A very disgusting woman.

his proud heart has come down to Harris's proposals; so he is filching a tale out of one of Defoe's novels, and has made me write him hints.   Floreat Tertia!——

Margate, Wednesday, *September* 16,
    where I stay a week longer.

And now farewell, Master Secretary!—and if your Diplomatic Majesty has any commissions for tape or bone lace, etc. in London, depend upon a faithful performance of the same.   I could find matter for a longer Letter, and will another day, if you will find time to read it.   Meantime believe me, yours sincerely.   Mary sends her kindest remembrances.   No hurry for the Pork.   C. LAMB.

John Rickman, Esq.,
    Dublin Castle.

To WILLIAM GODWIN.

LETTER C.]   *Margate, September* 17, 1801.

[Fragment.]

I shall be glad to come home and talk these matters over with you.   I have read your scheme very attentively. That Arabella has been mistress to King Charles is sufficient to all the purposes of the story.   It can only diminish that respect we feel for her to make her turn whore to one of the Lords of his Bedchamber.   Her son must not know that she has been a whore: it matters not that she has been whore to a *King:* equally in both cases, it is against decorum and against the delicacy of a son's respect that he should be privy to it.   No doubt, many sons might feel a wayward pleasure in the honourable guilt of their mothers; but is it a true feeling?   Is it the best sort of feeling?   Is it a feeling to be exposed on theatres to mothers and daughters?   Your conclusion (or

rather Defoe's) comes far short of the tragic ending, which
is always expected ; and it is not safe to disappoint. A
tragic auditory wants *blood*. They care but little about
a man and his wife parting. Besides, what will you do
with the son, after all his pursuits and adventures? Even
quietly leave him to take guinea-and-a-half lodgings with
mamma in Leghorn ! O impotent and pacific measures !
. . . I am certain that you must mix up some strong
ingredients of distress to give a savour to your pottage.
I still think that you may, and must, graft the story of
Savage upon Defoe. Your hero must *kill* a *man* or *do
something*. Can't you bring him to the gallows or some
great mischief, out of which she *must* have recourse to an
explanation with her husband to save him. Think on this.
The husband, for instance, has great friends in Court at
Leghorn. The son is condemned to death. She cannot
tease him for a stranger. She must tell the whole truth.
Or she *may* tease him, as for a stranger, till (like Othello
in Cassio's case) he begins to suspect her for her impor-
tunity. Or, being pardoned, can she not tease her
husband to get him banished? Something of this I
suggested before. *Both* is best. The murder and the
pardon will make business for the fourth act, and the
banishment and explanation (by means of the *Friend* I
want you to draw) the fifth. You must not open any of
the truth to Dawley by means of a letter. A letter is a
feeble messenger on the stage. Somebody, the son or his
friend, must, as a *coup de main*, be exasperated, and
obliged to tell the husband. Damn the husband and his
" gentlemanlike qualities." Keep him out of sight, or he
will trouble all. Let him be in England on trade, and
come home as Biron does in *Isabella*, in the fourth act,
when he is wanted. I am for introducing situations, sort
of counterparts to situations which have been tried in
other plays—*like*, but not the *same*. On this principle I
recommended a friend like Horatio in the "Fair Penitent,"
and on this principle I recommend a situation like Othello,
with relation to Desdemona's intercession for Cassio.

Bye-scenes may likewise receive hints. The son may see his mother at a mask or Feast, as Romeo, Juliet. The festivity of the company contrasts with the strong perturbations of the individuals. Dawley may be told his wife's past unchastity at a mask by some witch-character, as Macbeth upon the heath, in dark sentences. This may stir his brain, and be forgot, but come in aid of stronger proof hereafter. From this what you will perhaps call whimsical way of counterparting, this honest stealing, and original mode of plagiarism, much yet, I think, remains to be sucked. Excuse these abortions. I thought you would want the draught soon again, and I would not send it empty away.—Yours truly,

WILLIAM GODWIN!!!

Somers Town, September 17, 1801.

To JOHN RICKMAN, Esq.

LETTER CI.]   *October* 9, 1801.

I called lately upon our common friend G. Dyer of Cliffords Inn. I found him inconsolable and very dirty. It seems that Gilbert Wakefield is dead, and George had not got his tribute ready for Mr. Phillips's magazine this month, and Dr. Aikin had sent a little tribute, and Miss Aikin had also sent a *tribute,* and the world would expect a tribute from his pen. At first I imagined that George was touched with some sense of kindred mortality, such as Methusaleh himself must have felt, when he was qualmish; but no, all that disturbed George was, that he had not got a *tribute. George* the *second,* George Burnett, supt with me last night. He is not got quite well of the metaphyz, but I hope and trust that last night's paroxysm will be the last, and that his disorder has come to its crisis. He maintained that if a highwayman, who is going to kill you, *spares* your *life* on your expressly promising to *spare his*, that is, not to prosecute, you are under no obligation to keep your word, because you were in a state of violence, when the promise was made, and the Good of the Whole, which may be partially endangered by suffering that man to live, is to be preferred to any such promise in such circumstances made. If I ever turn freebooter, and light upon George Burnett in my travels, I shall remember what I have to trust to. But saving his metaphyz (which goes off after the first heats of youth like the green sickness) George the 2nd has good parts. He only wants fortune. He as ill becomes adversity, as George the first would do prosperity, if any one should leave him a rich legacy. Another of fortune's *humble servants* is a visitor of mine, who in the language of antiquity would have been nominated Simonds-with-the-slit-lip. I cannot say his linen was of Tarsus, nor quite so robust as Russian, but it certainly craved bleaching, but saving his dirty shirt, and his physiognomy and his 'bacco box, together with a certain kiddy air in his walk, a man would have gone near to have mistaken him for a gentleman. He has a sort of ambition to be so misunderstood. It seems the Treasury does not pay with that weekly promptitude, and accommodating periodicalness, it was wont; and some constitutions *cannot wait*. He craved the loan of a half guinea; could I refuse a GENTLEMAN who seemed in distress? He dropt some words, as if he were desirous of trying what effect the Irish air would have upon a *poor* constitution. Couldn't you make him a door-keeper, or a game-keeper, or find some post for him, not altogether so brilliant as useful? Some situation under the *mint-master ?*—I leave him to your mercy and ability. There is no hurry, for what you have given him will keep him in *work* some time, and for *pay*, why 'tis just as his Majesty's ministers shall please. So, Cottle's Psalms are come out hot press'd for six shillings. Of course I shall send you a copy. " Poetry is never more delightfully employed than when in the service of its Creator."

Vide Preface to the Translation (if he had writ one, but he has not).

Quid majus!—the Professor is not married, the *Plough* is yet *in posse*—peace is all the cry here—fireworks, lights, etc., abound—White stationed himself at Temple Bar among the boys, and threw squibs ; burned one man's cravat.—This is the cream of London intelligence—you shall have the earliest tidings of all new movements.   C. L.

John Rickman, Esq.,
    Dublin Castle.

LETTER CII.]   *Tuesday, November* 24, 1801.

Dr Rickman—I have just put my finishing hand to my play to alter it for publishing. I have made a thorough change in the structure of the latter part, omitting all those scenes which shew'd John under the first impression of his father's death. I have done this, because I had made him too weak, and to expose himself before his servants, which was an indecorum ; and from a theory that poetry has nothing to do to give *pain ;* the imbecilities, and deformities, the dotages of human nature, are not fit objects to be shewn. Instead of these rejected scenes I have told his feelings in a *narrative* of the old servant to Margaret, which is a relief to the oppression of John so often *talking* in his own person.—I have cut out all the interview of John and Simon, and they do not meet at all, and I have expunged Simon's bloody resolution, which offended you so much from him. I have sent him to *improve himself* by travel, and it is explained that his presence (who is the *good son* in my *parable*) would have been too much of a reproach and a pain to *my prodigal* in the first hour of his grief.—The whole ends with Margaret's Consolation, where it *should* end, without any pert incident of surprise and trick to make a catastrophe. Moreover,

I have excluded the two tales of the Witch and the Gentleman who died for love, having since discovered by searching the parish register of St. Mary Ottery, that his disorder was a stranguary, tho' some rimes upon his grave-stone did a little lean to my hypothesis.—Moreover, I have gone through and cut out all the Ahs! and Ohs! and sundry weak parts, which I thought so fine three or four years ago. When it comes out you must let me know in what manner I can transmit you a copy or two. I have been so particular, because you have shewn more liking to my Margaret than most people, and my alterations were *in part* the offspring of your suggestions; not wholly, for I have long smelt a jumble. I hope you will find it now nearly all of a piece. I am to christen it "John Woodvil" simply—not "Pride's Cure."—As Dyer says, "I am no enemy to candid and ingenuous criticism, I only deprecate the arrows of calumny": *vide* most of the prefaces of G. Dyer. Dyer regularly dines with me when he does not go a visiting and brings his shilling. He has pick'd up amazingly. I never saw him happier. He has had his doors listed and his casements puttied, and bought a handsome *screen* of the last century. Only his poems do not get finished. One volume is printing, but the second wants a good deal doing to it. I do not expect that he will make much progress with his Life and Opinions, till his detestable Lyric Poetry is delivered to subscribers. I shall make him not deliver one vol. till both are ready, else he would infallibly have made two troubles and two expences of it. He talks of marrying, but this *en passant* (as he says) and *entre nous*, for God's sake don't mention it to him, for he has not forgiven me for betraying to you his purpose of writing his own Life. He says, that if it once spreads, so many people will expect and wish to have a place in it, that he is sure he shall disoblige all his friends.——

G. Burnett shewed me your rouzing Letter. If I had not known your theory and design, I must have called it a very cruel Letter, and sure as I was that your general idea of the treatment, which is best for Burnetts and George the Seconds, was right, I could not help thinking you had gone too far, even so far that he could not put up with it or you ever after, without doing a moral injury to himself. But you must pursue your own course, which 9 times out of ten will be more judicious than mine. The less of interference in these cases, the better. I was principally (if not only) sorry, that you assured him of Southey's opinion of the mediocrity of his understanding perfectly agreeing with your own. Southey was the last plank of the scaffold which propt up George in his opinion of himself. But I dare not affirm you did wrong. I am not a teacher in Israel. Yours truly,

C. LAMB.

John Rickman, Esq.,
    Dublin Castle.

LETTER CIII.]

    For John Rickman, Esq.,
        Dublin Castle.   [1801.]

I was the moon-struck man, that was inspired to write on the pacquet "for John Rickman," and must hasten to clear Burnett of that part of his *Indictment*. He brought to me his Letter and his Essay, or rather two Essays, and desired me to write myself and put up all together in a parcel. I had no leisure to write then, but I did up his things, and when I had done so the enormous bulk staggered me, and I preferred that obnoxious indorsement to enlarging it with another cover. I was guided by the usages of the India House, where I have often received superscriptions similar, and escaped shot-free. I will never practise upon your pocket in the like manner again, but Burnett stands acquitted. None but the Bishop could have composed that illustrious specimen of ignorance which you extract, and he alone, in all England, would not understand the absurdity of it, if it were to be pointed out. Still I wish something could be done for him, even if he waited six weeks, *or a day over,* for it. Methinks! (as the Poets say) I see Preferment waiting at the door, *afraid to come in,* 'till his Worship has finished his Introduction, that she may not deprive the World of his matchless labours.

I have nothing to communicate, but my thanks. I do assure you that I retain a very lively memory of our old Smoking Evenings in Southampton Buildings. G. Dyer, our illustrious Co-Puffer, has emigrated to Enfield, where some rich man, that has got two Country Houses, allows him the use of a very large one, with a library, where he is getting the final vol. of his Poems ready, and then I shall set him about his Life : by *use* in a sentence back, I mean dirting and littering.

Southey is not arrived.

Yours sincerely,

C. LAMB.

I forgot to notice an anachronism in your 1st Letter, which I am glad to see you correct in a subsequent—you accost me my dear SIR. By what twist of association in your unlucky Pericranium have you connected that Honor with my cognomen?

Mary thanks you, but she prefers *Rum.*

I have literally *this moment* rec[d] your packet for Southey. I mean Burnett's History of his own times. And your letter. For your kind mention of Slit-lips take my warmest thanks. He will have no objection to wait six weeks or *a day over,* tho' it may be damnably more inconvenient for him to *wait,* than for the Bishop. The fact of the "strange flesh" which he is reported to have eaten, astounds me, but I can believe and tremble.— Never mind the ceremony of franking to me. John Company pays.

LETTER CIV.]   [No date or post-mark, 1801.]

I sincerely thank you for your repeated offer, but I have just received as much as £50, an old debt which I told you of, and that will a good deal and more than cover the expences of printing. I expect to be able to send you some copies in a few weeks. I have not had a proof sheet yet. I have nothing to claim upon Dyer's account. He paid me from the beginning as near as I can calculate, and I solemnly protest it, to a penny for all the expences he put me to, and whenever he dines with us he regularly brings his shilling, which is a fair average for what his gluttony devours. To be sure he has occasionally an eleemosynary whiff of tobacco, for which I cannot sconse the Poet. I am afraid he sometimes does not come when he has not got a shilling. I cannot force him, for now his health is come back, he is the most unmanageable of God's creatures. He goes about fetching and carrying for Ladies, and always thinking he *must* call upon this Lady and t'other Gentleman. His first vol. is nearly printed, but he is projecting new odes and impertinences for the 2d, and I cannot foresee a period. Still he seems by fits bent upon writing his Life, and will do it if the Prototype is not overtaken with death. I quite give up any hope of reducing him to common sense and human conduct. All that can be done is to bolster up his carcase by a daily habit of Dining, until he finishes his mortal pilgrimage. Poor G. Burnett is very ill and reduced. You would deposit your fierce anger if you saw the metaphysician. He has brought his Introduction to a finish at last, but he is not in a capacity to go on. Coleridge has recommended him to the Editor of the *Morning Post*, who has promised to employ him. But a Lion is in his foot-path, and he cannot *begin yet*. I suppose he will write to you, and it will be needless to say more of him here. The goul has a gouless and two,

if not three young gouls. The goul has not paid me the
pittance, for 'twas not much, he borrowed of me, but I
have reason to believe his circumstances are so squalid,
that it would be more to expect of him than can be
expected from man or goul, to divert his Comings in from
the service of genuine hunger and thirst.——Fenwick's
Plough (how one idea of Poverty introduces another!) is
degenerated already from a daily to a weekly paper. I
wish it may not vanish into thin air, or come out the
same day as Burnett's Historia Romana issues from the
press. I meantime have made some overtures to the
Editor of the *Morning Post* thro' Coleridge, who writes
for that paper, and hope I am on the point of being
engaged.——I have seen Southey several times. His wife
is considerably improved, and will talk if she is talked
to, but she bitterly complains that when literary men
get together, they never speak to the women. Mrs.
Lovel is also in town and Southey's mother, who is
DYING :——"So am not I, said the foolish fat scullion."
Do you remember our unfeeling behaviour at the funeral
of that dear young Lady, who was withered in her bloom
by the untimely stroke of Death, and lies in what-d'ye-call-
'em Church yard? The tear is falling while I remember——
don't you perceive the Ink is rather *brackish?* as G.
Burnett asked in a company at my brother's the other
day, whether the Thames Water at Blackfriars Bridge
was not a little Brackish.——The Professor has not yet
thrown himself away. I am sorry to find he is about
to commit a folly, for I hear that She has no fortune and
has one child, and they propose that she shall ease the
burden of the family expences by translating from the
French.——Fell, the inevitable shadow of everything which
Godwin does, is absolutely writing a Play. It is a
Comedy. It is just finished, and I go this evening in
the hope to see it. It will have one trait in it. There
can be no mirth in it. An Owl making a Pun would be
no bad emblem of the unnatural attempt. To your
enquiry whether Mary swallows certain mixed Liquors,

she answers that I unfortunately misunderstood that
advice, as if it had been addrest to me, and have almost
killed myself by the Blunder.   But she will profit by the
correction.   She desires her love and remembrance.
White often enquires after you, and as often desires to
be mentioned to you, which I as regularly forget.
Stoddart is going to begin the study of Civil Law at the
Commons.

Farewell, old Comrade and new Secretary,
Thine,   C. L.

You must send up your St. Helena letter *immediately*,
and I will drop it in our Box.   I can't frank it, John
Company never franks *outwards*.   A ship, the *Marquis
of Ely*, goes at Xmas.   The *Armston* goes next
Wednesday.

Since I wrote last Leaf, I have read Fell's Comedy,
and am surprized to find it contain, if not sterling wit
or character, a liveliness and knowledge of the present
popular taste, which has astonish'd me.   The serious
parts are damn'd flat.   But I should not at all wonder,
he having a pretty good introduction, even if it should
please highly.   He has been a minute observer of what
takes in Reynolds's plays, and has had real actors
continually in his view.—Who knows, but Owls *do* make
Puns, when they hoot by moonshine?   I shall hear from
the *Morning Post* this day, and shall endeavour to get
the Theatrical Reports, not *all*, but Kemble's chief
characters, and Cooke's, etc.

John Rickman, Esq.,
     Dublin Castle.

January 9, 1802.

Please to send me *one* Letter with the *Broad Seal*, for a friend who is curious in impressions.

I am to be sure much gratified with your use of Margaret as a kind of rack to extract confession from women. But don't give me out as your Rack-maker, lest the women retort upon me the fate of Perillus, which you may read in your Ainsworth under the article Phalaris; or you may find the story more at large by perusing the Controversy between Bentley and Boyle. I have delayed to write (I believe I am telling a Lye) until I should get a book ready to send (but I believe this has been all along a pretext recurred to, a kind of after-motive, when the resolution was taken a priori, rather than the true cause, which was mixed up of busy days and riotous nights, doing the Company's business in a morning, straining for Jokes in the afternoon, and retailing them (not being yet published) over punch at night. The Lungs of Stentor could not long sustain the Life I have led. I get into parties, or treat them with Pope Joan four times in a week. You have dropt in ere now when Norris was courting at such a Party, and you know the game. I stick to it like any *Papist*. 'Tis better than Poetry, Mechanics, Politics, or Metaphysics. That's a stop—there's pope—you did not take your ace—what a magic charm in sounds. . . . I begin not to wonder at the bloodshed which dyed Christian Europe concerning Omousia and Omoiousia.—A party of people's *faces* about a fire grinning over cards and forgetting that they have got to go home is the supreme felicity, the Maximum Bonum. White has or is about to write you at my suggestion. We desire nothing so vigorously as to see Master Secretary in these parts. There are Liquors and fumes extant, which have power to detain a Bachelor from his cold Bed till cock crow.

Fenwick gives routs and balls and suppers (not balls) but splendid entertainments out of the first fruits of the *Plow*—he had some hundreds of pounds from unthinking Nobility.   It is no breach of charity to suppose that part is expended—his wife and daughter have got magnificent Hats, which Mary waggishly has christen'd Northumberland Hats, from his great Patron at Charing Cross.

Dyer has at last met with a madman more mad than himself—the Earl of Buchan, brother to the Erskines and eccentric biographer of Fletcher of Saltoun.   This old man of near eighty is come to London in his way to France, and George and he go about everywhere.   George brought the mad Lord up to see me—I wan't at home but Mary was washing—a pretty pickle to receive an Earl in !   Lord have mercy upon us ! a Lord in my garret !   My utmost ambition was some time or other to receive a Secretary !   Well, I am to breakfast with this mad Lord on Sunday.   I am studying manners. George and my Lord of Buchan went on Thursday last to Richmond in the Long Coach to pay their devotions to the shrine of Thomson ! The coldest day in the year. Enough to cool a Jerusalem-Padder.   George is as proud as a Turkey Cock and can talk of nothing else ; always taking care to hedge in at the end that he don't value Lords, and that the Earl has nothing of the Lord about him.   O human nature ! human Nature ! for my part I have told every Body, how I had an Earl come to see me. . . . George describes the Earl as a very worthy man, who has his hobby horses ; for instance, George says, he will stop you in the street, when you are walking with him, and hold you by the button, and talk so loud, that all the Passers by look at you.   So you may guess *why* he cleaves to George the first.   If you have read the *Post,* you may have seen a dissertation on Cooke's Richard the 3d. which is the best thing I have done.   It was in last Monday ; stray Jokes I will not *mark*, hoping you

George deposes, that he was Teaching them their Lesson, when he was called down by Ld. Stanhope to be introduced to his Lordship's Mother; when he returned his Pupils were flown. They had gone out of Window with their best Coats and Linen.—The Eldest Son of Ld. S. served him exactly the same Trick, and his Lordship sets it down, that these striplings as well as the former (who never came back) were spirited away by the Pitt and Grenville Party, to whom he is allied by marriage. He says, that Pitt will make them Villains. Ministers have already bought off his Son and his Son-in-Law: and he meant to bring up these young ones (the eldest 16) to mechanics or manufactures. It is very probable what he says—for the P's and G's (writing to a Secretary I dare not be more explicit) would go some steps to stop the growth of Democratic Peers.—George declares that he is only sorry on Ld. Stanhope's account, who is much agitated, but on his own he don't care at all: nay I have no doubt he is ready to leap at his heart, for Lord S. desires he will stay in his house, and he will try to get him something. So George has got his old desirable prospect of food and clothing with no Duty to perform for it. I could fill vols. with a History of his absurdities since the date of my Last. . . . Take one or 2.—Imprimis, he overstay'd his 3 weeks—then he wrote to Lord S. from town to write to him, but forgot to mention his own address—then he was forced to write again to say he forgot, and begg'd his Lordship to tell him the Exact situation where his Lordship's House stood, that he might have no trouble in finding it ! ! ! to write to a Peer of the Realm to tell the number of his house ! Then he determines to set off for Chevening next morning, and writes that he will come down by the 3 o'clock stage— then he comes to us the night before at 11 and complains bitterly of the difficulty of getting up so early—then he goes away, and White and I lay wagers that he won't go at all. Next morning 11 o'clock—enter Geo. the 2nd in a dirty neckcloth—he could not go because he had no

Linen, and he had not time to go to Southey and borrow it, and inadvertently slips out that to be sure there was a Coach went at ½ past 10. Then my Tutor gapes, and stares, and borrows a neckcloth and sets off with all proper humility to My Lord's in a Post Chaise—drives up to the Door in Style—and there I leave him bowing and gaping to see the fine Pictures.

Yours truly,   C. LAMB.

Mary's grateful thanks for your indulgence by which she reads my works.

To John Rickman, Esq.,
    Dublin Castle.

LETTER CIX.]   *February* 4, 1802.

Dear Rickman—I send you three Copies. Keep one yourself, and distribute the others. Perhaps you will send one to her, "whom you in sport do call your Margaret," but this is mere conjecture.

G. Dyer is sitting by me, he begs to be kindly remembered. He has brought news, that a Mr. Wainewright, with a Mr. Frend the Pamphleteer, and Mr. Perry the Chronicleer, have set up as a Committee to procure him an annuity by subscription. Ld. Stanhope has sent £50.

Talking of money, you owe me £22—which I paid in advance for your father's Papers.

Yours truly,   C. L.

To John Rickman, Esq.
    Dublin Castle.

LETTER CX.]   *February* 14, 1802.

"I take thy groat in earnest of Revenge." One-and-twenty Margarets fall to the disposal of your dainty Cousin. I sup with him at Southey's on Tuesday, God willing.—Your guineas (which, let me tell you, are too much, but you shall have your way) are not absolutely mal-a-pros, for by a cruel reverse of Fortune, that Dame who is painted with a wheel to signify to you, that she is changes, and rollings, and mutabilities, I am no longer Paragraph spinner. The fact is, that Stuart was wonderfully polite and civil at first, I suppose because Coleridge recommended me, from whose assistance in the Paper he expected great things, but Coleridge from ill health and unsettlement having hung back, I gradually got out of favor, and Stuart has at last twice told me that I must take more pains about my paragraphs, for he has not been able to draw above one in five from what I have sent him. This in connection with his altered behaviour was hint quite enough for me, who do not require hints as big as St. Paul's Church to make me understand a coldness, excited my magnanimous spirit to endite a valorous Letter of Resignation, which I did with some qualms, when I remembered what I gave up : but to tell truth, all the little I have done has been very irksome, and rendered ten times more so from a sense of my employer not being fully satisfied : and that little has subtracted from my pleasure of walking, reading, idling, etc., which are as necessary to me as the "golden vapour" of Life itself. My health (silly as it seems to relate) has suffered bitterly. My Spirits absolutely require freedom and leisure, and I think I shall never engage to do task work any more, for I am sick.—I must cut closer. I am almost ashamed at my capriciousness, as must seem to you, but upon a serious review I do approve of what I've done. I've foolishly involved you (I fear) in an expense of 8 guineas a year, which I *think* was on my acct. but as it is for *whom* it is, I must not call it foolish. A Paper in a Country Town is a kind of London. But I would gladly purchase your acquiescence by paying half, which I know you won't accept. I have given this up only two days, and I feel myself at elbow room, free and happy. I can scribble now at my heart's Leisure, if I have an impulse, and tho' I know I speak as a fool, I am sure I can write better gratis. Say no more about it. I have weighed my loss and my gain, and I write *Profit*.

I may yet do the *Londoners* at my Leisure.

This Letter is short for I have got a bad headache. Mr. Abbot's elevation, you may be sure, surprized me. I take it for granted you will not be a Loser. I am sure I shall be a gainer, if an Easterly wind wafts you to England.

Frend was here yesterday. He desires me to set down every day Dyer dines with me, and the Committee will pay me, as George is to have no money of his own. George contrives constantly to dine here, when he says he shan't over night, which is very *convenient*, and vice versa. It is the damned Vanity of being supposed to be always engaged. Now he is got well, he is as freakish as King David at Gath. Nothing can be done with him; save that the Committee will preserve him from felo de se, that he shan't starve himself.

George the 2nd discharges his important Trust, of doing *nothing* for Ld. S. with fidelity and diligence. His Lordship sends him to town upon any fiddle-faddle errand, and George fancies himself essential to his Lordship's comfort. He looks more important than Mr. Dressin, King's messenger.

Mary always desires to be most kindly remembered by you. She bids me *not* tell you that an Epigram called *Helen*, in my little Book, is of her writing. But it is, every tittle of it. I hope you do not dislike it. We remain yours truly,

C. L., M. L.

To John Rickman, Esq.,
Dublin Castle.

To THOMAS MANNING.

LETTER CXI.] *February* 15, 1802.

Apropos, I think you wrong about my play. All the omissions are right. And the supplementary scene, in which Sandford narrates the manner in which his master is affected, is the best in the book. It stands where a hodge-podge of German puerilities used to stand. I insist upon it that you like that scene. Love me, love that scene. I will now transcribe the "Londoner" (No. 1), and wind up all with affection and humble servant at the end.

[Here was transcribed the essay called "The Londoner," see *Poems, Plays, and Essays* in this Edition.]

"What is all this about?" said Mrs. Shandy. "A story of a cock and a bull," said Yorick: and so it is; but Manning will take good-naturedly what *God will send him* across the water: only I hope he won't *shut* his *eyes*, and *open* his *mouth*, as the children say, for that is the way to *gape*, and not to *read*. Manning, continue your laudable purpose of making me your register. I will render you back all your remarks; and *I, not you*, shall have received usury by having read them. In the meantime, may the great Spirit have you in his keeping, and preserve our Englishman from the inoculation of frivolity and sin upon French earth.

Allons—or what is it you say, instead of *good-bye?*

Mary sends her kind remembrance, and covets the remarks equally with me.   C. LAMB.

LETTER CXII.]   *February* 1802.

Not a sentence, not a syllable of Trismegistus shall be lost through my neglect. I am his word-banker, his storekeeper of puns and syllogisms. You cannot conceive (and if Trismegistus cannot, no man can) the strange joy which I felt at the receipt of a letter from Paris. It seemed to give me a learned importance, which placed me above all who had not Parisian correspondents. Believe that I shall carefully husband every scrap, which will save you the trouble of memory, when you come back. You cannot write things so trifling, let them only be about Paris, which I shall not treasure. In particular, I must have parallels of actors and actresses. I must be told if any building in Paris is at all comparable to St. Paul's, which, contrary to the usual mode of that part of our nature called admiration, I have looked up to with un-fading wonder, every morning at ten o'clock, ever since it has lain in my way to business. At noon I casually glance upon it, being hungry; and hunger has not much taste for the fine arts. Is any night-walk comparable to a walk from St. Paul's to Charing Cross, for lighting and paving, crowds going and coming without respite, the rattle of coaches, and the cheerfulness of shops? Have you seen a man guillotined yet? Is it as good as hanging? Are the women *all* painted, and the men *all* monkeys? or are there not a *few* that look like *rational* of *both sexes?* Are you and the first consul *thick?* All this expense of ink I may fairly put you to, as your letters will not be solely for my proper pleasure.; but are to serve as

memoranda and notices, helps for short memory, a kind
of Rumfordising recollection, for yourself on your return.
Your letter was just what a letter should be, crammed,
and very funny. Every part of it pleased me till you
came to Paris; then your philosophical indolence, or
indifference, stung me. You cannot stir from your rooms
till you know the language! What the devil!—are men
nothing but word-trumpets? Are men all tongue and
ear? Have these creatures, that you and I profess to
know *something about,* no faces, gestures, gabble, no folly,
no absurdity, no induction of French education upon the
abstract idea of men and women, no similitude nor dis-
similitude to English! Why, thou cursed Smellfungus!
your account of your landing and reception, and Bullen,
(I forget how you spell it, it was spelt my way in Harry
the Eighth's time), was exactly in that minute style which
strong impressions INSPIRE (writing to a Frenchman, I
write as a Frenchman would). It appears to me as if I
should die with joy at the first landing in a foreign country.
It is the nearest pleasure which a grown man can substitute for that unknown one, which he can never know, the
pleasure of the first entrance into life from the womb.
I dare say, in a short time, my habits would come back
like a "stronger man" armed, and drive out that new
pleasure; and I should soon sicken for known objects.
Nothing has transpired here that seems to me of sufficient
importance to send dry-shod over the water: but I suppose you will want to be told some news. The best and
the worst to me is, that I have given up two guineas a
week at the *Post,* and regained my health and spirits,
which were upon the wane. I grew sick, and Stuart
unsatisfied. *Ludisti satis, tempus abire est;* I must cut
closer, that's all. Mister Fell, or as you, with your usual
facetiousness and drollery, call him, Mr. F + ll, has
stopped short in the middle of his play. Some *friend*
has told him that it has not the least merit in it. Oh
that I had the rectifying of the Litany! I would put in
a *libera nos (Scriptores videlicet) ab amicis!* That's all

the news.   *Apropos:* is it pedantry, writing to a French-man, to express myself sometimes by a French word, when an English one would not do as well? Methinks my thoughts fall naturally into it.

In all this time I have done but one thing, which I reckon tolerable, and that I will transcribe, because it may give you pleasure, being a picture of *my* humours. You will find it in my last page.   It absurdly is a first Number of a series, thus strangled in embryo.

More news! The Professor's Rib has come out to be a disagreeable woman, so much so as to drive me and some more old cronies from his house.   He must not wonder if people are shy of coming to see him because of the "snakes."   C. L.

To Mr. RICKMAN.

Letter CXIII.]   *April* 10, 1802.

Dear Rickman—The enclosed letter explains itself. It will save me the danger of a corporal interview with the man-eater, who, if very sharp set, may take a fancy to me, if you will give me a short note, declaratory of probabilities.   These from him who hopes to see you once or twice more before he goes hence, to be no more seen : for there is no tipple nor tobacco in the grave, whereunto he hasteneth.   C. Lamb.

16, Mitre Court Buildings,
    Inner Temple.

How clearly the Ghoul writes, and like a gentleman!

To SAMUEL TAYLOR COLERIDGE.

Letter CXIV.]   *September* 8, 1802.

Dear Coleridge—I thought of not writing till we had performed some of our commissions ; but we have been hindered from setting about them, which yet shall be done to a tittle.   We got home very pleasantly on Sunday. Mary is a good deal fatigued, and finds the difference of going *to* a place, and coming *from* it. I feel that I shall remember your mountains to the last day I live. They haunt me perpetually. I am like a man who has been falling in love unknown to himself, which he finds out when he leaves the lady. I do not remember any very strong impression while they were present; but, being gone, their mementos are shelved in my brain. We passed a very pleasant little time with the Clarksons. The Wordsworths are at Montagu's rooms, near neighbours to us. They dined with us yesterday, and I was their guide to Bartlemy Fair!

To Mrs. GODWIN.

LETTER CXV.] [Early in *September* 1802?]

Dear Mrs. G.—Having observed with some concern that Mr. Godwin is a little fastidious in what he eats for supper, I herewith beg to present his palate with a piece of dried salmon. I am assured it is the best that swims in Trent. If you do not know how to dress it, allow me to add, that it should be cut in thin slices and broiled in paper *previously prepared in butter*. Wishing it exquisite, I remain,—Much as before, yours sincerely, C. LAMB.

Some add *mashed potatoes*.

To THOMAS MANNING.

LETTER CXVI.] *London, September* 24, 1802.

My dear Manning—Since the date of my last letter I have been a traveller. A strong desire seized me of visiting remote regions. My first impulse was to go and see Paris. It was a trivial objection to my aspiring mind, that I did not understand a word of the language, since I certainly intend some time in my life to see Paris, and equally certainly intend never to learn the language; therefore that could be no objection. However, I am very glad I did not go, because you had left Paris (I see) before I could have set out. I believe, Stoddart promising to go with me another year prevented that plan. My

next scheme (for to my restless, ambitious mind London
was become a bed of thorns) was to visit the far-famed
peak in Derbyshire, where the Devil sits, they say, without breeches. *This* my purer mind rejected as indelicate.
And my final resolve was, a tour to the Lakes. I set
out with Mary to Keswick, without giving Coleridge any
notice, for my time, being precious, did not admit of it.
He received us with all the hospitality in the world, and
gave up his time to show us all the wonders of the country.
He dwells upon a small hill by the side of Keswick, in a
comfortable house, quite enveloped on all sides by a net
of mountains : great floundering bears and monsters they
seemed, all couchant and asleep. We got in in the evening, travelling in a post-chaise from Penrith, in the midst
of a gorgeous sunshine, which transmuted all the mountains into colours, purple, etc. etc. We thought we had
got into fairyland. But that went off (as it never came
again ; while we stayed we had no more fine sunsets),
and we entered Coleridge's comfortable study just in the
dusk, when the mountains were all dark with clouds upon
their heads. Such an impression I never received from
objects of sight before, nor do I suppose I can ever again.
Glorious creatures, fine old fellows, Skiddaw, etc. I
never shall forget ye, how ye lay about that night, like
an intrenchment ; gone to bed, as it seemed for the night,
but promising that ye were to be seen in the morning.
Coleridge had got a blazing fire in his study ; which is a
large antique, ill-shaped room, with an old-fashioned organ,
never played upon, big enough for a church, shelves of
scattered folios, an Æolian harp, and an old sofa, half
bed, etc. And all looking out upon the last fading view
of Skiddaw, and his broad-breasted brethren : what a
night ! Here we stayed three full weeks, in which time
I visited Wordsworth's cottage, where we stayed a day
or two with the Clarksons (good people, and most hospit-
able, at whose house we tarried one day and night), and
saw Lloyd. The Wordsworths were gone to Calais.
They have since been in London, and past much time

with us : he is now gone into Yorkshire to be married.
So we have seen Keswick, Grasmere, Ambleside, Ulswater
(where the Clarksons live), and a place at the other end
of Ulswater; I forget the name; to which we travelled
on a very sultry day, over the middle of Helvellyn. We
have clambered up to the top of Skiddaw, and I have
waded up the bed of Lodore. In fine, I have satisfied
myself that there is such a thing as that which tourists
call *romantic*, which I very much suspected before : they
make such a spluttering about it, and toss their splendid
epithets around them, till they give as dim a light as at
four o'clock next morning the lamps do after an illumination. Mary was excessively tired when she got about
half-way up Skiddaw, but we came to a cold rill (than
which nothing can be imagined more cold, running over
cold stones), and with the reinforcement of a draught of
cold water she surmounted it most manfully. Oh, its
fine black head, and the bleak air atop of it, with a prospect of mountains all about and about, making you giddy;
and then Scotland afar off, and the border countries so
famous in song and ballad ! It was a day that will stand
out, like a mountain, I am sure, in my life. But I am
returned (I have now been come home near three weeks ;
I was a month out), and you cannot conceive the degradation I felt at first, from being accustomed to wander free
as air among mountains, and bathe in rivers without
being controlled by any one, to come home and *work*. I
felt very *little*. I had been dreaming I was a very great
man. But that is going off, and I find I shall conform
in time to that state of life to which it has pleased God
to call me. Besides, after all, Fleet Street and the Strand
are better places to live in for good and all than amidst
Skiddaw. Still, I turn back to those great places where
I wandered about, participating in their greatness. After
all, I could not *live* in Skiddaw. I could spend a year,
two, three years among them, but I must have a prospect
of seeing Fleet Street at the end of that time, or I should
mope and pine away, I know. Still, Skiddaw is a fine

creature. My habits are changing, I think, *i.e.* from drunk to sober. Whether I shall be happier or not remains to be proved. I shall certainly be more happy in a morning ; but whether I shall not sacrifice the fat, and the marrow, and the kidneys, *i.e.* the night, glorious care-drowning night, that heals all our wrongs, pours wine into our mortifications, changes the scene from indifferent and flat to bright and brilliant ! O Manning, if I should have formed a diabolical resolution, by the time you come to England, of not admitting any spirituous liquors into my house, will you be my guest on such shameworthy terms ? Is life, with such limitations, worth trying ? The truth is, that my liquors bring a nest of friendly harpies about my house, who consume me. This is a pitiful tale to be read at St. Gothard, but it is just now nearest my heart. Fenwick is a ruined man. He is hiding himself from his creditors, and has sent his wife and children into the country. Fell, my other drunken companion (that has been : *nam hic cœstus artemque repono*), is turned editor of a Naval Chronicle. Godwin continues a steady friend, though the same facility does not remain of visiting him often. That . . . has detached Marshall from his house ; Marshall, the man who went to sleep when the "Ancient Mariner" was reading ; the old, steady, unalterable friend of the Professor. Holcroft is not yet come to town. I expect to see him, and will deliver your message. Things come crowding in to say, and no room for 'em. Some things are too little to be told, *i.e.* to have a preference ; some are too big and circumstantial. Thanks for yours, which was most delicious. Would I had been with you, be-nighted, etc.! I fear my head is turned with wandering. I shall never be the same acquiescent being. Farewell. Write again quickly, for I shall not like to hazard a letter, not knowing where the fates have carried you. Farewell, my dear fellow.   C. LAMB.

To SAMUEL TAYLOR COLERIDGE.

LETTER CXVII.]   *October* 9, 1802.

CAROLUS AGNUS COLERIDGIO SUO S.

Carissime—Scribis, ut nummos scilicet epistolarios
solvam et postremo in Tartara abeam : immo tu potius
Tartaricum (ut aiunt) deprehendisti, qui me vernaculâ
meâ linguâ pro scribâ conductitio per tot annos satis
eleganter usum ad Latinè impure et canino fere ore
latrandum per tuasmet epistolas benè compositas et con-
cinnatas percellere studueris.   Conabor tamen : Attamen
vereor, ut Ædes istas nostri Christi, inter quas tantâ
diligentiâ magistri improbâ bonis literulis, quasi per
clysterem quendam injectis, infrà supràque olim penitùs
imbutus fui, Barnesii et Marklandii doctissimorum virorum
nominibus adhuc gaudentes, barbarismis meis peregrinis
et aliunde quæsitis valde dehonestavero.   Sed pergere
quocunque placet.   Adeste igitur, quotquot estis, conju-
gationum declinationumve turmæ, terribilia spectra, et tu
imprimis ades, Umbra et Imago maxima obsoletæ (Diis
gratiæ) Virgæ, quâ novissime in mentem receptâ, horres-
cunt subito natales, et parum deest quo minùs braccas
meas ultro usque ad crura demittam, et ipse puer pueriliter
ejulem.

Ista tua Carmina Chamouniana satis grandia esse
mihi constat ; sed hoc mihi nonnihil displicet, quòd in iis
illæ montium Grisosonum inter se responsiones totidem
reboant anglicè, *God, God,* haud aliter atque temet audivi
tuas montes Cumbrianas resonare docentem, *Dodd, Dodd,*
nempe Doctorem infelicem : vocem certe haud Deum
Sonantem.   Pro cæteris plaudo.

Itidem comparationes istas tuas satis callidas et lepidas
certè novi : sed quid hoc ad verum ? cum illi Consulari
viro et *mentem irritabilem* istum Julianum : et etiam
astutias frigidulas quasdam Augusto propriores, nequa-

quam congruenter uno afflatu comparationis causâ insedisse affirmaveris : necnon nescio quid similitudinis etiam cum Tiberio tertio in loco solicite produxeris.   Quid tibi equidem cum uno vel altero Cæsare, cùm universi Duodecim ad comparationes tuas se ultro tulerint ?   Præterea, vetustati adnutans, comparationes iniquas odi.

Istas Wordsworthianas nuptias (vel potius cujusdam *Edmundii* tui) te retulisse mirificum gaudeo.   Valeas, Maria, fortunata nimium, et antiquæ illæ Mariæ Virgini (comparatione plusquam Cæsareanâ) forsitan comparanda, quoniam "beata inter mulieres :" et etiam fortasse Wordsworthium ipsum tuum maritum Angelo Salutatori æquare fas erit, quoniam e Cœlo (ut ille) descendunt et Musæ et ipsi Musicolæ : at Wordsworthium Musarum observantissimum semper novi.   Necnon te quoque affinitate hâc novâ, Dorothea, gratulor : et tu certe alterum *donum Dei.*

Istum Ludum, quem tu, Coleridgi, Americanum garris, a Ludo (ut Ludi sunt) maximè abhorrentem prætereo : nempe quid ad Ludum attinet, totius illæ gentis Columbianæ, a nostrâ gente, eadem stirpe ortâ, ludi singuli causa voluntatem perperam alienare?   Quæso ego materiam ludi : tu Bella ingeris.

Denique valeas, et quid de Latinitate meâ putes, dicas : facias ut opossum illum nostrum volantem vel (ut tu malis) quendam Piscem errabundum, a me salvum et pulcherrimum esse jubeas.   Valeant uxor tua cum Hartleiio nostro.   Soror mea salva est et ego : vos et ipsa salvere jubet.   Ulterius progrediri non liquet : homo sum æratus.

P.S.—Pene mihi exciderat, apud me esse Librorum a Johanno Miltono Latinè scriptorum volumina duo, quæ (Deo volente) cum cæteris tuis libris ocyùs citiùs per Mariam ad te missura curabo ; sed me in hoc tali genere rerum nullo modo *festinantem* novisti : habes confitentem reum.   Hoc solum dici restat, prædicta volumina pulchra esse et omnia opera Latina J. M. in se continere.   Circa

defensionem istam Pro Pop⁰. Ang⁰. acerrimam in præsens
ipse præclaro gaudio moror.

Jussa tua Stuartina faciam ut diligenter colam.

Iterum iterumque valeas :

Et facias memor sis nostri.

LETTER CXVIII.]   *October* 11, 1802.

Dear Coleridge—Your offer about the German poems
is exceedingly kind : but I do not think it a wise speculation, because the time it would take you to put them
into prose would be nearly as great as if you versified
them.   Indeed I am sure you could do the one nearly as
soon as the other ; so that instead of a division of labour,
it would be only a multiplication.   But I will think of
your offer in another light.   I daresay I could find many
things, of a light nature, to suit that paper, which you
would not object to pass upon Stuart as your own, and I
should come in for some light profits, and Stuart think
the more highly of your assiduity.   "Bishop Hall's
Characters " I know nothing about, having never seen
them.   I will reconsider your offer, which is very
plausible ; but as to the drudgery of going every day to
an editor with my scraps, like a pedler, for him to pick
out and tumble about my ribbons and posies, and to wait
in his lobby, etc., no money could make up for the
degradation.   You are in too high request with him to
have anything unpleasant of that sort to submit to.

It was quite a slip of my pen, in my Latin letter, when
I told you I had Milton's Latin Works.   I ought to have
said his Prose Works, in two volumes, Birch's edition,
containing all, both Latin and English, a fuller and better
edition than Lloyd's of Toland.   It is completely at your
service, and you must accept it from me ; at the same
time I shall be much obliged to you for your Latin
Milton, which you think you have at Howitt's ; it will
leave me nothing to wish for but the *History of England,*
which I shall soon pick up for a trifle.   But you must

write me word whether the Miltons are worth paying carriage for. You have a Milton; but it is pleasanter to eat one's own pease out of one's own garden, than to buy them by the peck at Covent Garden; and a book reads the better, which is our own, and has been so long known to us, that we know the topography of its blots and dog's-ears, and can trace the dirt in it to having read it at tea with buttered muffins, or over a pipe, which I think is the maximum. But, Coleridge, you must accept these little things, and not think of returning money for them, for I do not set up for a factor or general agent. As for the fantastic debt of £15, I'll think you were dreaming, and not trouble myself seriously to attend to you. My bad Latin you properly correct; but *natales* for *nates* was an inadvertency: I knew better. *Progrediri*, or *progredi*, I thought indifferent, my authority being Ainsworth. However, as I have got a fit of Latin, you will now and then indulge me with an *epistola*. I pay the postage of this, and propose doing it by turns. In that case I can now and then write to you without remorse; not that you would mind the money, but you have not always ready cash to answer small demands, the *epistolarii nummi*.

Your "Epigram on the Sun and Moon in Germany" is admirable. Take 'em all together, they are as good as Harrington's. I will muster up all the conceits I can, and you shall have a packet some day. You and I together can answer all demands surely: you, mounted on a terrible charger (like Homer, in the Battle of the Books), at the head of the cavalry: I will lead the light horse. I have just heard from Stoddart. Allen and he intend taking Keswick in their way home. Allen wished particularly to have it a secret that he is in Scotland, and wrote to me accordingly very urgently. As luck was, I had told not above three or four; but Mary had told Mrs. Green, of Christ's Hospital! For the present, farewell: never forgetting love to Pipos and his friends.

C. LAMB.

LETTER CXIX.]   *October* 23, 1802.

I read daily your political essays. I was particularly pleased with " Once a Jacobin :" though the argument is obvious enough, the style was less swelling than your things sometimes are, and it was plausible *ad populum.* A vessel has just arrived from Jamaica with the news of poor Sam Le Grice's death. He died at Jamaica of the yellow fever. His course was rapid, and he had been very foolish ; but I believe there was more of kindness and warmth in him than in almost any other of our schoolfellows. The annual meeting of the Blues is to-morrow, at the London Tavern, where poor Sammy dined with them two years ago, and attracted the notice of all by the singular foppishness of his dress. When men go off the stage so early, it scarce seems a noticeable thing in their epitaphs, whether they had been wise or silly in their lifetime.

I am glad the snuff and Pi-pos's books please. " Goody Two Shoes " is almost out of print. Mrs. Barbauld's stuff has banished all the old classics of the nursery ; and the shopman at Newberry's hardly deigned to reach them off an old exploded corner of a shelf, when Mary asked for them. Mrs. Barbauld's and Mrs. Trimmer's nonsense lay in piles about. Knowledge insignificant and vapid as Mrs. Barbauld's books convey, it seems, must come to a child in the *shape of knowledge;* and his empty noddle must be turned with conceit of his own powers when he has learnt that a horse is an animal, and Billy is better than a horse, and such like ; instead of that beautiful interest in wild tales, which made the child a man, while all the time he suspected himself to be no bigger than a child. Science has succeeded to poetry no less in the little walks of children than with men. Is there no possibility of averting this sore evil ? Think what you would have been now, if, instead of being fed with tales and old wives' fables in childhood, you had been crammed with geography and natural history !

Hang them !—I mean the cursed Barbauld crew, those blights and blasts of all that is human in man and child.

As to the translations, let me do two or three hundred lines, and then do you try the nostrums upon Stuart in any way you please. If they go down I will bray more. In fact, if I got or could but get £50 a year only, in addition to what I have, I should live in affluence.

Have you anticipated it, or could you not give a parallel of Buonaparte with Cromwell, particularly as to the contrast in their deeds affecting *foreign* States ? Cromwell's interference for the Albigenses, Buonaparte's against the Swiss. Then religion would come in ; and Milton and you could rant about our countrymen of that period. This is a hasty suggestion, the more hasty because I want my supper. I have just finished Chapman's Homer. Did you ever read it ? it has the continuous power of interesting you all along, like a rapid original, more than any ; and in the uncommon excellence of the more finished parts goes beyond Fairfax or any of 'em. The metre is fourteen syllables, and capable of all sweetness and grandeur. Cowper's blank verse detains you every step with some heavy Miltonism ; Chapman gallops off with you his own free pace. Take a simile for example. The council breaks up—

> " Being abroad, the earth was overlaid
> With flockers to them, that came forth ; as when of frequent bees
> Swarms rise out of a hollow rock, repairing the degrees
> *Of their egression endlessly, with ever rising new*
> From forth their sweet nest ; as their store, still as it faded, grew,
> *And never would cease sending forth her clusters to the spring,*
> They still crowd out so ; this flock here, that there, belabouring
> The loaded flowers. So," etc. etc.

What *endless egression of phrases* the dog commands !

Take another, Agamemnon wounded, bearing his wound heroically for the sake of the army (look below), to a woman in labour.

> " He, with his lance, sword, mighty stones, pour'd his heroic wreak
> On other squadrons of the foe, whiles yet warm blood did break

Thro' his cleft veins ; but when the wound was quite exhaust
    and crude,
The eager anguish did approve his princely fortitude.
As when most sharp and bitter pangs distract a labouring dame,
Which the divine Ilithiæ, that rule the painful frame
Of human childbirth, pour on her ; the Ilithiæ that are
The daughters of Saturnia ; with whose extreme repair
The woman in her travail strives, to take the worst it gives ;
With thought, it *must be, 'tis love's fruit, the end for which she*
    lives ;
The mean to make herself new born, what comforts will redound :
So," etc.

I will tell you more about Chapman and his pecu-
liarities in my next.   I am much interested in him.

Yours ever affectionately, and Pi-Pos's.   C. L.

LETTER CXX.]   *November* 4, 1802.

Observe, there comes to you, by the Kendal waggon
to-morrow, the illustrious 5th of November, a box, containing the Miltons, the strange American Bible, with
White's brief note, to which you will attend ; *Baxter's
Holy Commonwealth*, for which you stand indebted to
me 3s. 6d. ; an odd volume of Montaigne, being of no
use to me, I having the whole ; certain books belonging
to Wordsworth, as do also the strange thick-hoofed shoes,
which are very much admired in London.   All these
sundries I commend to your most strenuous looking after.
If you find the Miltons in certain parts dirtied and soiled
with a crumb of right Gloucester, blacked in the candle
(my usual supper), or peradventure a stray ash of tobacco
wafted into the crevices, look to that passage more
especially ; depend upon it, it contains good matter.   I
have got your little Milton, which, as it contains " Sal-
masius," and I make a rule of never hearing but one side
of the question (why should I distract myself ?), I shall
return to you when I pick up the *Latina opera*.   The
first Defence is the greatest work among them, because
it is uniformly great, and such as is befitting the very
mouth of a great nation, speaking for itself.   But the

second Defence, which is but a succession of splendid episodes, slightly tied together, has one passage, which, if you have not read, I conjure you to lose no time, but read it : it is his consolations in his blindness, which had been made a reproach to him. It begins whimsically, with poetical flourishes about Tiresias and other blind worthies (which still are mainly interesting as displaying his singular mind, and in what degree poetry entered into his daily soul, not by fits and impulses, but engrained and innate), but the concluding page, *i.e.* of *this passage* (not of the *Defensio*), which you will easily find, divested of all brags and flourishes, gives so rational, so true an enumeration of his comforts, so human, that it cannot be read without the deepest interest. Take one touch of the religious part :—" Et sane haud ultima Dei cura cæci —*we blind folks*, I understand it (not *nos* for *ego ;*)— sumus ; qui nos, quominus quicquam aliud præter ipsum cernere valemus, eo clementius atque benignius respicere dignatur. Væ qui illudit nos, væ qui lædit, execratione publica devovendo ; nos ab injuriis hominum non modo incolumes, sed pene sacros, divina lex reddidit, divinus favor : nec tam *oculorum hebetudine* quam *cœlestium alarum umbrâ* has nobis fecisse tenebras videtur, factas illustrare rursus interiore ac longe præstabiliore lumine haud raro solet. Huc refero, quod et amici officiosius nunc etiam quam solebant, colunt, observant, adsunt, quod et nonnulli sunt, quibuscum Pyladeas atque Theseas alternare voces verorum amicorum liceat.

" Vade gubernaculum mei pedis.
Da manum ministro amico
Da collo manum tuam, ductor autem viæ ero tibi ego."

All this, and much more, is highly pleasing to know. But you may easily find it ; and I don't know why I put down so many words about it but for the pleasure of writing to you, and the want of another topic.

Yours ever,   C. LAMB.

To-morrow I expect with anxiety S. T. C.'s letter to Mr. Fox.

To THOMAS MANNING.

My dear Manning—I must positively write, or I shall miss you at Toulouse. I sit here like a decayed minute hand; (I lie: *that* does not *sit;*) and being myself the exponent of no time, take no heed how the clocks about me are going. You possibly by this time may have explored all Italy, and toppled, unawares, into Etna, while you went too near those rotten-jawed, gaptoothed, old worn-out chaps of hell,—while I am meditating a quiescent letter to the honest post-master of Toulouse. But in case you should not have been *felo de se*, this is to tell you, that your letter was quite to my palate: in particular your just remarks upon Industry, cursed Industry (though indeed you left me to explore the reason), were highly relishing. I have often wished I had lived in the golden age, when shepherds lay stretched upon flowers, and roused themselves at their leisure,—the genius there is in a man's natural idle face, that has not learned his multiplication table! before doubt, and propositions, and corollaries, got into the world!

Now, as Joseph Cottle, a Bard of Nature, sings, going up Malvern Hills,

> "How steep! how painful the ascent!
> It needs the evidence of *close deduction*
> To know that ever I shall gain the top."

You must know that Joe is lame, so that he had some reason for so singing. These two lines, I assure you, are taken *totidem literis* from a very *popular* poem. Joe is also an Epic Poet as well as a Descriptive, and has written a tragedy, though both his drama and epopoiea are strictly *descriptive*, and chiefly of the *Beauties of Nature*, for Joe thinks *man* with all his passions and frailties not a proper subject of the *Drama*. Joe's tragedy hath the following surpassing speech in it. Some king is told that his enemy has engaged twelve archers to come over in a

boat from an enemy's country and waylay him ; he
thereupon pathetically exclaims—

"*Twelve*, dost thou say ?   Curse on those dozen villains ! "

Cottle read two or three acts out to us, very gravely on
both sides till he came to this heroic touch,—and then
he asked what we laughed at ?   I had no more muscles
that day.   A poet that chooses to read out his own verses
has but a limited power over you.   There is a bound
where his authority ceases.   *Apropos*, if you should go
to Florence or to Rome, inquire what works are extant
in gold, silver, bronze, or marble, of Benvenuto Cellini, a
Florentine artist, whose life, doubtless, you have read, or
if not, without controversy you must read—so haste ye,
send for it immediately from Lane's circulating Library.
It is always put among the Romances, but you have read
it I suppose.   In particular, inquire at Florence for his
colossal bronze statue (in the Grand Square, or somewhere) of Perseus.   You may read the story in Tooke's
Pantheon.   Nothing material has transpired in these
parts.   Coleridge has indited a violent Philippic against
Mr. Fox in the *Morning Post,* which is a compound of
expressions of humility, gentleman-ushering-in most
arrogant charges.   It will do Mr. Fox no real injury
among those that know him.

LETTER CXXII.]   *February* 19, 1803.

My dear Manning—The general scope of your letter
afforded no indications of insanity, but some particular
points raised a scruple.   For God's sake don't think any
more of "Independent Tartary."   What are you to do
among such Ethiopians ?   Is there no *lineal descendant*
of Prester John ?   Is the chair empty ?   Is the sword
unswayed ?   Depend upon it they'll never make you their
king, as long as any branch of that great stock is remaining.   I tremble for your Christianity.   They will certainly
circumcise you.   Read Sir John Mandeville's travels to
cure you, or come over to England.   There is a Tartar-

man now exhibiting at Exeter Change. Come and talk with him, and hear what he says first. Indeed he is no very favourable specimen of his countrymen! But perhaps the best thing you can do is to *try* to get the idea out of your head. For this purpose repeat to yourself every night, after you have said your prayers, the words Independent Tartary, Independent Tartary, two or three times, and associate with them the *idea* of *oblivion* ('tis Hartley's method with obstinate memories), or say, Independent, Independent, have I not already got an *independence?* That was a clever way of the old puritans, pun-divinity. My dear friend, think what a sad pity it would be to bury such *parts* in heathen countries, among nasty, unconversable, horse - belching, Tartar - people! Some say, they are Cannibals; and then, conceive a Tartar - fellow *eating* my friend, and adding the *cool malignity* of mustard and vinegar! I am afraid 'tis the reading of Chaucer has misled you; his foolish stories about Cambuscan, and the ring, and the horse of brass. Believe me, there are no such things, 'tis all the poet's *invention;* but if there were such darling things as old Chaucer sings, I would *up* behind you on the horse of brass, and frisk off for Prester John's country. But these are all tales; a horse of brass never flew, and a king's daughter never talked with birds! The Tartars, really, are a cold, insipid, smouchy set. You'll be sadly moped (if you are not eaten) among them. Pray *try* and cure yourself. Take hellebore (the counsel is Horace's, 'twas none of my thought *originally*). Shave yourself oftener. Eat no saffron, for saffron-eaters contract a terrible Tartar-like yellow. Pray, to avoid the fiend. Eat nothing that gives the heart-burn. *Shave the upper lip.* Go about like an European. Read no books of voyages (they are nothing but lies), only now and then a romance, to keep the fancy *under*. Above all, don't go to any sights of *wild beasts. That has been your ruin.* Accustom yourself to write familiar letters, on common subjects, to your friends in England, such as are of a moderate understand-

ing. And think about common things more. There's
your friend Holcroft, now, has written a Play. You used
to be fond of the drama. Nobody went to see it. Notwithstanding this, with an audacity perfectly original,
he faces the town down in a preface that they *did* like it
very much. I have heard a waspish punster say, " Sir,
why did you not laugh at my jest?" But for a man
boldly to face one out with " Sir, I maintain it, you *did*
laugh at my jest," is a little too much. I have seen H.
but once. He spoke of you to me in honourable terms.
H. seems to me to be drearily dull. G———— is dull,
then he has a dash of affectation, which smacks of the
coxcomb, and your coxcombs are always agreeable. I
supped last night with Rickman, and met a merry *natural*
captain, who pleases himself vastly with once having
made a pun at Otaheite in the O. language. 'Tis the
same man who said Shakspeare he liked, because he was
so much of the gentleman. Rickman is a man " absolute
in all numbers." I think I may one day bring you
acquainted, if you do not go to Tartary first ; for you'll
never come back. Have a care, my dear friend, of Anthropophagi! their stomachs are always craving. 'Tis terrible
to be weighed out at fivepence a-pound ; to sit at table (the
reverse of fishes in Holland) not as a guest, but as a meat.

God bless you : do come to England. Air and exercise
may do great things. Talk with some minister. Why
not your father ?

God dispose all for the best. I have discharged my duty.

Your sincere friend,   C. LAMB.

LETTER CXXIII.]   *March* 1803.

Dear Manning—I send you some verses I have made
on the death of a young Quaker you may have heard me
speak of as being in love with for some years while I
lived at Pentonville, though I had never spoken to her in
my life. She died about a month since. If you have
interest with the Abbé de Lisle, you may get 'em translated ; he has done as much for the Georgics.

To SAMUEL TAYLOR COLERIDGE.

LETTER CXXIV.]   *March* 20, 1803.

Mary sends love from home.

Dear Coleridge—I do confess that I have not sent your books as I ought to have done; but you know how the human free will is tethered, and that we perform promises to ourselves no better than to our friends. A watch is come for you. Do you want it soon, or shall I wait till some one travels your way? You, like me, I suppose, reckon the lapse of time from the waste thereof, as boys let a cock run to waste; too idle to stop it, and rather amused with seeing it dribble. Your poems have begun printing; Longman sent to me to arrange them, the old and the new together. It seems you have left it to him; so I classed them, as nearly as I could, according to dates. First, after the Dedication (which must march first), and which I have transplanted from before the Preface (which stood like a dead wall of prose between), to be the first poem; then comes " The Pixies," and the things most juvenile; then on " To Chatterton," etc.,—on, lastly, to the " Ode on the Departing Year," and " Musings,"—which finish. Longman wanted the Ode first, but the arrangement I have made is precisely that marked out in the Dedication, following the order of time. I told Longman I was sure that you would omit a good portion of the first edition. I instanced several sonnets, etc.; but that was not his plan, and, as you have done nothing in it, all I could do was to arrange 'em on the supposition that all were to be retained. A few I positively rejected; such as that of " The Thimble," and that of " Flicker and Flicker's Wife," and that *not* in the manner of Spenser, which you yourself had stigmatised—and the " Man of Ross,"—I doubt whether I should this last. It is not too late to save it. The first proof is only just come. I have been forced to call that Cupid's Elixir, " Kisses." It stands in your first volume, as an Effusion, so that, instead of prefixing "The Kiss" to that of "One Kiss, dear Maid," etc., I have ventured to entitle it "To Sara." I am aware of the nicety of changing even so mere a trifle as a title to so short a piece, and subverting old associations; but two called "Kisses" would have been absolutely ludicrous, and "Effusion" is no name, and these poems come close together. I promise you not to alter one word in any poem whatever, but to take your last text, where two are. Can you send any wishes about the book? Longman, I think, should have settled with you; but it seems you have left it to him. Write as soon as you possibly can; for, without making myself responsible, I feel myself, in some sort, accessory to the selection, which I am to proof-correct; but I decidedly said to Biggs that I was sure you would omit more. Those I have positively rubbed off, I can swear to *individually* (except the "Man of Ross," which is too familiar in Pope), but no others—you have your cue. For my part, I would rather all the *Juvenilia* were kept—*memoriæ causâ*.

Robert Lloyd has written me a masterly letter, containing a character of his father. See how different from Charles he views the old man! (*Literatim*): "My father smokes, repeats Homer in Greek, and Virgil, and is learning, when from business, with all the vigour of a young man, Italian. He is, really, a wonderful man. He mixes public and private business, the intricacies of disordering life, with his religion and devotion. No one more rationally enjoys the romantic scenes of Nature, and the chit-chat and little vagaries of his children; and, though surrounded with an ocean of affairs, the very neatness of his most obscure cupboard in the house passes not unnoticed. I never knew any one view with such clearness, nor so well satisfied with things as they are, and make such allowance for things which must appear perfect Syriac to him." By the last he means the Lloydisms of the younger branches. His portrait of Charles (exact as far as he has had opportunities of noting him) is most exquisite :—" Charles is become steady as a church, and as straightforward as a Roman road. It would distract him to mention anything that was not as plain as sense ; he seems to have run the whole scenery of life, and now rests as the formal precisian of non-existence." Here is genius, I think, and 'tis seldom a young man, a Lloyd, looks at a father (so differing) with such good-nature while he is alive. Write—

I am in post-haste, C. LAMB.

Love, etc., to Sara, P., and H.

LETTER CXXV.] *April* 13, 1803.

My dear Coleridge—Things have gone on better with me since you left me. I expect to have my old house-keeper home again in a week or two. She has mended most rapidly. My health too has been better since you took away that Montero cap. I have left off cayenned eggs and such bolsters to discomfort. There was death in that cap. I mischievously wished that by some inauspicious jolt the whole contents might be shaken, and the coach set on fire ; for you said they had that property. How the old gentleman, who joined you at Grantham, would have clapp'd his hands to his knees, and not know-ing but it was an immediate visitation of God that burnt him, how pious it would have made him !—him, I mean, that brought the Influenza with him, and only took places for one—an old sinner ; he must have known what he had got with him ! However, I wish the cap no harm for the sake of the *head it fits*, and could be content to see it disfigure my healthy sideboard again.

What do you think of smoking ? I want your sober, *average, noon opinion* of it. I generally am eating my dinner about the time I should determine it.

Morning is a girl, and can't smoke—she's no evidence one way or the other ; and Night is so evidently *bought over*, that he can't be a very upright judge. May be the truth is, that *one* pipe is wholesome, *two* pipes toothsome, *three* pipes noisome, *four* pipes fulsome, *five* pipes quarrelsome, and that's the *sum* on't. But that is deciding rather upon rhyme than reason. . . . After all, our instincts *may* be best. Wine, I am sure—good mellow, generous Port—can hurt nobody, unless those who take it to excess, which they may easily avoid if they observe the rules of temperance.

Bless you, old sophist, who next to human nature taught me all the corruption I was capable of knowing! And bless your Montero cap, and your trail (which shall come after you whenever you appoint), and your wife and children—Pipos especially.

When shall we two smoke again? Last night I had been in a sad quandary of spirits, in what they call the evening; but a pipe, and some generous Port, and *King Lear* (being alone), had their effects as solacers. I went to bed pot-valiant. By the way, may not the Ogles of Somersetshire be remotely descended from King Lear?

C. L.

To THOMAS MANNING.

Letter CXXVI.]   *April 23*, 1803.

My dear Manning—Although something of the latest, and after two months' waiting, your letter was highly gratifying. Some parts want a little explication; for example, " the god-like face of the first consul." *What god* does he most resemble, Mars, Bacchus, or Apollo? or the god Serapis, who, flying (as Egyptian chronicles deliver) from the fury of the dog Anubis (the hieroglyph of an English mastiff), lighted upon Monomotapa (or the land of apes), by some thought to be Old France, and there set up a tyranny, etc. Our London prints of him represent him gloomy and sulky, like an angry Jupiter. I hear that he is very small, even less than me. I envy you your access to this great man, much more than your séances and conversaziones, which I have a shrewd suspicion must be something dull. What you assert concerning the actors of Paris, that they exceed our comedians, bad as ours are, is *impossible*. In one sense it may be true, that their fine gentlemen, in what is called genteel comedy, may possibly be more brisk and *dégagé* than Mr. Caulfield, or Mr. Whitfield; but have any of them the power to move *laughter in excess?* or can a Frenchman *laugh?* Can they batter at your judicious ribs till they *shake*, nothing loth to be so shaken? This is John Bull's criterion, and it shall be mine. You are Frenchified. Both your tastes and morals are corrupt and perverted. By and by you will come to assert that Buonaparte is as great a general as the old Duke of Cumberland, and deny that one Englishman can beat three Frenchmen. Read *Henry the Fifth* to restore your orthodoxy.

All things continue at a stay-still in London. I cannot repay your new novelties with my stale reminiscences. Like the prodigal, I have spent my patrimony, and feed upon the superannuated chaff and dry husks of repentance; yet sometimes I remember with pleasure the hounds and horses, which I kept in the days of my prodigality. I find nothing new, nor anything that has so much of the gloss and dazzle of novelty as may rebound in narrative, and cast a reflective glimmer across the channel. Something I will say about people that you and I know. Fenwick is still in debt, and the Professor has not done making love to his new spouse. I think he never looks into an almanack, or he would have found by the calendar that the honeymoon was extinct a moon ago. Southey is Secretary to the Chancellor of the Irish Exchequer; £400 a year. Stoddart is turned Doctor of Civil Law, and dwells in Doctors' Commons. I fear *his* commons are short, as they say. Did I send you an epitaph I scribbled upon a poor girl who died at nineteen?—a good girl, and a pretty girl, and a clever girl, but strangely neglected by all her friends and kin.

" Under this cold marble stone
  Sleep the sad remains of one
Who, when alive, by few or none
  Was loved, as loved she might have been,
If she prosperous days had seen,
  Or had thriving been, I ween.
Only this cold funeral stone
  Tells she was beloved by one,
Who on the marble graves his moan."

Brief, and pretty, and tender, is it not? I send you this, being the only piece of poetry I have *done* since the Muses all went with T. M. to Paris. I have neither stuff in my brain, nor paper in my drawer, to write you a longer letter. Liquor and company and wicked tobacco, a'nights, have quite dispericraniated me, as one may say; but you, who spiritualise upon Champagne, may continue to write long letters, and stuff 'em with amusement to the end. Too long they cannot be, any more than a codicil to a will, which leaves me sundry parks and manors not specified in the deed. But don't be *two months* before you write again. These from merry old England, on the day of her valiant patron St. George.

C. LAMB.

To SAMUEL TAYLOR COLERIDGE.

LETTER CXXVII.]   *May* 27, 1803.

My dear Coleridge—The date of my last was one day prior to the receipt of your letter, full of foul omens. I explain this lest you should have thought mine too light a reply to such sad matter. I seriously hope by this time you have given up all thoughts of journeying to the green Islands of the Bless'd—(voyages in time of war are very precarious)—or at least, that you will take them in your way to the Azores. Pray be careful of this letter till it has done its duty, for it is to inform you that I have booked off your watch (laid in cotton like an untimely fruit), and with it Condillac, and all other books of yours which were left here. These will set out on Monday next, the 29th May, by Kendal waggon, from White Horse, Cripplegate. You will make seasonable inquiries, for a watch mayn't come your way again in a hurry. I have been repeatedly after Tobin, and now hear that he is in the country, not to return till the middle of June. I will take care and see him with the earliest. But cannot you write pathetically to him, enforcing a speeding mission of your books for literary purposes? He is too good a retainer to Literature to let her interests suffer through his default. And why, in the name of Beelzebub, are your books to travel from Barnard's Inn to the Temple, and thence circuitously to Cripplegate, when their business is to take a short cut down Holborn Hill, up Snow ditto, on to Wood Street, etc.? The former mode seems a sad superstitious sub-division of labour. Well! the "Man of Ross" is to stand; Longman begs for it; the printer stands with a wet sheet in one hand, and a useless Pica in the other, in tears, pleading for it; I relent. Besides, it was a *Salutation* poem, and has the mark of the beast "Tobacco" upon it. Thus much I have done; I have swept off the lines about *widows* and *orphans* in second edition, which (if you remember) you most awkwardly and illogically caused to be inserted between two *Ifs*, to the great breach and disunion of said *Ifs*, which now meet again (as in first edition), like two clever lawyers arguing a case. Another reason for subtracting the pathos was, that the "Man of Ross" is too familiar to need telling what he did, especially in worse lines than Pope told it, and it now stands simply as "Reflections at an Inn about a known Character," and sucking an old story into an accommodation with present feelings. Here is no breaking spears with Pope, but a new, independent, and really a very pretty poem. In fact 'tis as I used to admire it in the first volume, and I have even dared to restore

"If neath this roof thy *wine cheer'd* moments pass,"

for

"Beneath this roof if thy cheer'd moments pass."

"Cheer'd" is a sad general word, "*wine-cheer'd*" I'm sure you'd give me, if I had a speaking-trumpet to sound to you 300 miles. But I am your *factotum ;* and that (save in this instance, which is a single case, and I can't get at you) shall be next to a *fac-nihil*—at most a *fac-simile.* I have ordered "Imitation of Spenser" to be restored on Wordsworth's authority ; and now, all that you will miss will be "Flicker and Flicker's Wife," "The Thimble," "Breathe *dear harmonist,*" and *I believe,* "The Child that was fed with Manna." Another volume will clear off all your Anthologic Morning-Postian Epistolary Miscellanies ; but pray don't put "Christabel" therein ; don't let that sweet maid come forth attended with Lady Holland's mob at her heels. Let there be a separate volume of Tales, Choice Tales, "Ancient Mariners," etc. A word of your health will be richly acceptable.   C. LAMB.

To Mr. RICKMAN.

LETTER CXXVIII.]   *Saturday Morning, July* 16, 1803.

Dear Rickman—I enclose you a wonder, a letter from the shades. A dead body wants to return, and be inrolled *inter vivos.* 'Tis a gentle ghost, and in this Galvanic age it may have a chance.

Mary and I are setting out for the Isle of Wight. We make but a short stay, and shall pass the time betwixt that place and Portsmouth, where Fenwick is. I sadly wanted to explore the Peak this Summer ; but Mary is against steering without card or compass, and we should be at large in Darbyshire.

We shall be at home this night and to-morrow, if you can come and take a farewell pipe.

I regularly transmitted your Notices to the *Morning Post,* but they have not been duly honoured. The fault lay not in me.—Yours truly,   C. LAMB.

To RICKMAN.

July 27, 1803.

(The earlier part of this letter is by Captain Burney, and is in his handwriting.)

Dear Rickman—We are at Cowes the whole flock, Sheep and Lambs—and in good pasturage—for notwithstanding that I joined, or rather acquiesced, in your dispraise of Cowes, in a dry summer like this it is a very pleasant place. We were much harassed by hot travelling and uncertainties till we fixed at this haven; and now I could feel myself thoroughly well disposed to indulge in a week of compleat idleness, if my senses were not invaded by the din of preparation, and the account which every day's paper brings of the universal bustle that prevails everywhere.

We purpose however to stay here one week longer reckoning from this date, and then to return to the defence of the Capital after so well having guarded the sea coast. We have visited Newport and Carisbrook Castle where we saw a deep well and a cross old woman. We went by water, and friend Lamb (to give a specimen of his Seamanship) very ingeniously and unconsciously cast loose the fastenings of the mast, so that mast, sprit, sails, and all the rest tumbled overboard with a crash, and not less to his surprise than to the surprise of every other person in the boat. I doubt whether any of us will muster up sufficient activity to go to the South part of the Island. We do everything that is idle, such as reading books from a circulating library, sauntering, hunting little crabs among the rocks, reading Church yard poetry which is as bad at Cowes as any Church yard in the Kingdom can produce. Miss Lamb is the only person among us who is not idle. All the cares she takes into her keeping. At night however we do a little business in the smoking line, and Martin endeavours to make Conundrums, but alas! he is not equal to the achieve-

ment.   Such is the edifying life we lead at the Isle of
Wight.   Let us know how you take care of the Capital.
An old sea saying is, " Give a sprat to catch a Mackarel,"
so pray send us your Mackarel and accept this sprat.

[Lamb's part begins here.]

I testify that this is a pretty good outline of our
doings, but the filling it up requires the hand of a Master.
A volume might be made of Martin's blunders which
parental tenderness omits.   Such as his letting the packet-
boat's boat go without him from the quay at Southampton,
while he stood hiatusing, smit with the love of a Naiad ;
his tumbling back over a stone twice the height of
himself, and daubing himself ; his getting up to bathe
at six o'clock, and forgetting it, and in consequence staying
in his room in a process of annihilation, etc., etc., then
the time expended in *Martin being scolded* would serve
as great a sinner as Judas to repent in.   In short nothing
in this house goes right till after supper, then a gentle
circumambience of the weed serves to shut out Isle of
Wight impertinent scenery and brings us back in fancy
to Mutton Lane and the romantic alleys ever green of
nether-Holborn, green that owes nothing to grass, but
the simple effect of cabbage-water, tripe-cauls, etc.   The
fact of my setting the mast upside down is partly true.
Indeed it was never properly nailed down, or the accident
could not have happened.—Capt. Burney does nothing
but teach his children bad habits.   He surfeits them with
cherries and black currants till they can eat no supper
and then claps down the fruit expended to the common
stock, and deducts what the surfeit saves from his part.
There's a little girl he's brought with him that has cost
I don't know what in codlings.—No ordinary orchard
would be a jointure for her.—To add to our difficulties
Martin has brought down a Terence, which he renders
out loud into canine Latin at Breakfast and other meals,
till the eyes of the infatuated Parent let slip water for

joy, and the ears of every body beside shed their wax for being tired.   More I could add but it is unsafe.

From the White Isle (date unknown).   C. L.

To John Rickman, Esq.,
   Dublin Castle.

To WILLIAM GODWIN.

LETTER CXXX.]   *November* 8, 1803.

My dear Sir—I have been sitting down for three or four days successively to the review, which I so much wished to do well, and to your satisfaction.   But I can produce nothing but absolute flatness and nonsense.   My health and spirits are so bad, and my nerves so irritable, that I am sure, if I persist, I shall tease myself into a fever.   You do not know how sore and weak a brain I have, or you would allow for many things in me which you set down for whims.   I solemnly assure you that I never more wished to prove to you the value which I have for you than at this moment; but although so seemingly trifling a service, I cannot get through with it : I pray you to impute it to this one sole cause, ill health. I hope I am above subterfuge, and that you will do me this justice to think so.

You will give me great satisfaction by sealing my pardon and oblivion in a line or two, before I come to see you, or I shall be ashamed to come.—Your, with great truth,   C. LAMB.

LETTER CXXXI.]   *November* 10, 1803.

Dear Godwin—You never made a more unlucky and perverse mistake than to suppose that the reason of my not writing that cursed thing was to be found in your book.   I assure you most sincerely that I have been greatly delighted with " Chaucer."   I may be wrong, but I think there is one considerable error runs through it, which is a conjecturing spirit, a fondness for filling out the picture by supposing what Chaucer did and how

he felt, where the materials are scanty. So far from
meaning to withhold from you (out of mistaken tenderness) this opinion of mine, I plainly told Mrs. Godwin
that I did find a *fault*, which I should reserve naming
until I should see you and talk it over. This she may very
well remember, and also that I declined naming this fault
until she drew it from me by asking me if there was not
too much fancy in the work. I then confessed generally
what I felt, but refused to go into particulars until I had
seen you. I am never very fond of saying things before
third persons, because in the relation (such is human
nature) something is sure to be dropped. If Mrs. Godwin has been the cause of your misconstruction, I am
very angry, tell her; yet it is not an anger unto death.
I remember also telling Mrs. G. (which she may have
dropt) that I was by turns considerably more delighted
than I expected. But I wished to reserve all this until
I saw you. I even had conceived an expression to meet
you with, which was thanking you for some of the most
exquisite pieces of criticism I had ever read in my life.
In particular, I should have brought forward that on
" Troilus and Cressida" and Shakspeare which, it is little
to say, delighted me, and instructed me (if not absolutely
instructed me, yet put into *full-grown sense* many conceptions which had arisen in me before in my most dis-
criminating moods). All these things I was preparing
to say, and bottling them up till I came, thinking to
please my friend and host the author, when lo! this
deadly blight intervened.

I certainly ought to make great allowances for your
misunderstanding me. You, by long habits of composition
and a greater command gained over your own powers,
cannot conceive of the desultory and uncertain way in
which I (an author by fits) sometimes cannot put the
thoughts of a common letter into sane prose. Any work
which I take upon myself as an engagement will act upon
me to torment, *e.g.* when I have undertaken, as three or
four times I have, a schoolboy copy of verses for Merchant

Taylors' boys, at a guinea a copy, I have fretted over them in perfect inability to do them, and have made my sister wretched with my wretchedness for a week together. The same, till by habit I have acquired a mechanical command, I have felt in making paragraphs. As to reviewing, in particular, my head is so whimsical a head, that I cannot, after reading another man's book, let it have been never so pleasing, give any account of it in any methodical way. I cannot follow his train. Something like this you must have perceived of me in conversation. Ten thousand times I have confessed to you, talking of my talents, my utter inability to remember in any comprehensive way what I read. I can vehemently applaud, or perversely stickle, at *parts ;* but I cannot grasp at a whole. This infirmity (which is nothing to brag of) may be seen in my two little compositions, the tale and my play, in both which no reader, however partial, can find any story. I wrote such stuff about Chaucer, and got into such digressions, quite irreducible into $1\frac{1}{5}$ column of a paper, that I was perfectly ashamed to show it you. However, it is become a serious matter that I should convince you I neither slunk from the task through a wilful deserting neglect, or through any (most imaginary on your part) distaste of "Chaucer"; and I will try my hand again, I hope with better luck. My health is bad and my time taken up; but all I can spare between this and Sunday shall be employed for you, since you desire it : and if I bring you a crude, wretched paper on Sunday, you must burn it, and forgive me ; if it proves anything better than I predict, may it be a peace-offering of sweet incense between us. C. LAMB.

To ROBERT LLOYD.

LETTER CXXXII.]   *March* 13, 1804.

Dear Robert—I received your notes safe, and thank you for them. It seems you are about to be married. Joy to you and uninterrupted satisfaction in that state. But who is the Lady? It is the character of your letters that you omit facts, dates, names, and matter, and describe nothing but feelings, in which, as I cannot always partake, as being more intense in degree or different in kind from my own tranquil ones, I cannot always well tell how to reply. Your dishes are too much sauced and spiced and flavoured for me to suppose that you can relish my plain meats and vulgar aliment. Still, Robert, if I cannot always send you of the same, they have a smack and a novelty, a Robert-ism about them, that make them a dainty stimulus to my palate at times. I have little to tell you of. You are mistaken, I am disengaged from all newspaper connections, and breathe a freer air in consequence. I was bound, like Gulliver, in a multitude of little chains, which, by quotidian leasing swelled to a rack and a gibbet in the year's account. I am poorer but happier. Your three pounds came seasonably, but I doubt whether I am fairly entitled to them as a debt.

I am obliged to break off here, and would not send this unfinished, but that you might otherwise be uneasy about the moneys.

Am I ever to see you? for it is like letters to the dead, or for a friend to write to his friend in the Fortunate Isles, or the Moon, or at the Antipodes, to address a line to ONE in Warwickshire that I am never to see in London. I shall lose the very face of Robert by disuse, and I question, if I were a painter, if I could now paint it from memory.

I could tell you many things, but you are so spiritual and abstracted, that I fear to insult you with tidings of this world. But may your approaching husband-hood humanise you. I think I see a dawn. I am sure joy is rising upon you, and I stand a tiptoe to see the sun ascending till it gets up and up, and "while a man tells the story," shows at last a fair face and a full light.

God bless you, Robt.   C. L.

LETTER CXXXIII.]   *September* 13, 1804.

Dear Robert—I was startled in a very pleasant manner by the contents of your letter. It was like your good self to take so handsome an opportunity of renewing an old friendship. I thank you kindly for your offers to bring me acquainted with Mrs. Ll. I cannot come now, but assuredly I will some time or other, to see how this new relation sits upon you. I am naturally shy of new faces ; but the Lady who has chosen my old friend Robert cannot have a repelling one. Assure her of my sincere congratulations and friendly feelings. Mary joins in both with me, and considers herself as only left out of your kind invitation by some LAPSUS STYLI. We have already had all the holydays we can have this year. We have been spending our usual summer month at Richmond, from which place we traced the banks of the old Thames for ten and twenty miles, in daily walks or rides, and found beauties which may compare with Ulswater and Windermere. We visited Windsor, Hampton, etc. etc.—but this is a deviation from the subject with which I began my letter.

Some day I certainly shall come and see you in your new light ; no longer the restless (but good) [? single] Robert ; but now the staid, sober (and not less good) married Robert. And how does Plumstead, the impetuous, take your getting the start of him? When will he subside into matrimony? Priscilla has taken a long time indeed to think about it. I will suppose that her first choice is now her final; though you do not expressly say that she is to be a Wordsworth. I wish her, and dare promise her, all happiness.

All these new nuptials do not make me unquiet in the perpetual prospect of celibacy. There is a quiet dignity in old bachelorhood, a leisure from cares, noise, etc., an enthronisation upon the armed-chair of a man's feeling that he may sit, walk, read, unmolested, to none accountable—but hush! or I shall be torn in pieces like a churlish Orpheus by young married women and bridemaids of Birmingham. The close is this, to every man that way of life, which in his election is best. Be as happy in yours as I am determined to be in mine, and we shall strive lovingly who shall sing best the praises of matrimony, and the praises of singleness.

Adieu, my old friend in a new character, and believe me that no "wounds" have pierced our friendship; only a long want of seeing each other has disfurnished us of topics on which to talk. Is not your new fortunes a topic which may hold us for some months (the honey months at least)?   C. LAMB.

To ROBERT SOUTHEY.

LETTER CXXXIV.]   *November* 7, 1804.

Dear Southey—You were the last person from whom we heard of Dyer, and if you know where to forward to him the news I now send I shall be obliged to you to lose no time. Dyer's sister-in-law, who lives in St. Dunstan's Court, wrote to him about three weeks ago to the Hoop Inn, Cambridge, to inform him that Squire Houlbert, or some such name, of Denmark Hill, has died, and left her husband a thousand pounds, and two or three hundred to Dyer. Her letter got no answer, and she does not know where to direct to him; so she came to me, who am equally in the dark. Her story is, that Dyer's immediately coming to town now, and signing some papers, will save him a considerable sum of money; how, I don't understand; but it is very right he should hear of this. She has left me barely time for the post; so I conclude with love to all at Keswick.

Dyer's brother, who by his wife's account has got £1000 left him, is father of the little dirty girl, Dyer's niece and factotum.—In haste,

Yours truly,   C. LAMB.

If you send George this, cut off the last paragraph.

D.'s laundress had a letter a few days since; but George never dates.

To THOMAS MANNING.

LETTER CXXXV.]   16, *Mitre Court Buildings,*
Saturday, February 24, 1805.

Dear Manning—I have been very unwell since I saw you: a sad depression of spirits, a most unaccountable nervousness; from which I have been partially relieved by an odd accident. You knew Dick Hopkins, the swearing scullion of Caius? This fellow, by industry and agility, has thrust himself into the important situations (no sinecures, believe me) of cook to Trinity Hall and Caius College: and the generous creature has contrived, with the greatest delicacy imaginable, to send me a present of Cambridge brawn. What makes it the more extraordinary is, that the man never saw me in his life that I know of. I suppose he has *heard* of me. I did not immediately recognise the donor; but one of Richard's cards, which had accidentally fallen into the

straw, detected him in a moment.   Dick, you know, was
always remarkable for flourishing. His card imports, that
" orders (to wit, for brawn) from any part of England,
Scotland, or Ireland, will be duly executed," etc.   At
first, I thought of declining the present ; but Richard
knew my blind side when he pitched upon brawn.   'Tis
of all my hobbies the supreme in the eating way.   He
might have sent sops from the pan, skimmings, crumpets,
chips, hog's lard, the tender brown judiciously scalped from
a fillet of veal (dexterously replaced by a salamander), the
tops of asparagus, fugitive livers, runaway gizzards of
fowls, the eyes of martyred pigs, tender effusions of laxa-
tive woodcocks, the red spawn of lobsters, leverets' ears,
and such pretty filchings common to cooks ; but these
had been ordinary presents, the everyday courtesies of
dish-washers to their sweethearts.   Brawn was a noble
thought.   It is not every common gullet-fancier that can
properly esteem it.   It is like a picture of one of the
choice old Italian masters.   Its gusto is of that hidden
sort.   As Wordsworth sings of a modest poet,—" you
must love him, ere to you he will seem worthy of your
love ;" so brawn, you must taste it ere to you it will
seem to have any taste at all.   But 'tis nuts to the adept :
those that will send out their tongue and feelers to find
it out.   It will be wooed, and not unsought be won.
Now, ham-essence, lobsters, turtle, such popular minions,
absolutely *court you*, lay themselves out to strike you at
first smack, like one of David's pictures (they call him
Darveed) compared with the plain russet-coated wealth
of a Titian or a Correggio, as I illustrated above.   Such
are the obvious glaring heathen virtues of a corporation
dinner, compared with the reserved collegiate worth of
brawn.   Do me the favour to leave off the business
which you may be at present upon, and go immediately
to the kitchens of Trinity and Caius, and make my most
respectful compliments to Mr. Richard Hopkins, and
assure him that his brawn is most excellent ; and that I
am moreover obliged to him for his innuendo about salt

water and bran, which I shall not fail to improve. I
leave it to you whether you shall choose to pay him the
civility of asking him to dinner while you stay in Cambridge, or in whatever other way you may best like to
show your gratitude to *my friend*. Richard Hopkins,
considered in many points of view, is a very extraordinary
character. Adieu. I hope to see you to supper in
London soon, where we will taste Richard's brawn, and
drink his health in a cheerful but moderate cup. We
have not many such men in any rank of life as Mr. R.
Hopkins. Crisp, the barber, of St. Mary's, was just such
another. I wonder *he* never sent me any little token,
some chestnuts, or a puff, or two pound of hair : just to
remember him by. Gifts are like nails. *Præsens ut
absens ;* that is, your *present* makes amends for your
absence.

    Yours,   C. LAMB.

To Miss WORDSWORTH.

LETTER CXXXVI.]   *June* 14, 1805.

My dear Miss Wordsworth—Your long kind letter
has not been thrown away (for it has given me great
pleasure to find you are all resuming your old occupations,
and are better) ; but poor Mary, to whom it is addressed,
cannot yet relish it. She has been attacked by one of
her severe illnesses, and is at present *from home*. Last
Monday week was the day she left me, and I hope I may
calculate upon having her again in a month or little more.
I am rather afraid late hours have in this case contributed
to her indisposition. But when she discovers symptoms
of approaching illness, it is not easy to say what is best
to do. Being by ourselves is bad, and going out is bad.
I get so irritable and wretched with fear, that I constantly hasten on the disorder. You cannot conceive the
misery of such a foresight. I am sure that, for the week
before she left me, I was little better than light-headed.

I now am calm, but sadly taken down and flat. I have every reason to suppose that this illness, like all her former ones, will be but temporary; but I cannot always feel so. Meantime she is dead to me, and I miss a prop. All my strength is gone, and I am like a fool, bereft of her co-operation. I dare not think, lest I should think wrong; so used am I to look up to her in the least and the biggest perplexity. To say all that I know of her would be more than I think anybody could believe, or even understand; and when I hope to have her well again with me, it would be sinning against her feelings to go about to praise her; for I can conceal nothing that I do from her. She is older and wiser and better than I, and all my wretched imperfections I cover to myself by resolutely thinking on her goodness. She would share life and death, heaven and hell, with me. She lives but for me; and I know I have been wasting and teasing her life for five years past incessantly with my cursed drinking and ways of going on. But even in this upbraiding of myself I am offending against her, for I know that she has cleaved to me for better, for worse; and if the balance has been against her hitherto, it was a noble trade. I am stupid, and lose myself in what I write. I write rather what answers to my feelings (which are sometimes sharp enough) than express my present ones, for I am only flat and stupid. I am sure you will excuse my writing any more, I am so very poorly.

I cannot resist transcribing three or four lines which poor Mary made upon a picture (a Holy Family) which we saw at an auction only one week before she left home. She was then beginning to show signs of ill boding. They are sweet lines and upon a sweet picture; but I send them only as the latest memorial of her.

"VIRGIN AND CHILD, L. DA VINCI.

"Maternal Lady, with thy virgin grace,
  Heaven-born, thy Jesus seemeth sure,
  And thou a virgin pure.
  Lady most perfect, when thy angel face

Men look upon, they wish to be
A Catholic, Madonna fair, to worship thee."

You had her lines about the "Lady Blanch." You have not had some which she wrote upon a copy of a girl from Titian, which I had hung up where that print of Blanch and the Abbess (as she beautifully interpreted two female figures from L. da Vinci) had hung in our room. 'Tis light and pretty :—

" Who art thou, fair one, who usurp'st the place
Of Blanch, the lady of the matchless grace ?
Come, fair and pretty, tell to me
Who in thy lifetime thou mightst be ?
Thou pretty art and fair,
But with the Lady Blanch thou never must compare.
No need for Blanch her history to tell,
Whoever saw her face, they there did read it well ;
But when I look on thee, I only know
There lived a pretty maid some hundred years ago."

This is a little unfair, to tell so much about ourselves, and to advert so little to your letter, so full of comfortable tidings of you all. But my own cares press pretty close upon me, and you can make allowance. That you may go on gathering strength and peace is my next wish to Mary's recovery.

I had almost forgot your repeated invitation. Supposing that Mary will be well and able, there is another *ability* which you may guess at, which I cannot promise myself. In prudence we ought not to come. This illness will make it still more prudential to wait. It is not a balance of this way of spending our money against another way, but an absolute question of whether we shall stop now, or go on wasting away the little we have got beforehand, which my wise conduct has already encroach'd upon one half. My best love, however, to you all ; and to that most friendly creature, Mrs. Clarkson, and better health to her, when you see or write to her.

CHARLES LAMB.

To THOMAS MANNING.

LETTER CXXXVII.]   [*July* 27, 1805.]

Dear Archimedes—Things have gone on badly with thy ungeometrical friend ; but they are on the turn. My old housekeeper has shown signs of convalescence, and will shortly resume the power of the keys, so I shan't be cheated of my tea and liquors. Wind in the West, which promotes tranquillity. Have leisure now to anticipate seeing thee again. Have been taking leave of tobacco in a rhyming address. Had thought *that vein* had long since closed up. Find I can rhyme and reason too. Think of studying mathematics, to restrain the fire of my genius, which G. D. recommends. Have frequent bleedings at the nose, which shows plethoric. Maybe shall try the sea myself, that great scene of wonders. Got incredibly sober and regular ; shave oftener, and hum a tune, to signify cheerfulness and gallantry.

Suddenly disposed to sleep, having taken a quart of pease with bacon and stout. Will not refuse Nature, who has done such things for me !

Nurse ! don't call me unless Mr. Manning comes.— What ! the gentleman in spectacles ?—Yes.

Dormit.   C. L.

Saturday,
   Hot Noon.

To WILLIAM WORDSWORTH.

LETTER CXXXVIII.]   *September* 28, 1805.

My dear Wordsworth (or Dorothy rather, for to you appertains the biggest part of this answer by right)— I will not again deserve reproach by so long a silence. I have kept deluding myself with the idea that Mary would write to you, but she is so lazy (or, which I believe is the true state of the case, so diffident), that it must revert to me as usual. Though she writes a pretty good style, and has some notion of the force of words, she is not always so certain of the true orthography of them; and that, and a poor handwriting (in this age of female calligraphy), often deters her, where no other reason does.

We have neither of us been very well for some weeks past. I am very nervous, and she most so at those times when I am; so that a merry friend, adverting to the noble consolation we were able to afford each other, denominated us, not unaptly, Gum-boil and Tooth-Ache, for they used to say that a gum-boil is a great relief to a tooth-ache.

We have been two tiny excursions this Summer, for three or four days each, to a place near Harrow, and to Egham, where Cooper's Hill is: and that is the total history of our rustications this year. Alas! how poor a round to Skiddaw and Helvellyn, and Borrowdale, and the magnificent sesquipedalia of the year 1802! Poor old Molly! to have lost her pride, that "last infirmity of noble minds," and her cow. Fate need not have set her wits to such an old Molly. I am heartily sorry for her. Remember us lovingly to her; and in particular remember us to Mrs. Clarkson in the most kind manner.

I hope, by "southwards," you mean that she will be at or near London, for she is a great favourite of both of us, and we feel for her health as much as possible for any one to do. She is one of the friendliest, comfortablest women we know, and made our little stay at your cottage one of the pleasantest times we ever past. We were quite strangers to her. Mr. C. is with you too; our kindest separate remembrances to him. As to our special affairs, I am looking about me. I have done nothing since the beginning of last year, when I lost my newspaper job; and having had a long idleness, I must do something, or we shall get very poor. Sometimes I think of a farce, but hitherto all schemes have gone off; an idle brag or

two of an evening, vapouring out of a pipe, and going off
in the morning; but now I have bid farewell to my
"sweet enemy," Tobacco, I shall perhaps set nobly to
work.   Hang work!

I wish that all the year were holiday; I am sure that
indolence—indefeasible indolence—is the true state of
man, and business the invention of the old Teazer, whose
interference doomed Adam to an apron and set him a
hoeing.   Pen and ink, and clerks and desks, were the
refinements of this old torturer some thousand years after,
under pretence of "Commerce allying distant shores,
promoting and diffusing knowledge, good," etc. etc.

I wish you may think this a handsome farewell to
my "Friendly Traitress."   Tobacco has been my evening
comfort and my morning curse for these five years; and
you know how difficult it is from refraining to pick one's
lips even, when it has become a habit.   This poem is
the only one which I have finished since so long as when
I wrote "Hester Savory."   I have had it in my head to
do it these two years, but tobacco stood in its own light
when it gave me headaches that prevented my singing
its praises.   Now you have got it, you have got all my
store, for I have absolutely not another line.   No more
has Mary.   We have nobody about us that cares for
poetry; and who will rear grapes when he shall be the
sole eater?   Perhaps if you encourage us to show you
what we may write, we may do something now and then
before we absolutely forget the quantity of an English
line for want of practice.   The "Tobacco," being a little
in the way of Wither (whom Southey so much likes),
perhaps you will somehow convey it to him with my kind
remembrances.   Then, everybody will have seen it that
I wish to see it, I having sent it to Malta.

I remain, dear W. and D., yours truly,

C. LAMB.

To WILLIAM HAZLITT.

LETTER CXXXIX.]   *November* 10, 1805.

Dear Hazlitt—I was very glad to hear from you, and that your journey was so *picturesque*. We miss you, as we foretold we should. One or two things have happened, which are beneath the dignity of epistolary communication, but which, seated about our fireside at night (the winter hands of pork have begun), gesture and emphasis might have talked into some importance. Something about Rickman's wife; for instance, how tall she is, and that she visits pranked up like a Queen of the May, with green streamers: a good-natured woman though, which is as much as you can expect from a friend's wife, whom you got acquainted with a bachelor. Some things too about Monkey, which can't so well be written: how it set up for a fine lady, and thought it had got lovers, and was obliged to be convinced of its age from the parish register, where it was proved to be only twelve; and an edict issued, that it should not give itself airs yet these four years; and how it got leave to be called Miss, by grace; these, and such like hows, were in my head to tell you; but who can write? Also how Manning is come to town in spectacles, and studies physic; is melancholy, and seems to have something in his head, which he don't impart. Then, how I am going to leave off smoking. O la! your Leonardos of Oxford made my mouth water. I was hurried through the gallery, and they escaped me. What do I say? I was a Goth then, and should not have noticed them. I had not settled my notions of beauty: I have now for ever!—the small head, the long eye,—that sort of peering curve,—the wicked Italian mischief; the stick-at-nothing, Herodias's daughter kind of grace. You understand me? But you disappoint me in passing over in absolute silence the Blenheim Leonardo. Didn't you see it? Excuse a lover's curiosity. I have seen no pictures of note since, except Mr. Dawe's gallery. It is curious to see how differently two great men treat the same subject, yet both excellent in their way. For instance, Milton and Mr. Dawe. Mr. D. has chosen to illustrate the story of Samson exactly in the point of view in which Milton has been most happy : the interview between the Jewish hero, blind and captive, and Delilah. Milton has imagined his locks grown again, strong as horse-hair or porcupine's bristles ; doubtless shaggy and black, as being hairs "which, of a nation armed, contained the strength." I don't remember he *says* black ; but could Milton imagine them to be yellow ? Do you ? Mr. Dawe, with striking originality of conception, has crowned him with a thin yellow wig, in colour precisely like Dyson's ; in curl and quantity, resembling Mrs. Professor's ; his limbs rather stout,—about such a man as my brother or Rickman,— but no Atlas nor Hercules, nor yet so long as Dubois, the clown of Sadler's Wells. This was judicious, taking the spirit of the story rather than the fact ; for doubtless God could communicate national salvation to the trust of flax and tow as well as hemp and cordage, and could draw down a temple with a golden tress as soon as with all the cables of the British navy.

Wasn't you sorry for Lord Nelson ? I have followed him in fancy ever since I saw him walking in Pall Mall (I was prejudiced against him before), looking just as a hero should look ; and I have been very much cut about it indeed. He was the only pretence of a great man we had. Nobody is left of any name at all. His secretary died by his side. I imagined him a Mr. Scott, to be the man you met at Hume's ; but I learnt from Mrs. Hume that it is not the same. I met Mrs. H. one day, and agreed to go on the Sunday to tea, but the rain prevented us, and the distance. I have been to apologise, and we are to dine there the first fine Sunday. Strange perverseness ! I never went while you stayed here ; and now I *go to find you !* What other news is there, Mary ? What puns have I made in the last fortnight ? You never remember them. You have no relish for the comic. "Oh! tell Hazlitt not to forget to send the *American Farmer*. I daresay it is not so good as he fancies; but a book's a book." I have not heard from Wordsworth or from Malta since. Charles Kemble, it seems, enters into possession to-morrow. We sup at 109 Russell Street, this evening. I wish your brother would not drink. 'Tis a blemish in the greatest characters. You send me a modern quotation poetical. How do you like this in an old play? Vittoria Corombona, a spunky Italian lady, a Leonardo one, nicknamed the White Devil, being on her trial for murder, etc.—and questioned about seducing a duke from his wife and the state, makes answer :—

> "Condemn you me for that the Duke did love me?
> So may you blame some fair and crystal river,
> For that some melancholic distracted man
> Hath drown'd himself in it."

N.B.—I shall expect a line from you, if but a bare line, whenever you write to Russell Street, and a letter often when you do not. I pay no postage; but I will have consideration for you until Parliament time and franks. Luck to Ned Search, and the new art of colouring. Monkey sends her love; and Mary especially.

Yours truly,   C. LAMB.

To THOMAS MANNING.

LETTER CXL.]   [*November* 15, 1805.]

Dear Manning—Certainly you could not have called at all hours from two till ten, for we have been only out of an evening Monday and Tuesday in this week. But if you think you have, your thought shall go for the deed. We did pray for you on Wednesday night. Oysters unusually luscious; pearls of extraordinary magnitude found in them. I have made bracelets of them; given them in clusters to ladies. Last night we went out in despite, because you were not come at your hour.

This night we shall be at home ; so shall we certainly, both, on Sunday, Monday, Tuesday, and Wednesday. Take your choice, mind I don't say of one : but choose which evening you will not come, and come the other four.   Doors open at five o'clock.   Shells forced about nine.   Every gentleman smokes or not as he pleases.

C. L.

To WILLIAM HAZLITT.

LETTER CXLI.]   *January* 15, 1806.

Dear Hazlitt—Godwin went to Johnson's yesterday about your business.   Johnson would not come down, or give any answer, but has promised to open the manuscript, and to give you an answer in one month.   Godwin will punctually go again (Wednesday is Johnson's open day) yesterday four weeks next : *i.e.* in one lunar month from this time ; till when, Johnson positively declines giving any answer.   I wish you joy on ending your Search. Mrs. H. was naming something about a " Life of Fawcett," to be by you undertaken : the great Fawcett, as she explained to Manning, when he asked, " *What Fawcett ?*"   He innocently thought *Fawcett the Player*.   But Fawcett the divine is known to many people, albeit unknown to the Chinese inquirer.   I should think, if you liked it, and Johnson declined it, that Phillips is the man. He is perpetually bringing out biographies,—Richardson, Wilks, Foot, Lee Lewis,—without number : little trim things in two easy volumes, price 12s. the two, made up of letters to and from, scraps, posthumous trifles, anecdotes, and about forty pages of hard biography.   You might dish up a Fawcettiad in three months, and ask £60 or £80 for it.   I should dare say that Phillips would catch at it.   I wrote to you the other day in a great hurry.   Did you get it ?   This is merely a letter of business at Godwin's request.   Lord Nelson is quiet at last. His ghost only keeps a slight fluttering in odes and elegies in newspapers, and impromptus, which could not be got ready before the funeral.

As for news, Fenwick is coming to town on Monday (if no kind angel intervene) to surrender himself to prison. He hopes to get the rules of the Fleet. On the same, or nearly the same day, Fell, my other quondam co-friend and drinker, will go to Newgate, and his wife and four children, I suppose, to the parish. Plenty of reflection and motives of gratitude to the wise Disposer of all things in *us*, whose prudent conduct has hitherto ensured us a warm fire and snug roof over our heads. *Nullum numen abest si sit Prudentia.* Alas! Prudentia is in the last quarter of her tutelary shining over me. A little time and I ——; but maybe I may, at last, hit upon some mode of collecting some of the vast superfluities of this money-voiding town. Much is to be got, and I do not want much. All I ask is time and leisure; and I am cruelly off for them. When you have the inclination, I shall be very glad to have a letter from you. Your brother and Mrs. H., I am afraid, think hardly of us for not coming oftener to see them; but we are distracted beyond what they can conceive with visitors and visitings. I never have an hour for my head to work quietly its own workings; which you know is as necessary to the human system as sleep. Sleep, too, I can't get for these winds of a night: and without sleep and rest what should ensue? Lunacy. But I trust it won't.

Yours, dear H.,   C. LAMB.

To Mr. RICKMAN.

LETTER CXLII.]   *January* 25, 1806.

Dear Rickman—You do not happen to have any place at your disposal which would suit a decayed Literatus? I do not much expect that you have, or that you will go much out of the way to serve the object, when you hear it is Fell. But the case is, by a *mistaking* of his *turn*, as they call it, he is reduced, I am afraid, to extremities, and would be extremely glad of a place in an office. Now it does sometimes happen, that just as a man wants a place, a place wants him; and though this is a lottery to which none but G. Burnett would choose to trust his all, there is no harm just to call in at Despair's office for a friend, and see if *his* number is come up (Burnett's further case I enclose by way of episode). Now, if you should happen, or anybody you know, to want a *hand*, here is a young man of solid but not brilliant genius, who would turn his hand to the making out of dockets, penning a manifesto, or scoring a tally, not the worse (I hope) for knowing Latin and Greek, and having in youth conversed with the philosophers. But from these follies I believe he is thoroughly awakened, and would bind himself by a terrible oath never to imagine himself an extraordinary genius again.

Yours, etc.,   C. LAMB.

To WILLIAM HAZLITT.

LETTER CXLIII.]   *February* 19, 1806.

Dear H.—Godwin has just been here in his way from Johnson's. Johnson has had a fire in his house; this happened about five weeks ago; it was in the daytime, so it did not burn the house down, but it did so much damage that the house must come down, to be repaired. His nephew that we met on Hampstead Hill put it out. Well, this fire has put him so back, that he craves one more month before he gives you an answer. I will certainly goad Godwin (if necessary) to go again this very day four weeks; but I am confident he will want no goading. Three or four most capital auctions of pictures are advertised: in May, *Wellbore Ellis Agar's*, the first private collection in England, so Holcroft says; in March, Sir George Young's in Stratford Place (where Cosway lives), and a Mr. Hulse's at Blackheath, both very capital collections, and have been announced for some months. Also the Marquis of Lansdowne's pictures in March; and though inferior to mention, lastly, the Tructhsessian Gallery. Don't your mouth water to be here? T'other night Loftus called, whom we have not seen since you went before. We meditate a stroll next Wednesday, fast-day. He happened to light upon Mr. Holcroft, wife, and daughter, their first visit at our house. Your brother called last night. We keep up our intimacy. He is going to begin a large Madonna and child from Mrs. H. and baby. I fear he goes astray after *ignes fatui*. He is a clever man. By the by, I saw a miniature of his as far excelling any in his show cupboard (that of your sister not excepted) as that show cupboard excels the show things you see in windows—an old woman (damn her name!), but most superlative; he has it to clean—I'll ask him the name—but the best miniature I ever saw. But for oil pictures!—what has he to do with Madonnas? If the Virgin Mary were alive and visitable, he would not hazard himself in a Covent Garden pit-door crowd to see her. It isn't his style of beauty, is it? But he will go on painting things he ought not to paint, and not painting things he ought to paint. Manning is not gone to China, but talks of going this Spring. God forbid! Coleridge not heard of. I am going to leave off smoke. In the meantime I am so smoky with last night's ten pipes, that I must leave off. Mary begs her kind remembrances. Pray write to us. This is no letter; but I supposed you grew anxious about Johnson.

N.B.—Have taken a room at three shillings a week, to be in between five and eight at night, to avoid my *nocturnal*, alias *knock-eternal*, visitors. The first-fruits of my retirement has been a farce, which goes to manager to-morrow. *Wish my ticket luck.* God bless you; and do write.—Yours, *fumosissimus*, C. LAMB.

To Mr. RICKMAN.

March 1806.

Dear Rickman—I send you some papers about a salt water soap, for which the inventor is desirous of getting a parliamentary reward, like Dr. Jenner. Whether such a project be feasible, I mainly doubt, taking for granted the equal utility. I should suppose the usual way of paying such projectors is by patent and contracts. The patent, you see, he has got. A contract he is about with the Navy Board. Meantime, the projector is hungry. Will you answer me two questions, and return them with the papers as soon as you can? Imprimis, is there any chance of success in application to Parliament for a reward? Did you ever hear of the invention? You see its benefits and saving to the nation (always the first motive with a true projector) are feelingly set forth : the last paragraph but one of the estimate, in enumerating the shifts poor seamen are put to, even approaches to the pathetic. But, agreeing to all he says, is there the remotest chance of Parliament giving the projector anything? And *when* should application be made, now, or after a report (if he can get it) from the Navy Board? Secondly, let the infeasibility be as great as you will, you will oblige me by telling me the way of introducing such an application in Parliament, without buying over a majority of members, which is totally out of projector's power. I vouch nothing for the soap myself ; for I always wash in *fresh water*, and find it answer tolerably well for all purposes of cleanliness ; nor do I know the projector ; but a relation of mine has put me on writing to you, for whose parliamentary knowledge he has great veneration.

P. S.—The Capt. and Mrs. Burney and Phillips take their chance at cribbage here on Wednesday. Will you and Mrs. R. join the party? Mary desires her compliments to Mrs. R., and joins in the invitation.

Yours truly,

C. Lamb.

To WILLIAM HAZLITT.

LETTER CXLV.]   *March* 15, 1806.

Dear H.—I am a little surprised at no letter from you. This day week, to wit, Saturday, the 8th of March, 1806, I booked off by the Wem coach, Bull and Mouth Inn, directed to *you*, at the Rev. Mr. Hazlitt's, Wem, Shropshire, a parcel containing, besides a book, etc., a rare print, which I take to be a Titian ; begging the said W. H. to acknowledge the receipt thereof ; which he not having done, I conclude the said parcel to be lying at the inn, and may be lost ; for which reason, lest you may be a Wales-hunting at this instant, I have authorised any of your family, whosoever first gets this, to open it, that so precious a parcel may not moulder away for want of looking after.

What do you in Shropshire when so many fine pictures are a-going a-going every day in London ? Monday I visit the Marquis of Lansdowne's, in Berkeley Square. Catalogue 2s. 6d. Leonardos in plenty. Some other day this week I go to see Sir Wm. Young's, in Stratford Place. Hulse's, of Blackheath, are also to be sold this month ; and in May, the first private collection in Europe, Welbore Ellis Agar's. And there are you, perverting Nature in lying landscapes, filched from old rusty Titians, such as I can scrape up here to send you, with an additament from Shropshire Nature thrown in to make the whole look unnatural. I am afraid of your mouth watering when I tell you that Manning and I got into Angerstein's on Wednesday. *Mon Dieu !* Such Claudes ! Four Claudes bought for more than £10,000 ; (those who talk of Wilson being equal to Claude are either mainly ignorant or stupid ;) one of these was perfectly miraculous. What colours short of *bonâ fide* sunbeams it could be painted in, I am not earthly colourman enough to say ; but I did not think it had been in the possibility of things. Then, a music piece by Titian, a thousand-pound picture, five figures standing behind a piano, the sixth playing—none of the heads, as M. observed, indicating great men, or affecting it, but so sweetly disposed —all leaning separate ways, but so easy—like a flock of some divine shepherd ; the colouring, like the economy of the picture, so sweet and harmonious—as good as Shakspeare's *Twelfth Night,*—*almost,* that is. It will give you a love of order, and cure you of restless, fidgety passions for a week after——more musical than the music which it would, but cannot, yet in a manner *does,* show. I have no room for the rest. Let me say, Angerstein sits in a room—his study (only that and the library are shown), when he writes a common letter, as I am doing, surrounded with twenty pictures worth £60,000. What a luxury ! Apicius and Heliogabalus, hide your diminished heads !

Yours, my dear painter,   C. LAMB.

Mr. Wm. Hazlitt,
    Wem, Shropshire.
In his absence, to be opened immediately.

To THOMAS MANNING.

LETTER CXLVI.]   *May* 10, 1806.

My dear Manning—I didn't know what your going was till I shook a last fist with you, and then 'twas just like having shaken hands with a wretch on the fatal scaffold, for when you are down the ladder you can never stretch out to him again. Mary says you are dead, and there's nothing to do but to leave it to time to do for us in the end what it always does for those who mourn for people in such a case. But she'll see by your letter you are not quite dead. A little kicking and agony, and then ——. Martin Burney *took me out* a walking that evening, and we talked of Manning ; and then I came home and smoked for you ; and at twelve o'clock came home Mary and Monkey Louisa from the play, and there was more talk and more smoking, and they all seemed first-rate characters, because they knew a certain person. But what's the use of talking about 'em? By the time you'll have made your escape from the Kalmuks, you'll have stayed so long I shall never be able to bring to your mind who Mary was, who will have died about a year before, nor who the Holcrofts were! Me perhaps you will mistake for Phillips, or confound me with Mr. Dawe, because you saw us together. Mary (whom you seem to remember yet) is not quite easy that she had not a formal parting from you. I wish it had so happened. But you must bring her a token, a shawl or something, and remember a sprightly little mandarin for our mantel-piece, as a companion to the child I am going to purchase at the museum. She says you saw her writings about the other day, and she wishes you should know what they are. She is doing for Godwin's bookseller twenty of Shakspeare's plays, to be made into children's tales. Six are already done by her; to wit, the *Tempest*, the *Winter's Tale*, *Midsummer Night's Dream*, *Much Ado about Nothing*, the *Two Gentlemen of Verona*, and *Cymbeline*. The *Merchant of Venice* is in forwardness. I have done *Othello* and *Macbeth*, and mean to do all the tragedies. I think it will be popular among the little people, besides money. It is to bring in sixty guineas. Mary has done them capitally, I think you'd think. These are the humble amusements we propose, while you are gone to plant the cross of Christ among barbarous pagan anthropophagi. Quam homo homini præstat! but then, perhaps, you'll get murdered, and we shall die in our beds with a fair literary reputation. Be sure, if you see any of those people whose heads do grow beneath their shoulders, that you make a draught of them. It will be very curious. Oh Manning, I am serious to sinking almost, when I think that all those evenings which you have made so pleasant, are gone perhaps for ever. Four years, you talk of, may be ten, and you may

come back and find such alterations! Some circumstances may grow up to you or to me, that may be a bar
to the return of any such intimacy. I daresay all this is
hum! and that all will come back; but indeed we die
many deaths before we die, and I am almost sick when
I think that such a hold as I had of you is gone. I have
friends, but some of 'em are changed. Marriage, or some
circumstance, rises up to make them not the same. But
I felt sure of you. And that last token you gave
me of expressing a wish to have my name joined with
yours, you know not how it affected me: like a
legacy.

God bless you in every way you can form a wish.
May He give you health, and safety, and the accomplishment of all your objects, and return you again to us, to
gladden some fireside or other (I suppose we shall be
moved from the Temple). I will nurse the remembrance
of your steadiness and quiet, which used to infuse something like itself into our nervous minds. Mary called
you our ventilator. Farewell, and take her best wishes
and mine.

Good-bye.   C. L.

To WILLIAM WORDSWORTH.

LETTER CXLVII.]   *June* 26, 1806.

Mary is just stuck fast in "All's Well that Ends
Well." She complains of having to set forth so many
female characters in boys' clothes. She begins to think
Shakspeare must have wanted—imagination! I, to encourage her (for she often faints in the prosecution of
her great work), flatter her with telling her how well
such a play and such a play is done. But she is stuck
fast, and I have been obliged to promise to assist her.

To do this it will be necessary to leave off tobacco. But I had some thoughts of doing that before, for I sometimes think it does not agree with me. Wm. Hazlitt is in town. I took him to see a very pretty girl, professedly, where there were two young girls (the very head and sum of the girlery was two young girls); they neither laughed, nor sneered, nor giggled, nor whispered —but they were young girls—and he sat and frowned blacker and blacker, indignant that there should be such a thing as youth and beauty, till he tore me away before supper, in perfect misery, and owned he could not bear young girls; they drove him mad. So I took him home to my old nurse, where he recovered perfect tranquillity. Independent of this, and as I am not a young girl myself, he is a great acquisition to us. He is, rather imprudently I think, printing a political pamphlet on his own account, and will have to pay for the paper, etc. The first duty of an author, I take it, is never to pay anything. But *non cuivis contigit adire Corinthum.* The managers, I thank my stars, have settled that question for me.

Yours truly,

C. LAMB.

LETTER CXLVIII.] *June* 1806

Dear Wordsworth—We are pleased, you may be sure, with the good news of Mrs. W——. Hope all is well over by this time. "A fine boy. Have you any more? —one more and a girl—poor copies of me!" vide *Mr. H.*, a farce which the proprietors have done me the honour——; but I will set down Mr. Wroughton's own words. *N.B.*—The ensuing letter was sent in answer to one which I wrote, begging to know if my piece had any chance, as I might make alterations, etc. I writing on Monday, there comes this letter on the Wednesday. Attend!

[Copy of a Letter from Mr. R. Wroughton.]

" Sir—Your piece of *Mr. H.*, I am desired to say, is accepted at Drury Lane Theatre, by the proprietors, and, if agreeable to you, will be brought forwards when the proper opportunity serves. The piece shall be sent to you, for your alterations, in the course of a few days, as the same is not in my hands, but with the proprietors.

" I am, sir, your obedient servant,

" RICHARD WROUGHTON.

[Dated]
" 66, Gower Street,
" Wednesday, June 11, 1806."

On the following Sunday Mr. Tobin comes. The scent of a manager's letter brought him. He would have gone further any day on such a business. I read the letter to him. He deems it authentic and peremptory. Our conversation naturally fell upon pieces, different sorts of pieces ; what is the best way of offering a piece, how far the caprice of managers is an obstacle in the way of a piece, how to judge of the merits of a piece, how long a piece may remain in the hands of the managers before it is acted ; and my piece, and your piece, and my poor brother's piece—my poor brother was all his life endeavouring to get a piece accepted. I am not sure that, when my poor brother bequeathed the care of his pieces to Mr. Tobin, he did not therein convey a legacy which in some measure mollified the otherwise first stupefactions of grief. It cannot be expected that the present Earl Nelson passes all his time in watering the laurels of the admiral with Right-Reverend Tears. Certainly he steals a fine day now and then to plot how to lay out the grounds and mansion at Burnham most suitable to the late Earl's taste, if he had lived, and how to spend the hundred thousand pounds which Parliament has given him in erecting some little neat monument to his memory.

I wrote that in mere wantonness of triumph. Have

nothing more to say about it. The managers, I thank my stars, have decided its merits for ever. They are the best judges of pieces, and it would be insensible in me to affect a false modesty after the very flattering letter which I have received.

ADMIT
TO
B O X E S.
Mr. H.
Ninth Night.

CHARLES LAMB.

I think this will be as good a pattern for orders as I can think on. A little thin flowery border, round, neat, not gaudy, and the Drury Lane Apollo, with the harp at the top. Or shall I have no Apollo?—simply nothing? Or perhaps the comic muse?

The same form, only I think without the Apollo, will serve for the pit and galleries. I think it will be best to write my name at full length; but then if I give away a a great many, that will be tedious. Perhaps *Ch. Lamb* will do.

BOXES, now I think on it, I'll have in capitals. The rest, in a neat Italian hand. Or better, perhaps 𝕭𝖔𝖝𝖊𝖘, in old English characters, like "Madoc" or "Thalaba?"

A-propos of Spenser (you will find him mentioned a page or two before, near enough for an *a-propos*), I was discoursing on poetry (as one's apt to deceive one's self, and when a person is willing to *talk* of what one likes, to believe that he also likes the same, as lovers do) with a young gentleman of my office, who is deep read in Anacreon Moore, Lord Strangford, and the principal modern poets, and I happened to mention Epithalamiums, and that I could show him a very fine one of Spenser's. At the mention of this, my gentleman, who is a very fine gentleman, and is brother to the Miss Evans whom

Coleridge so narrowly escaped marrying, pricked up his ears and expressed great pleasure, and begged that I would give him leave to copy it : he did not care how long it was (for I objected the length), he should be very happy to see *anything by him.* Then pausing, and looking sad, he ejaculated " POOR SPENCER !" I begged to know the reason of his ejaculation, thinking that time had by this time softened down any calamities which the bard might have endured. " Why, poor fellow," said he, " he has lost his wife !" " Lost his wife !" said I, " whom are you talking of ?" " Why, Spencer," said he ; " I've read the *Monody* he wrote on the occasion, and *a very pretty thing it is.*" This led to an explanation (it could be delayed no longer) that the sound *Spenser,* which, when poetry is talked of, generally excites an image of an old bard in a ruff, and sometimes with it dim notions of Sir P. Sydney, and perhaps Lord Burleigh, had raised in my gentleman a quite contrary image of the Honourable William Spencer, who has translated some things from the German very prettily, which are published with Lady Di. Beauclerk's designs. Nothing like defining of terms when we talk. What blunders might I have fallen into of quite inapplicable criticism, but for this timely explanation !

N.B.—At the beginning of *Edm.* Spenser (to prevent mistakes), I have copied from my own copy, and primarily from a book of Chalmers's on Shakspeare, a sonnet of Spenser's never printed among his poems. It is curious, as being manly, and rather Miltonic, and as a sonnet of Spenser's with nothing in it about love or knighthood. I have no room for remembrances ; but I hope our doing your commission will prove we do not quite forget you.

C. L.

To THOMAS MANNING.

LETTER CXLIX.] *December* 5, 1806.

Manning, your letter dated Hottentots, August (the what-was-it?) came to hand. I can scarce hope that mine will have the same luck. China! Canton! Bless us—how it strains the imagination and makes it ache! I write under another uncertainty, whether it can go to-morrow by a ship which I have just learned is going off direct to your part of the world, or whether the despatches may not be sealed up and this have to wait, for if it is detained here, it will grow staler in a fortnight than in a five months' voyage coming to you. It will be a point of conscience to send you none but bran-new news (the latest edition), which, like oranges, will but grow the better for a sea voyage. Oh that you should be so many hemispheres off!—if I speak incorrectly you can correct me—why the simplest death or marriage that takes place here must be important to you as news in the old Bastile. There's your friend Tuthill has got away from France; you remember France?—and Tuthill—ten to one but he writes by this post, if he don't get my note in time, apprising him of the vessel's sailing. Know then that he has found means to obtain leave from Buonaparte (without making use of any *incredible romantic pretences* as some have done, who never meant to fulfil them) to come home, and I have seen him here and at Holcroft's. Arn't you glad about Tuthill? Now then, be sorry for Holcroft, whose new play, called the *Vindictive Man*, was damned about a fortnight since. It died in part of its own weakness, and in part for being choked up with bad actors. The two principal parts were destined to Mrs. Jordan and Mr. Bannister, but Mrs. J. has not come to terms with the managers; they have had some squabble; and Bannister shot some of his fingers off by the going off of a gun. So Miss Duncan had her part, and Mr. de Camp took his. His part, the principal comic hope of the play, was most unluckily *Goldfinch*, taken out of the *Road to Ruin*, not only the same character, but the identical *Goldfinch*—the same as *Falstaff* is in two plays of Shakspeare's. As the devil of ill-luck would have it, half the audience did not know that Holcroft had written it, but were displeased at his stealing from the *Road to Ruin ;* and those who might have borne a gentlemanly coxcomb with his " That's your sort," " Go it "—such as Lewis is —did not relish the intolerable vulgarity and inanity of the idea stript of his manner. De Camp was hooted, more than hist, hooted and bellowed off the stage before the second act was finished ; so that the remainder of his part was forced to be, with some violence to the play, omitted. In addition to this, a whore was another principal character—a most unfortunate choice in this moral day. The audience were as scandalised as if you were to introduce such a personage to their private tea-tables. Besides, her action in the play was gross— wheedling an old man into marriage. But the mortal blunder of the play was that which, oddly enough, Holcroft took pride in, and exultingly told me of the night before it came out, that there were no less than eleven principal characters in it, and I believe he meant of the men only, for the play-bill expressed as much, not reckoning one woman, and one whore ; and true it was, for Mr. Powell, Mr. Raymond, Mr. Bartlett, Mr. H. Siddons, Mr. Barrymore, etc. etc., to the number of eleven, had all parts equally prominent, and there was as much of them in quantity and rank as of the hero and heroine— and most of them gentlemen who seldom appear but as the hero's friend in a farce, for a minute or two ; and here they all had their ten-minute speeches, and one of them gave the audience a serious account of how he was now a lawyer but had been a poet, and then a long enumeration of the inconveniences of authorship, rascally booksellers, reviewers, etc. ; which first set the audience a-gaping ; but I have said enough. You will be so sorry,

that you will not think the best of me for my detail;
but news is news at Canton. Poor Holcroft I fear will
feel the disappointment very seriously in a pecuniary
light. From what I can learn he has saved nothing.
You and I were hoping one day that he had, but I fear
he has nothing but his pictures and books, and a no very
flourishing business, and to be obliged to part with his
long-necked Guido that hangs opposite as you enter, and
the game-piece that hangs in the back drawing-room, and
all those Vandykes, etc. ! God should temper the wind
to the shorn connoisseur. I hope I need not say to you,
that I feel for the weather-beaten author, and for all his
household. I assure you his fate has soured a good deal
the pleasure I should have otherwise taken in my own
little farce being accepted, and I hope about to be acted :
it is in rehearsal actually, and I expect it to come out
next week. It is kept a sort of secret, and the rehearsals
have gone on privately, lest by many folks knowing it,
the story should come out, which would infallibly damn
it. You remember I had sent it before you went.
Wroughton read it, and was much pleased with it. I
speedily got an answer. I took it to make alterations,
and lazily kept it some months, then took courage and
furbished it up in a day or two and took it. In less
than a fortnight I heard the principal part was given to
Elliston, who liked it and only wanted a prologue, which
I have since done and sent, and I had a note the day
before yesterday from the manager, Wroughton (bless his
fat face ! he is not a bad actor in some things), to say
that I should be summoned to the rehearsal after the
next, which next was to be yesterday. I had no idea it
was so forward. I have had no trouble, attended no
reading or rehearsal, made no interest. What a contrast
to the usual parade of authors ! But it is peculiar to
modesty to do all things without noise or pomp. I have
some suspicion it will appear in public on Wednesday
next, for Wroughton says in his note, it is so forward
that if wanted it may come out next week, and a new

melodrame is announced for every day till then ; and "a new farce is in rehearsal," is put up in the bills. Now you'd like to know the subject. The title is *Mr. H.*, no more. How simple, how taking ! A great H. sprawling over the play-bill and attracting eyes at every corner. The story is a coxcomb appearing at Bath, vastly rich— all the ladies dying for him—all bursting to know who he is ; but he goes by no other name than Mr. H.—a curiosity like that of the dames of Strasburg about the man with the great nose. But I won't tell you any more about it. Yes, I will ; but I can't give you an idea how I have done it. I'll just tell you that after much vehement admiration, when his true name comes out, "Hogsflesh," all the women shun him, avoid him, and not one can be found to change their name for him. That's the idea. How flat it is here—but how whimsical in the farce ! And only think how hard upon me it is that the ship is despatched to-morrow, and my triumph cannot be ascertained till the Wednesday after ; but all China will ring of it by and by. *N.B.* (But this is a secret). The Professor has got a tragedy coming out, with the young Roscius in it, in January next, as we say —January last it will be with you—and though it is a profound secret now, as all his affairs are, it cannot be much of one by the time you read this. However, don't let it go any further. I understand there are dramatic exhibitions in China. One would not like to be fore- stalled. Do you find in all this stuff I have written any- thing like those feelings which one should send my old adventuring friend, that is gone to wander among Tartars and may never come again ? I don't ; but your going away, and all about you, is a threadbare topic. I have worn it out with thinking : it has come to me when I have been dull with anything, till my sadness has seemed more to have come from it than to have introduced it. I want you, you don't know how much ; but if I had you here in my European garret, we should but talk over such stuff as I have written—so. Those *Tales from*

Shakspeare are near coming out, and Mary has begun a new work. Mr. Dawe is turned author; he has been in such a way lately—Dawe, the painter, I mean—he sits and stands about at Holcroft's and says nothing; then sighs and leans his head on his hand. I took him to be in love; but it seems he was only meditating a work,—"The Life of Morland." The young man is not used to composition. Rickman and Captain Burney are well; they assemble at my house pretty regularly of a Wednesday—a new institution. Like other great men I have a public day, cribbage and pipes, with Phillips and noisy Martin.

Good God! what a bit only I've got left! How shall I squeeze all I know into this morsel! Coleridge is come home, and is going to turn lecturer on Taste at the Royal Institution. I shall get £200 from the theatre if *Mr. H.* has a good run, and I hope £100 for the copyright. Nothing if it fails; and there never was a more ticklish thing. The whole depends on the manner in which the name is brought out, which I value myself on, as a *chef-d'œuvre*. How the paper grows less and less! In less than two minutes I shall cease to talk to you, and you may rave to the great wall of China. *N.B.* Is there such a wall? Is it as big as old London Wall, by Bedlam? Have you met with a friend of mine, named Ball, at Canton? If you are acquainted, remember me kindly to him. May be you'll think I have not said enough of Tuthill and the Holcrofts. Tuthill is a noble fellow, as far as I can judge. The H.'s bear their disappointment pretty well, but indeed they are sadly mortified. Mrs. H. is cast down. It was well, if it were but on this account, that T. is come home. *N.B.* If my little thing don't succeed I shall easily survive, having, as it were, compared to H.'s venture, but a sixteenth in the lottery. Mary and I are to sit next the orchestra in the pit, next the tweedledees. She remembers you. You are more to us than five hundred farces, clappings, etc.

Come back one day. C. LAMB.

To Miss STODDART.

LETTER CL.]   *December* 11, 1806.

Don't mind this being a queer letter.   I am in haste, and taken up by visitors, condolers, etc.

God bless you.

Dear Sarah—Mary is a little cut at the ill success of *Mr. H.*, which came out last night and *failed.*   I know you'll be sorry, but never mind.   We are determined not to be cast down.   I am going to leave off tobacco, and then we must thrive.   A smoking man must write smoky farces.

Mary is pretty well, but I persuaded her to let me write.   We did not apprise you of the coming out of *Mr. H.* for fear of ill luck.   You were much better out of the house.   If it had taken, your partaking of our good luck would have been one of our greatest joys.   As it is, we shall expect you at the time you mentioned.   But whenever you come you shall be most welcome.

God bless you, dear Sarah,

Yours most truly,   C. L.

Mary is by no means unwell, but I made her let me write.

To WILLIAM WORDSWORTH.

LETTER CLI.]   *December* 11, 1806.

Mary's love to all of you—I wouldn't let her write.

Dear Wordsworth—*Mr. H.* came out last night, and failed.   I had many fears ; the subject was not substantial enough.   John Bull must have solider fare than a *letter.* We are pretty stout about it ; have had plenty of condoling friends ; but, after all, we had rather it should have succeeded.   You will see the prologue in most of the morning papers.   It was received with such shouts as I never witnessed to a prologue. It was attempted to be encored. How hard !—a thing I did merely as a task, because it was wanted, and set no great store by ; and *Mr. H. ! !* The number of friends we had in the house —my brother and I being in public offices, etc. — was astonishing, but they yielded at length to a few hisses.

A hundred hisses ! (Damn the word, I write it like kisses—how different !)—a hundred hisses outweigh a thousand claps. The former come more directly from the heart. Well, 'tis withdrawn, and there is an end.

Better luck to us. C. LAMB.

[Turn over.]

P.S.—Pray, when any of you write to the Clarksons, give our kind loves, and say we shall not be able to come and see them at Christmas, as I shall have but a day or two, and tell them we bear our mortification pretty well.

To WILLIAM GODWIN.

LETTER CLII.] 1806.

I repent. Can that God whom thy votaries say that thou hast demolished expect more? I did indite a splenetic letter, but did the black Hypocondria never gripe *thy* heart, till thou hast taken a friend for an enemy? The foul fiend Flibbertigibbet leads me over four-inched bridges, to course my own shadow for a traitor. There are certain positions of the moon, under which I counsel thee not to take anything written from this domicile as serious.

I rank thee with Alves,—*Latinè*, Helvetius, or any of his accursed crew? Thou art my friend, and henceforth my philosopher. Thou shalt teach Distinction to the junior branches of my household and Deception to the gray-haired Janitress at my door.

What ! Are these atonements? Can Arcadias be brought upon knees, creeping and crouching?

Come, as Macbeth's drunken porter says, knock, knock, knock, knock, knock, knock, knock—seven times a day shalt thou batter at my peace, and if I shut aught against thee, save the Temple of Janus, may Briareus, with his hundred hands, in each a brass knocker, lead me such a life.   C. LAMB.

To WILLIAM WORDSWORTH.

LETTER CLIII.]   *Thursday, January* 29, 1807.

Dear Wordsworth—We have book'd off from Swan and Two Necks, Lad Lane, this day (per Coach) the Tales from Shakspeare. You will forgive the plates, when I tell you they were left to the direction of Godwin, who left the choice of subjects to the bad baby, who from mischief (I suppose) has chosen one from damn'd beastly vulgarity (vide *Merch. Venice*) where no atom of authority was in the tale to justify it; to another has given a name which exists not in the tale, Nic Bottom, and which she thought would be funny, though in this I suspect *his* hand, for I guess her reading does not reach far enough to know Bottom's Christian name; and one of Hamlet and grave-digging, a scene which is not hinted at in the story, and you might as well have put King Canute the Great reproving his courtiers. The rest are giants and giantesses. Suffice it, to save our taste and damn our folly, that we left it all to a friend, W. G., who in the first place cheated me into putting a name to them, which I did not mean, but do not repent, and then wrote a puff about their *simplicity*, etc., to go with the advertisement as in my name! Enough of this egregious dupery. I will try to abstract the load of teasing circumstances from the stories and tell you that I am answerable for *Lear*, *Macbeth*, *Timon*, *Romeo*, *Hamlet*, *Othello*, for occasionally a tailpiece or correction of grammar, for none of the cuts and all of the spelling. The rest is my Sister's.——We think Pericles of hers the best, and Othello of mine; but

I hope all have some good. *As you like It*, we like least. So much, only begging you to tear out the cuts and give them to Johnny, as " Mrs. Godwin's fancy "! !—

C. L.

Our love to all.

I had almost forgot, My part of the Preface begins in the middle of a sentence, in last but one page, after a colon, thus—

:—*which if they be happily so done, etc.*

the former part hath a more feminine turn and does hold me up something as an instructor to young ladies : but upon my modesty's honour I wrote it not.

Godwin told my Sister that the Baby chose the subjects : a fact in taste.

To Rev. W. HAZLITT.

LETTER CLIV.] *Temple, February* 18, 1808.

Sir—I am truly concerned that any mistake of mine should have caused you uneasiness, but I hope we have got a clue to William's absence, which may clear up all apprehensions. The people where he lodges in town have received direction from him to forward some linen to a place called Winterslow, in the county of Wilts (not far from Salisbury), where the lady lives, whose cottage, pictured upon a card, if you opened my letter you have doubtless seen ; and though we have had no explanation of the mystery since, we shrewdly suspect that at the time of writing that letter which has given you all this trouble, a certain son of yours (who is both painter and author) was at her elbow, and did assist in framing that very cartoon which was sent to amuse and mislead us in town, as to the real place of his destination. And some words at the back of the said cartoon, which we had not marked so narrowly before, by the similarity of the handwriting to William's, do very much confirm the suspicion.

If our theory be right, they have had the pleasure of their jest, and I am afraid you have paid for it in anxiety. But I hope your uneasiness will now be removed, and you will pardon a suspense occasioned by LOVE, who does so many worse mischiefs every day.

The letter to the people where William lodges says, moreover, that he shall be in town in a fortnight.

My sister joins in respects to you and Mrs. Hazlitt, and in our kindest remembrances and wishes for the restoration of Peggy's health.

I am, Sir, your humble servant,   CH. LAMB.

Rev. W. Hazlitt, Wem, Shropshire.

To THOMAS MANNING.

LETTER CLV.]   *February* 26, 1808.

Dear Missionary—Your letters from the farthest ends of the world have arrived safe. Mary is very thankful for your remembrance of her ; and with the less suspicion of mercenariness, as the silk, the *symbolum materiale* of your friendship, has not yet appeared. I think Horace says somewhere, *nox longa*. I would not impute negligence or unhandsome delays to a person whom you have honoured with your confidence, but I have not heard of the silk, or of Mr. Knox, save by your letter. Maybe he expects the first advances ! or it may be that he has not succeeded in getting the article on shore, for it is among the *res prohibitæ et non nisi smuggle-ationis viâ fruendæ*. But so it is, in the friendships between *wicked men* the very expressions of their goodwill cannot but be sinful. I suppose you know my farce was damned. The noise still rings in my ears. Were you ever in the pillory ?—being damned is something like that. A treaty of marriage is on foot between William Hazlitt and Miss Stoddart. Something about settlements only retards it. She has somewhere about £80 a year, to be £120 when her mother dies. He has no settlement except what he

can claim from the Parish. *Pauper est Cinna, sed amat.*
The thing is therefore in abeyance. But there is love a-
both sides. Little Fenwick (you don't see the connection
of ideas here ; how the devil should you ?) is in the rules
of the Fleet. Cruel creditors ! operation of iniquitous
laws. Is Magna Charta then a mockery ? Why, in
general (here I suppose you to ask a question) my spirits
are pretty good ; but I have my depressions, black as a
smith's beard, Vulcanic, Stygian. At such times I have
recourse to a pipe, which is like not being at home to a
dun : he comes again with tenfold bitterness the next
day.—(Mind, I am not in debt ; I only borrow a similitude from others ; it shows imagination.) I have done
two books since the failure of my farce ; they will both
be out this Summer. The one is a juvenile book—the
Adventures of Ulysses, intended to be an introduction to
the reading of *Telemachus !* It is done out of the
Odyssey, not from the Greek (I would not mislead you),
nor yet from Pope's *Odyssey,* but from an older translation of one Chapman. The *Shakspeare Tales* suggested
the doing of it. Godwin is in both those cases my bookseller. The other is done for Longman, and is *Specimens
of English Dramatic Poets contemporary with Shakspeare.*
Specimens are becoming fashionable. We have " Specimens of Ancient English Poets," " Specimens of Modern
English Poets," " Specimens of Ancient English Prose
Writers," without end. They used to be called "Beauties."
You have seen " Beauties of Shakspeare " ? so have many
people that never saw any beauties in Shakspeare. Longman is to print it, and be at all the expense and risk, and
I am to share the profits after all deductions ; *i.e.* a year
or two hence I must pocket what they please to tell me
is due to me. But the book is such as I am glad there
should be. It is done out of old plays at the Museum,
and out of Dodsley's collection, etc. It is to have notes.
So I go creeping on since I was lamed with that cursed
fall from off the top of Drury Lane Theatre into the
pit, something more than a year ago. However, I have

been free of the house ever since, and the house was pretty free with me upon that occasion. Damn 'em, how they hissed ! It was not a hiss neither, but a sort of a frantic yell, like a congregation of mad geese, with roaring sometimes, like bears, mows and mops like apes, sometimes snakes, that hiss'd me into madness. 'Twas like St. Anthony's temptations. Mercy on us, that God should give his favourite children, men, mouths to speak with, to discourse rationally, to promise smoothly, to flatter agreeably, to encourage warmly, to counsel wisely, to sing with, to drink with, and to kiss with, and that they should turn them into mouths of adders, bears, wolves, hyenas, and whistle like tempests, and emit breath through them like distillations of aspic poison, to asperse and vilify the innocent labours of their fellow-creatures who are desirous to please them ! Heaven be pleased to make the breath stink and teeth rot out of them all therefore : make them a reproach, and all that pass by them to loll out their tongue at them ! Blind mouths ! as Milton somewhere calls them. Do you like Braham's singing ? The little Jew has bewitched me. I follow him like as the boys followed Tom the Piper. He cures me of melancholy as David cured Saul : but I don't throw stones at him as Saul did at David in payment. I was insensible to music till he gave me a new sense. Oh that you could go to the new opera of *Kais* to-night ! 'Tis all about Eastern manners ; it would just suit you. It describes the wild Arabs, wandering Egyptians, lying dervises, and all that sort of people, to a hair. You needn't ha' gone so far to see what you see, if you saw it as I do every night at Drury Lane Theatre. Braham's singing, when it is impassioned, is finer than Mrs. Siddons's or Mr. Kemble's acting ! and when it is not impassioned, it is as good as hearing a person of fine sense talking. The brave little Jew ! Old Sergeant Hill is dead. Mrs. Rickman is in the family way. It is thought that Hazlitt will have children if he marries Miss Stoddart. I made a pun the other day, and palmed it upon Holcroft, who grinned like a Cheshire cat. (Why do cats grin in Cheshire?—Because it was once a county palatine, and the cats cannot help laughing whenever they think of it, though I see no great joke in it.) I said that Holcroft, on being asked who were the best dramatic writers of the day, replied, "Hook AND I." Mr. Hook is author of several pieces, *Tekeli*, etc. You know what *hooks and eyes* are, don't you? They are what little boys do up their breeches with. Your letter had many things in it hard to be understood: the puns were ready and Swift-like; but don't you begin to be melancholy in the midst of Eastern customs? "The mind does not easily conform to foreign usages, even in trifles: it requires something that it has been familiar with." That begins one of Dr. Hawkesworth's papers in the *Adventurer*, and is, I think, as sensible a remark as ever fell from the Doctor's mouth. White is at Christ's Hospital, a wit of the first magnitude, but would rather be thought a gentleman, like Congreve. You know Congreve's repulse which he gave to Voltaire, when he came to visit him as a *literary man*, that he wished to be considered only in the light of a private gentleman. I think the impertinent Frenchman was properly answered. I should just serve any member of the French Institute in the same manner, that wished to be introduced to me. Buonaparte has voted 5000 livres to Davy, the great young English Chemist! but it has not arrived. Coleridge has delivered two lectures at the Royal Institution; two more were attended, but he did not come. It is thought he has gone sick upon them. He isn't well, that's certain. Wordsworth is coming to see him. He sits up in a two pair of stairs room at the *Courier* Office, and receives visitors. . . .

Does any one read at Canton? Lord Moira is President of the Westminster Library. I suppose you might have interest with Sir Joseph Banks to get to be president of any similar institution that should be set up at Canton. I think public reading-rooms the best mode of educating young men. Solitary reading is apt to give

the headache.   Besides, who knows that you *do* read?
There are ten thousand institutions similar to the Royal
Institution which have sprung up from it.   There is
the London Institution, the Southwark Institution, the
Russell Square Rooms Institution, etc.—*College quasi
Conlege*, a place where people read together.   Wordsworth, the great poet, is coming to town ; he is to have
apartments in the Mansion House.   He says he does not
see much difficulty in writing like Shakspeare, if he had
a mind to try it.   It is clear, then, nothing is wanting
but the mind.   Even Coleridge a little checked at this
hardihood of assertion.   Dyer came to me the other
evening at 11 o'clock, when there was a large room full
of company, which I usually get together on a Wednesday
evening (all great men have public days), to propose to
me to have my face done by a Miss Beetham (or Betham),
a miniature painter, some relation to Mrs. Beetham the
Profilist or Pattern Mangle woman opposite St. Dunstan's,
to put before my book of Extracts.   I declined it.

Well, my dear Manning, talking cannot be infinite.
I have said all I have to say ; the rest is but remembrances of you, which we shall bear in our heads while
we have heads.   Here is a packet of trifles nothing
worth ; but it is a trifling part of the world where I
live : emptiness abounds.   But in fulness of affection, we
remain yours,   C. L.

To WILLIAM GODWIN.

LETTER CLVI.]   *March* 11, 1808.

Dear Godwin—The giant's vomit was perfectly nauseous, and I am glad you pointed it out.   I have removed
the objection.   To the other passages I can find no other
objection but what you may bring to numberless passages
besides, such as of Scylla snatching up the six men, etc.,
—that is to say, they are lively images of *shocking* things.
If you want a book, which is not occasionally to *shock*,
you should not have thought of a tale which was so full

of anthropophagi and wonders. I cannot alter these things without enervating the Book, and I will not alter them if the penalty should be that you and all the London booksellers should refuse it. But speaking as author to author, I must say that I think *the terrible* in those two passages seems to me so much to preponderate over the nauseous, as to make them rather fine than disgusting. Who is to read them, I don't know : who is it that reads "Tales of Terror" and "Mysteries of Udolpho"? Such things sell. I only say that I will not consent to alter such passages, which I know to be some of the best in the book. As an author, I say to you, an author : touch not my work. As to a bookseller I say, Take the work such as it is, or refuse it. You are as free to refuse it as when we first talked of it. As to a friend I say, Don't plague yourself and me with nonsensical objections. I assure you I will not alter one more word.

To GEORGE DYER.

LETTER CLVII.]
From my desk in Leadenhall Street,
December 5, 1808.

Dear Dyer—Coleridge is not so bad as your fears have represented him : it is true he is Bury'd, although he is not dead ; to understand this quibble you must know that he is at Bury St. Edmunds, relaxing after the fatigues of lecturing and Londonising. The little Rickmaness whom you inquire after so kindly, thrives and grows apace ; she is already a prattler, and 'tis thought that on some future day she may be a speaker. We hold our weekly meetings still at No. 16, where although we are not so high as the top of Malvern we are involved in almost as much mist. Miss B.'s merit "in every point of view" I am not disposed to question, although I have not been indulged with any view of that lady, back, side or front—fie, Dyer, to praise a female in such common market phrases—you who are so courtly and so attentive. My book is not yet out, that is, not my

Extracts; my *Ulysses* is, and waits your acceptance. When you shall come to town, I hope to present you both together, never thinking of your buying the *Extracts* —half a guinea books were never calculated for my friends. More poets have started up since your departure; William Hazlitt, your friend and mine, is putting to press a collection of verses, chiefly amatory, some of them pretty enough. How these painters encroach on our province! There's Hopner, Shee, Westall, and I don't know who beside, and Tresham. It seems, on confession, that they are not at the top of their own art, when they seek to eke out their fame with the assistance of another's; no large tea-dealer sells cheeses, and no great silversmith deals in razor-straps; it is only your petty dealers who mix commodities. If Nero had been a great emperor he would never have played the violoncello. Who ever caught you, Dyer, designing a landscape or taking a likeness? I have no more to add, who am a friend of virtue, poetry, and painting, therefore, in an especial manner, unalterably thine,   C. LAMB.

To G. Dyer, Esq.,
    Jas. Martin's Wood,
        Overbury, Worcestershire.

To MRS. HAZLITT.

LETTER CLVIII.]   *Saturday, December* 10, 1808.

There came this morning a printed Prospectus from "S. T. Coleridge, Grasmere," of a Weekly Paper, to be called *The Friend;* a flaming Prospectus. I have no time to give the heads of it. To commence the first Saturday in January. There came also notice of a turkey from Mr. Clarkson, which I am more sanguine in expecting the accomplishment of than I am of Coleridge's prophecy.   C. LAMB.

Mrs. Hazlitt, Winterslow,
    near Sarum, Wilts.

CHAPTER III.

1809–1816.

LETTERS TO MANNING, COLERIDGE, WORDSWORTH, AND OTHERS.

To ROBERT LLOYD.

LETTER CLIX.]   *Saturday, February* 25, 1809.

Dear Robert—A great gap has been filled up since our intercourse was broken off. We shall at least have some things to talk over when we meet. That you should never have been in London since I saw you last is a fact which I cannot account for on the principles of my own mental formation. You are worthy to be mentioned with Claudian's " Old Man of Verona." I forbear to ask you any questions concerning your family : *who* are dead, and *who* married ; I will not anticipate our meeting. I have been in total darkness respecting you all these years. I am just up ; and have heard, without being able to confirm the fact, that Drury Lane Theatre is burnt to the ground. Of Walton's *Angler* a new edition is just published with the original plates revived. I think of buying it. The old editions are two guineas, and two guineas and a half. I have not forgotten our ride from Saffron Walden, and the madness of young parson Thomson of Cambridge, that I took your brother to see.   He is gone as a missionary to the East.

I live at present at No. 16 Mitre Court Buildings, Inner Temple.   I shall move at Lady Day, or a little later : if you don't find me in M.C.B., I shall be at No. 2 *or* 4 Inner Temple Lane, at either of which places I shall be happy to shake my old friend Robert by the hand.   C. L.

To THOMAS MANNING.

LETTER CLX.]   34 *Southampton Buildings,*
                                                     March 28, 1809.

Dear Manning—I sent you a long letter by the ships which sailed the beginning of last month, accompanied with books, etc.   Since I last wrote Holcroft is dead. He died on Thursday last.   So there is one of your friends whom you will never see again !   Perhaps the next fleet may bring you a letter from Martin Burney, to say that he writes by desire of Miss Lamb, who is not well enough to write herself, to inform you that her brother died on Thursday last, 14th June, etc.   But I hope *not.*   I should be sorry to give occasion to open a correspondence between Martin and you.   This letter must be short, for I have driven it off to the very moment of doing up the packets ; and besides, that which I refer to above is a very long one ; and if you have received my books, you will have enough to do to read them. While I think on it, let me tell you, we are moved. Don't come any more to Mitre Court Buildings.   We are at 34, Southampton Buildings, Chancery Lane, and shall be here till about the end of May ; then we remove to No. 4, Inner Temple Lane, where I mean to live and die ; for I have such horror of moving, that I would not take a benefice from the King if I was not indulged with non-residence. What a dislocation of comfort is comprised in that word "moving"! Such a heap of little nasty things, after you think all is got into the cart: old dredging-boxes, worn-out brushes, gallipots, vials, things that it is impossible the most necessitous person can ever want, but which the women, who preside on these occasions, will not leave behind if it was to save your soul. They'd keep the cart ten minutes to stow in dirty pipes and broken matches, to show their economy. Then you can find nothing you want for many days after you get into your new lodgings. You must comb your hair with your fingers, wash your hands without soap, go about in dirty gaiters. Were I Diogenes, I would not move out of a kilderkin into a hogshead, though the first had had nothing but small beer in it, and the second reeked claret. Our place of final destination—I don't mean the grave, but No. 4, Inner Temple Lane—looks out upon a gloomy churchyard-like court, called Hare Court, with three trees and a pump in it. Do you know it? I was born near it, and used to drink at that pump when I was a Rechabite of six years old. If you see newspapers you will read about Mrs. Clarke. The sensation in London about this nonsensical business is marvellous. I remember nothing in my life like it: thousands of ballads, caricatures, lives of Mrs. Clarke, in every blind alley. Yet in the midst of this stir, a sublime abstracted dancing-master, who attends a family we know at Kensington, being asked a question about the progress of the examinations in the House, inquired who Mrs. Clarke was? He had heard nothing of it. He had evaded this omnipresence by utter insignificancy! The Duke should make that man his confidential valet. I proposed locking him up, barring him the use of his fiddle and red pumps, until he had minutely perused and committed to memory the whole body of the examinations, which employed the House of Commons a fortnight, to teach him to be more attentive to what concerns the public. I think I told you of Godwin's little book, and of Coleridge's prospectus, in my last; if I did not, remind me of it, and I will send you them, or an account of them, next fleet. I have no conveniency of doing it by this. Mrs. Godwin grows every day in disfavour with me. I will be buried with this inscription over me :—" Here lies C. L., the woman-hater : " I mean that hated one woman : for the rest, God bless them ! How do you like the Mandarinesses ? Are you on some little footing with any of them ? This is Wednesday. On Wednesdays is my levee. The Captain, Martin, Phillips (not the Sheriff), Rickman, and some more, are constant attendants, besides stray visitors. We play at whist, eat cold meat and hot potatoes, and any gentleman that chooses smokes. Why do you never drop in ? You'll come some day, won't you ?

C. LAMB, etc.

To SAMUEL TAYLOR COLERIDGE.

LETTER CLXI.] *June 7*, 1809.

Dear Coleridge—I congratulate you on the appearance of the *Friend*. Your first Number promises well, and I have no doubt the succeeding Numbers will fulfil the promise. I had a kind letter from you some time since, which I have left unanswered. I am also obliged to you, I believe, for a review in the Annual, am I not ? The *Monthly Review* sneers at me, and asks " if *Comus* is not *good enough* for Mr. Lamb ? " because I have said no good serious dramas have been written since the death of Charles the First, except *Samson Agonistes*. So because they do not know, or won't remember, that *Comus* was written long before, I am to be set down as an under-valuer of Milton ! O Coleridge, do kill those reviews, or they will kill us ; kill all we like. Be a friend to all else, but their foe. I have been turned out of my chambers in the Temple by a landlord who wanted them for himself, but I have got other at No. 4, Inner Temple Lane, far more commodious and roomy. I have two rooms on the third floor and five rooms above, with an inner staircase to myself, and all new painted, etc., and all for £30 a year! I came into them on Saturday week; and on Monday following Mary was taken ill with the fatigue of moving; and affected, I believe, by the novelty of the home she could not sleep, and I am left alone with a maid quite a stranger to me, and she has a month or two's sad distraction to go through. What sad large pieces it cuts out of life!—out of *her* life, who is getting rather old; and we may not have many years to live together. I am weaker, and bear it worse than I ever did. But I hope we shall be comfortable by and by. The rooms are delicious, and the best look backwards into Hare Court, where there is a pump always going. Just now it is dry. Hare Court trees come in at the window, so that 'tis like living in a garden. I try to persuade myself it is much pleasanter than Mitre Court; but, alas! the household gods are slow to come in a new mansion. They are in their infancy to me; I do not feel them yet; no hearth has blazed to them yet. How I hate and dread new places!

I was very glad to see Wordsworth's book advertised: I am to have it to-morrow lent me, and if Wordsworth don't send me an order for one upon Longman, I will buy it. It is greatly extolled and liked by all who have seen it. Let me hear from some of you, for I am desolate. I shall have to send you, in a week or two, two volumes of Juvenile Poetry, done by Mary and me within the last six months, and that tale in prose which Wordsworth so much liked, which was published at Christmas, with nine others, by us, and has reached a second edition. There's for you. We have almost worked ourselves out of child's work, and I don't know what to do. Sometimes I think of a drama, but I have no head for play-making; I can do the dialogue, and that's all. I am quite aground for a plan; but I must do something for money. Not that I have immediate wants, but I have prospective ones. O money, money, how blindly thou hast been worshipped, and how stupidly abused! Thou art health and liberty and strength; and he that has thee may rattle his pockets at the Devil.

Nevertheless, do not understand by this that I have not quite enough for my occasions for a year or two to come. While I think on it, Coleridge, I fetch'd away my books which you had at the *Courier* Office, and found all but a third volume of the old plays, containing the *White Devil*, Green's *Tu Quoque*, and the *Honest Whore*, perhaps the most valuable volume of them all—*that* I could not find. Pray, if you can, remember what you did with it, or where you took it out with you a walking perhaps; send me word, for, to use the old plea, it spoils a set. I found two other volumes (you had three), the *Arcadia*, and *Daniel*, enriched with manuscript notes. I wish every book I have were so noted. They have thoroughly converted me to relish *Daniel*, or to say I relish him, for after all, I believe I did relish him. You well call him sober-minded. Your notes are excellent. Perhaps you've forgot them. I have read a review in the *Quarterly*, by Southey, on the Missionaries, which is most masterly. I only grudge its being there. It is quite beautiful. Do remember my Dodsley; and, pray, do write, or let some of you write. Clarkson tells me you are in a smoky house. Have you cured it? It is hard to cure anything of smoking. Our little poems are but humble, but they have no name. You must read them, remembering they were task work; and perhaps you will admire the number of subjects, all of children, picked out by an old Bachelor and an old Maid. Many parents would not have found so many. Have you read *Cœlebs*? It has reached eight editions in so many weeks, yet literally it is one of the very poorest sort of common novels, with the draw-back of dull religion in it. Had the religion been high and flavoured, it would have been something.   I borrowed this *Cœlebs in Search of a Wife*, of a very careful, neat lady, and returned it with this stuff written in the beginning :—

> " If ever I marry a wife
> I'll marry a landlord's daughter,
> For then I may sit in the bar,
> And drink cold brandy and water."

I don't expect you can find time from your *Friend* to write to me much ; but write something, for there has been a long silence.   You know Holcroft is dead.   Godwin is well.   He has written a very pretty, absurd book about sepulchres.   He was affronted because I told him it was better than Hervey, but not so good as Sir T. Browne.   This letter is all about books ; but my head aches, and I hardly know what I write, but I could not let the *Friend* pass without a congratulatory epistle.   I won't criticise till it comes to a volume.   Tell me how I shall send my packet to you ?—by what conveyance ?— by Longman, Short-man, or how ?   Give my kindest remembrances to Wordsworth.   Tell him he must give me a book.   My kind love to Mrs. W. and to Dorothy separately and conjointly.   I wish you could all come and see me in my new rooms.   God bless you all.

C. L.

To CHARLES LLOYD, THE ELDER.

LETTER CLXII.]   *July* 31, 1809.

Dear Sir—The general impression made by your Translation on the mind of my friend who kept your MS. so unreasonably long, as well as on another friend who read over a good part of it with me, was that it gave a great deal more of the sense of Homer than either of his two great modern Translators have done.   In several expressions which they at first objected to, on

turning to the Greek they found it completely warranted
you in the use of them; and they were even surprised
that you could combine so much fidelity with so much of
the turn of the best modern improvements in the Couplet
versification. I think of the two, I rather prefer the
Book of the Iliad which you sent me, for the sound of
the verse; but the difference of subject almost in-
voluntarily modifies verse. I find Cowper is a favourite
with nobody. His injudicious use of the stately slow
Miltonic verse in a subject so very different, has given a
distaste. Nothing can be more unlike to my fancy than
Homer and Milton. Homer is perfect prattle, tho'
exquisite prattle, compared to the deep oracular voice of
Milton. In Milton you love to stop, and saturate your
mind with every great image or sentiment; in Homer
you want to go on, to have more of his agreeable narrative.
Cowper delays you as much, walking over a Bowling
Green, as the other does, travelling over steep Alpine
heights, where the labour enters into and makes a part
of the pleasure. From what I have seen, I would
certainly be glad to hear that you continued your employ-
ment quite through the Poem: that is, for an agreeable
and honourable recreation to yourself; though I should
scarce think that (Pope having got the ground) a translation in Pope's Couplet versification would ever supersede
his to the public, however faithfuller or in some respects
better. Pitt's Virgil is not much read, I believe, though
nearer to the Original than Dryden's. Perhaps it is,
that people do not like two Homers or Virgils—there is
a sort of confusion in it to an English reader, who has
not a centre of reference in the Original: when Tate and
Brady's Psalms came out in our Churches, many pious
people would not substitute them in the room of David's,
as they call'd Sternhold and Hopkins's. But if you
write for a relaxation from other sort of occupations I
can only congratulate you, Sir, on the noble choice, as
it seems to me, which you have made, and express my
wonder at the facility which you suddenly have arrived

at, if (as I suspect) these are indeed the first specimens of this sort which you have produced. But I cannot help thinking that you betray a more practised gait than a late beginner could so soon acquire. Perhaps you have only resumed what you had formerly laid aside as interrupting more necessary avocations.

I need not add how happy I shall be to see at any time what you may please to send me. In particular, I should be glad to see that you had taken up Horace, which I think you enter into as much as any man that was not born in his days, and in the *Via Longa* or *Flaminia*, or near the *Forum*.

With many apologies for keeping your MS. so long, which my friend's engagements in business must excuse, —I remain, Dear Sir, yours truly, C. L.

My kind respects to Mrs. Ll., and my remembrances to Robert, etc. etc.

To SAMUEL TAYLOR COLERIDGE.

LETTER CLXIII.] *Monday, October* 30, 1809.

Dear Coleridge—I have but this moment received your letter, dated the 9th instant, having just come off a journey from Wiltshire, where I have been with Mary on a visit to Hazlitt. The journey has been of infinite service to her. We have had nothing but sunshiny days, and daily walks from eight to twenty miles a day ; have seen Wilton, Salisbury, Stonehenge, etc. Her illness lasted but six weeks ; it left her weak, but the country has made us whole. We came back to our Hogarth Room. I have made several acquisitions since you saw them,—and found Nos. 8, 9, 10 of the *Friend*. The account of Luther in the Warteburg is as fine as anything I ever read. God forbid that a man who has such things to say should be silenced for want of £100. This

Custom-and-Duty Age would have made the Preacher on the Mount take out a licence, and St. Paul's Epistles would not have been missible without a stamp. O that you may find means to go on! But alas! where is Sir G. Beaumont?—Sotheby? What has become of the rich Auditors in Albemarle Street? Your letter has saddened me.

I am so tired with my journey, being up all night, that I have neither things nor words in my power. I believe I expressed my admiration of the pamphlet. Its power over me was like that which Milton's pamphlets must have had on his contemporaries, who were tuned to them. What a piece of prose! Do you hear if it is read at all? I am out of the world of readers. I hate all that do read, for they read nothing but reviews and new books. I gather myself up unto the old things.

I have put up shelves. You never saw a book-case in more true harmony with the contents than what I've nailed up in a room, which, though new, has more aptitudes for growing old than you shall often see—as one sometimes gets a friend in the middle of life, who becomes an old friend in a short time. My rooms are luxurious; one is for prints and one for books; a Summer and a Winter parlour. When shall I ever see you in them?

C. L.

To ROBERT LLOYD.

LETTER CLXIV.]   *January* 1, 1810.

Dear Robert—In great haste I write. The Turkey is down at the fire, and some pleasant friends are come in to partake of it. The Sender's Health shall not be forgot. What you tell me of your Father's perseverance in his honourable task gives me great pleasure. Seven Books are a serious earnest of the whole, which I hope to see finish'd.

We had a delightful month in Wiltshire, four weeks of uniform fine weather, the only fine days which had been all the summer. Saw Salisbury Cathedral, Stonehenge, Wilton, etc. etc. Mary is in excellent health, and sends her Love. Accept of mine, with my kind respects to Mrs. Ll—— and to your father and mother.

Coleridge's *Friend* is occasionally sublime. What do you think of that Description of Luther in his Study in one of the earlier numbers? The worst is, he is always promising something which never comes; it is now 18th Number, and continues introductory; the 17th (that stupid long letter) was nothing better than a Prospectus, and ought to have preceded the 1st Number. But I rejoice that it lives.

When you come to London, you will find us at No. 4, Inner Temple Lane, with a few old Books, a few old Hogarths round the room, and the Household Gods at last establish'd. The feeling of Home, which has been slow to come, has come at last. May I never move again, but may my next Lodging be my Coffin.

Yours truly, C. LAMB.

To THOMAS MANNING.

LETTER CLXV.] *January* 2, 1810.

Dear Manning—When I last wrote to you I was in lodgings. I am now in chambers, No. 4, Inner Temple Lane, where I should be happy to see you any evening. Bring any of your friends, the Mandarins, with you. I have two sitting-rooms: I call them so *par excellence*, for you may stand, or loll, or lean, or try any posture in them, but they are best for sitting; not squatting down Japanese fashion, but the more decorous use of the haunches which European usage has consecrated. I have two of these rooms on the third floor, and five sleeping, cooking,

etc., rooms, on the fourth floor.   In my best room is a
choice collection of the works of Hogarth, an English
painter of some humour.   In my next best are shelves
containing a small but well-chosen library.   My best
room commands a court, in which there are trees and a
pump, the water of which is excellent cold, with brandy,
and not very insipid without.   Here I hope to set up my
rest, and not quit till Mr. Powell, the undertaker, gives
me notice that I may have possession of my last lodging.
He lets lodgings for single gentlemen.   I sent you a
parcel of books by my last, to give you some idea of the
state of European literature.   There comes with this two
volumes, done up as letters, of minor poetry, a sequel to
"Mrs. Leicester"; the best you may suppose mine; the
next best are my coadjutor's.   You may amuse yourself
in guessing them out; but I must tell you mine are but
one-third in quantity of the whole.   So much for a very
delicate subject.   It is hard to speak of one's self, etc.
Holcroft had finished his life when I wrote to you, and
Hazlitt has since finished his life; I do not mean his own
life, but he has finished a life of Holcroft, which is going
to press.   Tuthill is Dr. Tuthill.   I continue Mr. Lamb.
I have published a little book for children on titles of
honour; and to give them some idea of the difference of
rank and gradual rising, I have made a little scale, supposing myself to receive the following various accessions
of dignity from the king, who is the fountain of honour—
As at first, 1, Mr. C. Lamb; 2, C. Lamb, Esq.; 3, Sir
C. Lamb, Bart.; 4, Baron Lamb, of Stamford; 5,
Viscount Lamb; 6, Earl Lamb; 7, Marquis Lamb; 8,
Duke Lamb.   It would look like quibbling to carry it on
further, and especially as it is not necessary for children
to go beyond the ordinary titles of sub-regal dignity in
our own country; otherwise I have sometimes in my
dreams imagined myself still advancing, as 9th, King
Lamb; 10th, Emperor Lamb; 11th, Pope Innocent;
higher than which is nothing upon earth.   Puns I have
not made many (nor punch much) since the date of my

last; one I cannot help relating. A constable in Salisbury Cathedral was telling me that eight people dined at the top of the spire of the cathedral; upon which I remarked, that they must be very sharp set. But in general I cultivate the reasoning part of my mind more than the imaginative. I am stuffed out so with eating turkey for dinner, and another turkey for supper yesterday (Turkey in Europe and Turkey in Asia), that I can't jog on. It is New Year here; that is, it was New Year half a year back, when I was writing this. Nothing puzzles me more than time and space; and yet nothing puzzles me less, for I never think about them. The Persian ambassador is the principal thing talked of now. I sent some people to see him worship the sun on Primrose Hill, at half-past six in the morning, 28th November; but he did not come, which makes me think the old fire-worshippers are a sect almost extinct in Persia. The Persian ambassador's name is Shaw Ali Mirza. The common people call him Shaw Nonsense. While I think of it, I have put three letters, besides my own three, into the India Post for you, from your brother, sister, and some gentleman whose name I forget. Will they, have they, did they come safe? The distance you are at, cuts up tenses by the root. I think you said you did not know Kate * * * * * * * * *. I express her by nine stars, though she is but one. You must have seen her at her father's. Try and remember her. Coleridge is bringing out a paper in weekly Numbers, called the *Friend*, which I would send if I could; but the difficulty I had in getting the packets of books out to you before, deters me; and you'll want something new to read when you come home. It is chiefly intended to puff off Wordsworth's poetry; but there are some noble things in it by the by. Except Kate, I have had no vision of excellence this year, and she passed by like the Queen on her coronation day; you don't know whether you saw her or not. Kate is fifteen: I go about moping, and sing the old pathetic ballad I used to like in my youth—

> "She's sweet fifteen,
> I'm *one year more.*"

Mrs. Bland sang it in boy's clothes the first time I heard it. I sometimes think the lower notes in my voice are like Mrs. Bland's. That glorious singer, Braham, one of my lights, is fled. He was for a season. He was a rare composition of the Jew, the gentleman, and the angel; yet all these elements mixed up so kindly in him, that you could not tell which preponderated; but he is gone, and one Phillips is engaged instead. Kate is vanished, but Miss B—— is always to be met with!

> "Queens drop away, while blue-legg'd Maukin thrives;
> And courtly Mildred dies while country Madge survives."

That is not my poetry, but Quarles's; but haven't you observed that the rarest things are the least obvious? Don't show anybody the names in this letter. I write confidentially, and wish this letter to be considered as *private.* Hazlitt has written a *grammar* for Godwin. Godwin sells it bound up with a treatise of his own on language; but the *gray mare is the better horse.* I don't allude to Mrs. Godwin, but to the word *grammar,* which comes near to *gray mare,* if you observe, in sound. That figure is called paronomasia in Greek. I am sometimes happy in it. An old woman begged of me for charity. "Ah! sir," said she, "I have seen better days." "So have I, good woman," I replied; but I meant, literally, days not so rainy and overcast as that on which she begged: she meant more prosperous days. Mr. Dawe is made associate of the Royal Academy. By what law of association I can't guess. Mrs. Holcroft, Miss Holcroft, Mr. and Mrs. Godwin, Mr. and Mrs. Hazlitt, Mrs. Martin and Louisa, Mrs. Lum, Capt. Burney, Mrs. Burney, Martin Burney, Mr. Rickman, Mrs. Rickman, Dr. Stoddart, William Dollin, Mr. Thompson, Mr. and Mrs. Norris, Mr. Fenwick, Mrs. Fenwick, Miss Fenwick, a man that saw you at our house one day, and a lady that heard me speak of you; Mrs. Buffam that heard

Hazlitt mention you, Dr. Tuthill, Mrs. Tuthill, Colonel
Harwood, Mrs. Harwood, Mr. Collier, Mrs. Collier, Mr.
Sutton, Nurse, Mr. Fell, Mrs. Fell, Mr. Marshall, are
very well, and occasionally inquire after you.

I remain yours ever,   CH. LAMB.

To CHARLES LLOYD, THE ELDER.

LETTER CLXVI.]   *March* 10, 1810.   *E. I. Ho.*

My dear Sir—The above are all the faults I, who
profess myself to be a mere English Reader, could find
after a scrupulous perusal twice over of your neat little
Book.   I assure you it gave me great pleasure in the
perusal, much more in this shape than in the Manuscript,
and I should be very sorry you should give up the
finishing of it on so poor pretence as your *Age* [sixty-
two], which is not so much by ten years as Dryden's
when he wrote his fables, which are his best works
allowed, and not more than Milton's when he had scarce
entered upon his original Epic Poem.   You have done
nearly a third ; persevere and let us see the whole.   I am
sure I should prize it for its Homeric plainness and truth
above the confederate jumble of Pope, Broome and Fenton
which goes under Pope's name, and is far inferior to his
ILIAD.   I have picked out what I think blemishes, but
they are but a score of words (I am a mere word-pecker)
in six times as many pages.   The rest all gave me
pleasure, and most of all the Book [the Sixth] in which
Ulysses and Nausicaa meet.   You have infused a kind of
biblical patriarchal manner into it, it reads like some
story of Jacob and Rachel, or some of those primitive
manners.   I am ashamed to carp at words, but I did
it in obedience to your desires, and the plain reason
why I did not acknowledge your kind present *sooner*
was that I had no criticisms of value to make.   I shall
certainly beg the opinion of my friend who read the two

first Books on this enlarged Performance. But he is so very much engaged that I cannot at present get at him, and besides him I have no acquaintance that takes much interest in Poetry, Greek or English. But I hope and adjure you to go on, and do not make excuses of Age till you have completed the Odyssey, and done a great part of Horace besides. Then you will be entitled to hang up your Harp.

I am, Dear Sir, with Love to all your family, your hble. Serv.,   C. LAMB.

To JOHN MATHEW GUTCH.

LETTER CLXVII.]   *April* 9, 1810.

Dear Gutch—I did not see your brother, who brought me Wither; but he understood, he said, you were daily expecting to come to town: this has prevented my writing. The books have pleased me excessively: I should think you could not have made a better selection. I never saw *Philarete* before—judge of my pleasure. I could not forbear scribbling certain critiques in pencil on the blank leaves. Shall I send them, or may I expect to see you in town? Some of them are remarks on the character of Wither and of his writings. Do you mean to have anything of that kind? What I have said on *Philarete* is poor, but I think some of the rest not so bad: perhaps I have exceeded my commission in scrawling over the copies; but my delight therein must excuse me, and pencil-marks will rub out. Where is the Life? Write, for I am quite in the dark.

Yours, with many thanks,   C. LAMB.

Perhaps I could digest the few critiques prefixed to the Satires, Shepherds Hunting, etc., into a short abstract of Wither's character and works, at the end of his Life. But, may be, you don't want anything, and have said all you wish in the Life.

To BASIL MONTAGU.

Winterslow, near Sarum,
July 12, 1810.

Dear Montagu—I have turned and twisted the MSS. in my head, and can make nothing of them. I knew when I took them that I could not, but I do not like to do an act of ungracious necessity at once; so I am ever committing myself by half engagements, and total failures. I cannot make anybody understand why I can't do such things; it is a defect in my occiput. I cannot put other people's thoughts together; I forget every paragraph as fast as I read it; and my head has received such a shock by an all-night journey on the top of the coach, that I shall have enough to do to nurse it into its natural pace before I go home. I must devote myself to imbecility; I must be gloriously useless while I stay here. How is Mrs. M. ? will she pardon my inefficiency ? The city of Salisbury is full of weeping and wailing. The bank has stopped payment; and everybody in the town kept money at it, or has got some of its notes. Some have lost all they had in the world. It is the next thing to seeing a city with the plague within its walls. The Wilton people are all undone; all the manufacturers there kept cash at the Salisbury bank; and I do suppose it to be the unhappiest county in England this, where I am making holiday. We propose setting out for Oxford Tuesday fortnight, and coming thereby home. But no more night travelling. My head is sore (understand it of the inside) with that deduction from my natural rest which I suffered coming down. Neither Mary nor I can spare a morsel of our rest : it is incumbent on us to be misers of it. Travelling is not good for us, we travel so seldom. If the sun be hell, it is not for the fire, but for the sempiternal motion of that miserable body of light. How much more dignified leisure hath a mussel glued to his unpassable rocky limit two inch square ! He hears the tide roll over him, backwards and forwards twice a day (as the Salisbury long coach goes and returns in eight-and-forty hours), but knows better than to take an outside night place a top on't. He is the owl of the sea —Minerva's fish—the fish of wisdom.

Our kindest remembrances to Mrs. M.

Yours truly,

C. LAMB.

To WILLIAM HAZLITT.

LETTER CLXIX.]   *Thursday* [*August* 9, 1810].

Dear H.—Epistemon is not well. Our pleasant excursion has ended sadly for one of us. You will guess I mean my sister. She got home very well (I was very ill on the journey) and continued so till Monday night, when her complaint came on, and she is now absent from home.

I am glad to hear you are all well. I think I shall be mad if I take any more journeys, with two experiences against it. I found all well here. Kind remembrances to Sarah,—have just got her letter.

H. Robinson has been to Blenheim. He says you will be sorry to hear that we should not have asked for the Titian Gallery there. One of his friends knew of it, and asked to see it. It is never shown but to those who inquire for it.

The pictures are all Titians, Jupiter and Ledas, Mars and Venuses, etc., all naked pictures, which may be a reason they don't show them to females. But he says they are very fine ; and perhaps they are shown separately to put another fee into the shower's pocket. Well, I shall never see it.

I have lost all wish for sights. God bless you. I shall be glad to see you in London.

Yours truly,

C. LAMB.

Mr. Hazlitt, Winterslow,
    near Salisbury.

To Miss WORDSWORTH.

Mary has left a little space for me to fill up with non-sense, as the geographers used to cram monsters in the voids of the maps, and call it Terra Incognita. She has told you how she has taken to water like a hungry otter. I too limp after her in lame imitation, but it goes against me a little at first. I have been acquaintance with it now for full four days, and it seems a moon. I am full of cramps and rheumatisms, and cold internally, so that fire won't warm me; yet I bear all for virtue's sake. Must I then leave you, gin, rum, brandy, aqua-vitæ, pleasant jolly fellows? Damn temperance and he that first invented it !—some Anti-Noahite. Coleridge has powdered his head, and looks like Bacchus, Bacchus ever sleek and young. He is going to turn sober, but his clock has not struck yet; meantime he pours down goblet after goblet, the second to see where the first is gone, the third to see no harm happens to the second, a fourth to say there is another coming, and a fifth to say he is not sure he is the last.

To WILLIAM WORDSWORTH.

Dear W.—Mary has been very ill, which you have heard, I suppose, from the Montagus. She is very weak and low-spirited now. I was much pleased with your continuation of the Essay on Epitaphs. It is the only sensible thing which has been written on that subject, and it goes to the bottom. In particular I was pleased with your translation of that turgid epitaph into the plain feeling under it. It is perfectly a test. But what is the reason we have no good epitaphs after all ?

A very striking instance of your position might be found in the churchyard of Ditton-upon-Thames, if you know such a place. Ditton-upon-Thames has been blessed by the residence of a poet, who for love or money—I do not well know which—has dignified every gravestone, for the last few years, with bran-new verses, all different, and all ingenious, with the author's name at the bottom of each.   This sweet Swan of Thames has so artfully diversified his strains and his rhymes, that the same thought never occurs twice ; more justly, perhaps, as no thought ever occurs at all, there was a physical impossibility that the same thought should recur.   It is long since I saw and read these inscriptions, but I remember the impression was of a smug usher at his desk in the intervals of instruction, levelling his pen.   Of death, as it consists of dust and worms, and mourners and uncertainty, he had never thought ; but the word "death" he had often seen separate and conjunct with other words, till he had learned to speak of all its attributes as glibly as Unitarian Belsham will discuss you the attributes of the word "God" in a pulpit ; and will talk of infinity with a tongue that dangles from a skull that never reached in thought and thorough imagination two inches, or further than from his hand to his mouth, or from the vestry to the sounding-board of the pulpit.

But the epitaphs were trim, and sprag, and patent, and pleased the survivors of Thames-Ditton above the old mumpsimus of "Afflictions Sore." . . . To do justice though, it must be owned that even the excellent feeling which dictated this dirge when new must have suffered something in passing through so many thousand applications, many of them no doubt quite misplaced, as I have seen in Islington churchyard (I think) an Epitaph to an infant who died " *Ætatis* four months," with this seasonable inscription appended, "Honour thy father and thy mother, that thy days may be long in the land," etc. Sincerely wishing your children long life to honour, etc.

I remain,

C. LAMB.

To Miss WORDSWORTH.

November 23, 1810.

We are in a pickle. Mary, from her affectation of physiognomy, has hired a stupid big country wench, who looked honest, as she thought, and has been doing her work some days, but without eating—eats no butter, nor meat, but prefers cheese with her tea for breakfast ; and now it comes out that she was ill when she came, with lifting her mother about (who is now with God) when she was dying, and with riding up from Norfolk, four days and nights in the waggon. She got advice yesterday, and took something which has made her bring up a quart of blood, and she now lies in her bed, a dead weight upon our humanity, incapable of getting up, refusing to go into an hospital, having nobody in town but a poor asthmatic uncle whose son lately married a drab who fills his house, and there is nowhere she can go, and she seems to have made up her mind to take her flight to heaven from our bed. Oh for the little wheel-barrow which trundled the hunchback from door to door to try the various charities of different professions of mankind ! Here's her uncle just crawled up. He is far liker Death than she. Oh the Parish, the Parish, the hospital, the infirmary, the charnel-house !—these are places meet for such guests, not our quiet mansion, where nothing but affluent plenty and literary ease should abound.—Howard's House, Howard's House, or where the Paralytic descended through the skylight (what a God's gift !) to get at our Saviour. In this perplexity such topics as Spanish papers and Monkhouses sink into comparative insignificance. What shall we do ? If she died, it were something : gladly would I pay the coffin-maker, and the bell-man and searchers.   C. L.

To Miss Wordsworth, Grasmere,
  near Kendal, Westmoreland.

To WILLIAM HAZLITT.

LETTER CLXXIII.]   *Wednesday, November* 28, 1810.

Dear Hazlitt—I sent you on Saturday a Cobbett, containing your reply to the *Edinburgh Review*, which I thought you would be glad to receive as an example of attention on the part of Mr. Cobbett to insert it so speedily. Did you get it? We have received your pig, and return you thanks; it will be dressed in due form, with appropriate sauce, this day. Mary has been very ill indeed since you saw her; that is, as ill as she can be to remain at home. But she is a good deal better now, owing to a very careful regimen. She drinks nothing but water, and never goes out; she does not even go to the Captain's. Her indisposition has been ever since that night you left town; the night Miss W[ordsworth] came. Her coming, and that d——d Mrs. Godwin coming and staying so late that night, so overset her that she lay broad awake all that night, and it was by a miracle that she escaped a very bad illness, which I thoroughly expected. I have made up my mind that she shall never have any one in the house again with her, and that no one shall sleep with her, not even for a night; for it is a very serious thing to be always living with a kind of fever upon her; and therefore I am sure you will take it in good part if I say that if Mrs. Hazlitt comes to town at any time, however glad we shall be to see her in the daytime, I cannot ask her to spend a night under our roof. Some decision we must come to, for the harassing fever that we have both been in, owing to Miss Wordsworth's coming, is not to be borne; and I would rather be dead than so alive. However, at present, owing to a regimen and medicines which Tuthill has given her, who very kindly volunteer'd the care of her, she is a great deal quieter, though too much harassed by company, who cannot or will not see how late hours and society teaze her.

Poor Phillips had the cup dash'd out of his lips as it were. He had every prospect of the situation, when about ten days since one of the council of the R—— Society started for the place himself, being a rich merchant who lately failed, and he will certainly be elected on Friday next. P. is very sore and miserable about it.

Coleridge is in town, or at least at Hammersmith. He is writing or going to write in the *Courier* against Cobbett, and in favour of paper money.

No news. Remember me kindly to Sarah. I write from the office.

Yours ever,   C. LAMB.

I just open'd it to say the pig, upon proof, hath turned out as good as I predicted. My fauces yet retain the sweet porcine odour. I find you have received the Cobbett. I think your paper complete.

Mrs. Reynolds, who is a sage woman, approves of the pig.

Mr. Hazlitt, Winterslow,
    near Salisbury, Wilts.

To HENRY CRABB ROBINSON.

LETTER CLXXIV.]   [1810.]

Dear R.—My brother, whom you have met at my rooms (a plump, good-looking man of seven-and-forty) has written a book about humanity, which I transmit to you herewith. Wilson, the publisher, has put it into his head that you can get it reviewed for him. I dare say it is not in the scope of your review; but if you could put it in any likely train, he would rejoice. For alas! our boasted humanity partakes of vanity. As it is, he teazes me to death with choosing to suppose that I could get it into all the reviews at a moment's notice. *I!!* who have been set up as a mark for them to throw at, and would willingly consign them all to Megæra's snaky locks.

But here's the book, and don't show it to Mrs. Collier, for I remember she makes excellent *eel* soup, and the leading points of the book are directed against that very process.

Yours truly,   C. LAMB.

To WILLIAM HAZLITT.

LETTER CLXXV.]   *October* 2, 1811.

Dear Hazlitt—I cannot help accompanying my sister's congratulations to Sarah with some of my own to you on this happy occasion of a man child being born.

Delighted fancy already sees him some future rich alderman or opulent merchant, painting perhaps a little in his leisure hours, for amusement, like the late H. Bunbury, Esq.

Pray, are the Winterslow estates entailed? I am afraid lest the young dog when he grows up should cut down the woods, and leave no groves for widows to take their lonesome solace in. The Wem estate of course can only devolve on him in case of your brother's leaving no male issue.

Well, my blessing and heaven's be upon him, and make him like his father, with something a better temper, and a smoother head of hair; and then all the men and women must love him.

Martin and the card-boys join in congratulations. Love to Sarah. Sorry we are not within caudle-shot.

C. LAMB.

If the widow be assistant on this notable occasion, give our due respects and kind remembrances to her.

Mr. Hazlitt, Winterslow,
    near Sarum, Wilts.

To WILLIAM GODWIN.

"Bis dat qui dat cito."

LETTER CLXXVI.]   [1811.]

I hate the pedantry of expressing that in another language which we have sufficient terms for in our own. So in plain English I very much wish you to give your vote to-morrow at Clerkenwell, instead of Saturday. It would clear up the brows of my favourite candidate, and stagger the hands of the opposite party. It commences at nine. How easy, as you come from Kensington (*à propos*, how is your excellent family?) to turn down Bloomsbury, through Leather Lane (avoiding Lay Stall St. for the disagreeableness of the name)! Why, it brings you in four minutes and a half to the spot renowned on northern milestones, "where Hicks' Hall formerly stood." There will be good cheer ready for every independent freeholder; where you see a green flag hang out, go boldly in, call for ham, or beef, or what you please, and a mug of Meux's best. How much more gentleman-like to come in the front of the battle, openly avowing one's sentiments, than to lag in on the last day, when the adversary is dejected, spiritless, laid low! Have the first cut at them. By Saturday you'll cut into the mutton. I'd go cheerfully myself, but I am no freeholder: (Fuimus Troes, fuit Ilium), but I sold it for £50. If they'd accept a copy-holder, we clerks are naturally *copy*-holders.

By the way, get Mrs. Hume, or that agreeable Amelia or Caroline, to stick a bit of green in your hat. Nothing daunts the adversary more than to wear the colours of your party. Stick it in cockade-like. It has a martial and by no means disagreeable effect.

Go, my dear freeholder, and if any chance calls you out of this transitory scene earlier than expected, the coroner shall sit lightly on your corpse. He shall not too anxiously inquire into the circumstances of blood found upon your razor. That might happen to any gentleman in shaving. Nor into your having been heard to express a contempt of life, or for scolding Louisa for what Julia did, and other trifling incoherencies.

Yours sincerely,   C. LAMB.

To SAMUEL TAYLOR COLERIDGE.

LETTER CLXXVII.]   *August* 13, 1814.

Dear Resuscitate—There comes to you by the vehicle from Lad Lane this day a volume of German ; what it is I cannot justly say, the characters of those northern nations having been always singularly harsh and unpleasant to me. It is a contribution of Dr. Southey's towards your wants, and you would have had it sooner but for an odd accident. I wrote for it three days ago, and the Doctor, as he thought, sent it me. A book of like exterior he did send, but being disclosed, how far unlike ! It was the *Well-bred Scholar*,—a book with which it seems the Doctor laudably fills up those hours which he can steal from his medical avocations. Chesterfield, Blair, Beattie, portions from the *Life of Savage*, make up a prettyish system of morality and the belles-lettres, which Mr. Mylius, a schoolmaster, has properly brought together, and calls the collection by the denomination above mentioned. The Doctor had no sooner discovered his error than he dispatched man and horse to rectify the mistake, and with a pretty kind of ingenuous modesty in his note, seemeth to deny any knowledge of the *Well-bred Scholar;* false modesty surely, and a blush misplaced : for what more pleasing than the consideration of professional austerity thus relaxing, thus improving ! But so, when a child, I remember blushing, being caught on my knees to my Maker, or doing otherwise some pious and praiseworthy action : *now* I rather love such things to be seen. Henry Crabb Robinson is out upon his circuit, and his books are inaccessible without his leave and key. He is attending the Norfolk Circuit,—a short term, but to him, as to many young lawyers, a long vacation, sufficiently dreary. I thought I could do no better than transmit to him, not extracts, but your very letter itself, than which I think I never read anything more moving, more pathetic, or more conducive to the purpose of persuasion. The Crab is a sour Crab if it does not sweeten him. I think it would draw another third volume of Dodsley out of me; but you say you don't want any English books. Perhaps, after all, that's as well; one's romantic credulity is for ever misleading one into misplaced acts of foolery. Crab might have answered by this time: his juices take a long time supplying, but they'll run at last—I know they will—pure golden pippin. A fearful rumour has since reached me that the Crab is on the eve of setting out for France. If he is in England your letter will reach him, and I flatter myself a touch of the persuasive of my own, which accompanies it, will not be thrown away; if it be, he is a sloe, and no true-hearted Crab, and there's an end. For that life of the German conjuror which you speak of, *Colerus de Vitâ Doctoris vix-Intelligibilis*, I perfectly remember the last evening we spent with Mrs. Morgan and Miss Brent, in London Street,— (by that token we had raw rabbits for supper, and Miss B. prevailed upon me to take a glass of brandy and water, which is not my habit),—I perfectly remember reading portions of that life in their parlour, and I think it must be among their packages. It was the very last evening we were at that house. What is gone of that frank-hearted circle, Morgan, and his cos-lettuces? He ate walnuts better than any man I ever knew. Friendships in these parts stagnate.

.   .   .   .   .

I am going to eat turbot, turtle, venison, marrow pudding,—cold punch, claret, Madeira,—at our annual feast, at half-past four this day. They keep bothering me (I'm at office), and my ideas are confused. Let me know if I can be of any service as to books. God forbid

the Architectonican should be sacrificed to a foolish
scruple of some book proprietor, as if books did not
belong with the highest propriety to those that understand 'em best.   C. LAMB.

To WILLIAM WORDSWORTH.

LETTER CLXXVIII.]   *August* 14, 1814.

Dear Wordsworth—I cannot tell you how pleased I
was at the receipt of the great armful of poetry which
you have sent me ; and to get it before the rest of the
world too ! I have gone quite through with it, and was
thinking to have accomplished that pleasure a second
time before I wrote to thank you, but M. Burney came
in the night (while we were out) and made holy theft of
it, but we expect restitution in a day or two. It is the
noblest conversational poem I ever read—a day in Heaven.
The part (or rather main body) which has left the sweetest
odour on my memory (a bad term for the remains of an
impression so recent) is the Tales of the Churchyard ; the
only girl among seven brethren, born out of due time, and
not duly taken away again,—the deaf man and the blind
man ;—the Jacobite and the Hanoverian, whom anti-
pathies reconcile ; the Scarron-entry of the rusticating
parson upon his solitude ;—these were all new to me
too.   My having known the story of Margaret (at the
beginning), a very old acquaintance, even as long back
as when I saw you first at Stowey, did not make her
reappearance less fresh. I don't know what to pick out
of this best of books upon the best subjects for partial
naming.   That gorgeous sunset is famous ; I think it
must have been the identical one we saw on Salisbury
Plain five years ago, that drew Phillips from the card-
table, where he had sat from rise of that luminary to its
unequalled set ; but neither he nor I had gifted eyes to
see those symbols of common things glorified, such as the
prophets saw them in that sunset—the wheel, the potter's

clay, the wash-pot, the wine-press, the almond-tree rod,
the basket of figs, the fourfold visaged head, the throne,
and Him that sat thereon.

One feeling I was particularly struck with, as what I
recognised so very lately at Harrow Church on entering in
it after a hot and secular day's pleasure, the instantaneous
coolness and calming, almost transforming, properties of
a country church just entered ; a certain fragrance which
it has, either from its holiness, or being kept shut all the
week, or the air that is let in being pure country, exactly
what you have reduced into words ; but I am feeling that
which I cannot express. Reading your lines about it
fixed me for a time, a monument in Harrow Church.
Do you know it ? with its fine long spire, white as washed
marble, to be seen, by vantage of its high site, as far as
Salisbury spire itself almost.

I shall select a day or two, very shortly, when I am
coolest in brain, to have a steady second reading, which
I feel will lead to many more, for it will be a stock book
with me while eyes or spectacles shall be lent me.
There is a great deal of noble matter about mountain
scenery, yet not so much as to overpower and discounte-
nance a poor Londoner or south-countryman entirely,
though Mary seems to have felt it occasionally a little too
powerfully, for it was her remark during reading it, that
by your system it was doubtful whether a liver in towns
had a soul to be saved. She almost trembled for that
invisible part of us in her.

Save for a late excursion to Harrow, and a day or two
on the banks of the Thames this Summer, rural images
were fast fading from my mind, and by the wise provi-
sion of the Regent, all that was country-fy'd in the
Parks is all but obliterated. The very colour of green
is vanished ; the whole surface of Hyde Park is dry
crumbling sand (*Arabia Arenosa*), not a vestige or hint
of grass ever having grown there. Booths and drinking-
places go all round it for a mile and half, I am confident
—I might say two miles in circuit. The stench of

liquors, *bad* tobacco, dirty people and provisions, conquers the air, and we are stifled and suffocated in Hyde Park.

Order after order has been issued by Lord Sidmouth in the name of the Regent (acting in behalf of his Royal father) for the dispersion of the varlets, but in vain. The *vis unita* of all the publicans in London, Westminster, Marylebone, and miles round, is too powerful a force to put down. The Regent has raised a phantom which he cannot lay. There they'll stay probably for ever. The whole beauty of the place is gone—that lake-look of the Serpentine—it has got foolish ships upon it; but something whispers to have confidence in Nature and its revival—

> At the coming of the *milder day*,
> These monuments shall all be overgrown.

Meantime I confess to have smoked one delicious pipe in one of the cleanliest and goodliest of the booths; a tent rather—

> " Oh call it not a booth ! "

erected by the public spirit of Watson, who keeps the Adam and Eve at Pancras (the ale-houses have all emigrated, with their train of bottles, mugs, corkscrews, waiters, into Hyde Park—whole ale-houses, with all their ale !), in company with some of the Guards that had been in France, and a fine French girl, habited like a princess of banditti, which one of the dogs had transported from the Garonne to the Serpentine. The unusual scene in Hyde Park, by candle-light, in open air,—good tobacco, bottled stout,—made it look like an interval in a campaign, a repose after battle. I almost fancied scars smarting, and was ready to club a story with my comrades of some of my lying deeds. After all, the fireworks were splendid ; the rockets in clusters, in trees and all shapes, spreading about like young stars in the making, floundering about in space (like unbroke horses), till some of Newton's calculations should fix them ; but then they went out. Any one who could see 'em, and the still finer showers of gloomy rain-fire that fell sulkily and angrily from 'em, and could go to bed without dreaming of the last day, must be as hardened an atheist as . . .

The conclusion of this epistle getting gloomy, I have chosen this part to desire *our* kindest loves to Mrs. Wordsworth and to Dorothea. Will none of you ever be in London again?

Again let me thank you for your present, and assure you that fireworks and triumphs have not distracted me from receiving a calm and noble enjoyment from it (which I trust I shall often), and I sincerely congratulate you on its appearance.

With kindest remembrances to you and your household, we remain, yours sincerely,

C. LAMB and Sister.

To SAMUEL TAYLOR COLERIDGE.

LETTER CLXXIX.] *August* 26, 1814.

Let the hungry soul rejoice, there is corn in Egypt. Whatever thou hast been told to the contrary by designing friends, who perhaps inquired carelessly, or did not inquire at all, in hope of saving their money, there is a stock of "Remorse" on hand—enough, as Pople conjectures, for seven years' consumption; judging from experience of the last two years. Methinks it makes for the benefit of sound literature, that the best books do not always go off best. Inquire in seven years' time for the *Rokebys* and the *Laras*, and where shall they be found?—fluttering fragmentally in some thread-paper; whereas thy *Wallenstein* and thy *Remorse* are safe on Longman's or Pople's shelves, as in some Bodleian; there they shall remain; no need of a chain to hold them fast —perhaps for ages—tall copies—and people shan't run about hunting for them as in old Ezra's shrievalty they did for a Bible, almost without effect till the great-great-

grand-niece (by the mother's side) of Jeremiah or Ezekiel
(which was it?) remembered something of a book, with
odd reading in it, that used to lie in the green closet in
her aunt Judith's bedchamber.

Thy caterer, Price, was at Hamburgh when last Pople
heard of him, laying up for thee like some miserly old
father for his generous-hearted son to squander.

Mr. Charles Aders, whose books also pant for that free
circulation which thy custody is sure to give them, is to
be heard of at his kinsmen, Messrs. Jameson and Aders,
No. 7, Laurence Pountney Lane, London, according to
the information which Crabius with his parting breath
left me. Crabius is gone to Paris. I prophesy he and
the Parisians will part with mutual contempt. His head
has a twist Allemagne, like thine, dear mystic.

I have been reading Madame Stael on Germany : an
impudent clever woman. But if *Faust* be no better than
in her abstract of it, I counsel thee to let it alone. How
canst thou translate the language of cat-monkeys? Fie
on such fantasies! But I will not forget to look for
Proclus. It is a kind of book which, when we meet
with it, we shut up faster than we opened it. Yet I
have some bastard kind of recollection that somewhere,
some time ago, upon some stall or other, I saw it. It
was either that or *Plotinus,* or Saint Augustine's *City of
God.* So little do some folks value, what to others, *sc.*
to you, "well used," had been the "Pledge of Immor-
tality." Bishop Bruno I never touched upon. Stuffing
too good for the brains of such a "Hare" as thou de-
scribest. May it burst his pericranium, as the gobbets of
fat and turpentine (a nasty thought of the seer) did that
old dragon in the Apocrypha! May he go mad in trying
to understand his author! May he lend the third volume
of him before he has quite translated the second, to a
friend who shall lose it, and so spoil the publication, and
may his friend find it and send it him just as thou or
some such less dilatory spirit shall have announced the
whole for the press. So I think I have answered all thy

questions except about Morgan's cos-lettuce. The first
personal peculiarity I ever observed of him (all worthy
souls are subject to 'em) was a particular kind of rabbit-
like delight in munching salads with oil without vinegar
after dinner—a steady contemplative browsing on them
—didst never take note of it? Canst think of any other
queries in the solution of which I can give thee satisfaction? Do you want any books that I can procure for
you? Old Jimmy Boyer is dead at last. Trollope has
got his living, worth £1000 a year net. See, thou
sluggard, thou heretic-sluggard, what mightest thou not
have arrived at! Lay thy animosity against Jimmy in
the grave. Do not *entail* it on thy posterity.

CHARLES LAMB.

To WILLIAM WORDSWORTH.

LETTER CLXXX.] *August* 29, 1814.

My dear W.—I have scarce time or quiet to explain
my present situation, how unquiet and distracted it is,
owing to the absence of some of my compeers, and to the
deficient state of payments at E. I. H., owing to bad
peace speculations in the calico market. (I write this to
W. W., Esq., Collector of Stamp Duties for the Conjoint
Northern Counties, not to W. W., Poet.) I go back,
and have for many days past, to evening work, generally
at the rate of nine hours a day. The nature of my work,
too, puzzling and hurrying, has so shaken my spirits, that
my sleep is nothing but a succession of dreams of business
I cannot do, of assistants that give me no assistance, of
terrible responsibilities. I reclaimed your book, which
Hazlitt has uncivilly kept, only two days ago, and have
made shift to read it again with shattered brain. It does
not lose—rather some parts have come out with a promi-
nence I did not perceive before—but such was my aching
head yesterday (Sunday), that the book was like a mountain landscape to one that should walk on the edge of a

precipice ; I perceive beauty dizzily. Now, what I would say is, that I see no prospect of a quiet half-day, or hour even, till this week and the next are past. I then hope to get four weeks' absence, and if *then* is time enough to begin, I will most gladly do what is required, though I feel my inability, for my brain is always desultory, and snatches off hints from things, but can seldom follow a "work" methodically. But that shall be no excuse. What I beg you to do is, to let me know from Southey, if that will be time enough for the *Quarterly, i.e.* suppose it done in three weeks from this date (19th Sept.) : if not, it is my bounden duty to express my regret, and decline it. Mary thanks you, and feels highly grateful for your "Patent of Nobility," and acknowledges the author of the *Excursion* as the legitimate Fountain of Honour. We both agree that, to our feeling, Ellen is best as she is. To us there would have been something repugnant in her challenging her Penance as a Dowry : the fact is explicable ; but how few are those to whom it would have been rendered explicit ! The unlucky reason of the detention of the *Excursion* was Hazlitt and we having a misunderstanding. He blowed us up about six months ago, since which the union hath snapt ; but M. Burney borrowed it for him, and after reiterated messages I only got it on Friday. His remarks had some vigour in them ; particularly something about an old ruin being *too modern for your Primeval Nature* and about *a lichen.* I forget the passage, but the whole wore a slovenly air of despatch. That objection which M. Burney had imbibed from him about Voltaire I explained to M. B. (or tried) exactly on your principle of its being a characteristic speech. That it was no settled comparative estimate of Voltaire with any of his own tribe of buffoons—no injustice, even if *you* spoke it, for I dared say you never could relish *Candide.* I know I tried to get through it about a twelvemonth since, and couldn't for the dulness. Now I think I have a wider range in buffoonery than you. Too much toleration perhaps.

I finish this after a raw ill-baked dinner fast gobbled up to set me off to office again, after working there till near four. Oh how I wish I were a rich man! even though I were squeezed camel-fashion at getting through that needle's eye that is spoken of in the *Written Word*. Apropos; are you a Christian? or is it the Pedler and the Priest that are?

I find I miscalled that celestial splendour of the mist going off, a *sunset*. That only shows my inaccuracy of head.

Do, pray, indulge me by writing an answer to the point of time mentioned above, or *let Southey*. I am ashamed to go bargaining in this way, but indeed I have no time I can reckon on till the first week in October. God send I may not be disappointed in that! Coleridge swore in a letter to me he would review the *Excursion* in the *Quarterly*. Therefore, though *that* shall not stop me, yet if I can do anything *when* done, I must know of him if he has anything ready, or I shall fill the world with loud exclaims.

I keep writing on, knowing the postage is no more for much writing, else so fagged and dispirited I am with cursed India House work, I scarce know what I do. My left arm reposes on the *Excursion*. I feel what it would be in quiet. It is now a sealed book. C. LAMB.

LETTER CLXXXI.] 1814.

Dear W.—Your experience about tailors seems to be in point blank opposition to Burton, as much as the author of the *Excursion* does, *toto cœlo*, differ in his notion of a country life from the picture which W. H. has exhibited of the same. But, with a little explanation, you and B. may be reconciled. It is evident that he confined his observations to the genuine native London tailor. What freaks tailor-nature may take in the country is not for him to give account of. And certainly some of the freaks recorded do give an idea of the persons in question being beside themselves, rather than in harmony with the common, moderate, self-enjoyment of the rest of mankind. A flying tailor, I venture to say, is no more *in rerum naturâ* than a flying horse or a gryphon. His wheeling his airy flight from the precipice you mention had a parallel in the melancholy Jew who toppled from the monument. Were his limbs ever found? Then, the man who cures diseases by words is evidently an inspired tailor. Burton never affirmed that the art of sewing disqualified the practiser of it from being a fit organ for supernatural revelation. He never enters into such subjects. 'Tis the common, uninspired tailor which he speaks of. Again, the person who makes his smiles to be *heard* is evidently a man under possession — a demoniac tailor. A greater hell than his own must have a hand in this. I am not certain that the cause which you advocate has much reason for triumph. You seem to me to substitute light-headedness for light-heartedness by a trick, or not to know the difference. I confess, a grinning tailor would shock me. Enough of tailors!

The "'scapes" of the great god Pan, who appeared among your mountains some dozen years since, and his narrow chance of being submerged by the swains, afforded me much pleasure. I can conceive the water-nymphs pulling for him. He would have been another Hylas— W. Hylas. In a mad letter which Capel Lofft wrote to M[onthly] M[agazine] Philips (now Sir Richard), I remember his noticing a metaphysical article on Pan, signed H., and adding, "I take your correspondent to be the same with Hylas." Hylas had put forth a pastoral just before. How near the unfounded conjecture of the certainly inspired Lofft (unfounded as we thought it) was to being realised! I can conceive him being "good to all that wander in that perilous flood." One J. Scott (I know no more) is editor of the *Champion*. Where is Coleridge?

That Review you speak of, I am only sorry it did not

appear last month. The circumstances of haste and
peculiar bad spirits under which it was written would
have excused its slightness and inadequacy, the full load
of which I shall suffer from its lying by so long, as it
will seem to have done, from its postponement. I
write with great difficulty, and can scarce command my
own resolution to sit at writing an hour together. I am
a poor creature, but I am leaving off gin. I hope you
will see good-will in the thing. I had a difficulty to perform not to make it all panegyric; I have attempted to
personate a mere stranger to you; perhaps with too much
strangeness. But you must bear that in mind when you
read it, and not think that I am, in mind, distant from
you or your poem, but that both are close to me, among
the nearest of persons and things. I do but act the
stranger in the Review. Then, I was puzzled about
extracts, and determined upon not giving one that had
been in the *Examiner;* for extracts repeated give an
idea that there is a meagre allowance of good things.
By this way, I deprived myself of *Sir Alfred Irthing,*
and the reflections that conclude his story, which are the
flower of the poem. Hazlitt had given the reflections
before me. *Then* it is the first review I ever did, and I
did not know how long I might make it. But it must
speak for itself, if Gifford and his crew do not put words
in its mouth, which I expect. Farewell. Love to all.
Mary keeps very bad. C. LAMB.

LETTER CLXXXII.] 1814.

Dear Wordsworth—I told you my Review was a very
imperfect one. But what you will see in the *Quarterly*
is a spurious one, which Mr. Baviad Gifford has palmed
upon it for mine. I never felt more vexed in my life
than when I read it. I cannot give you an idea of what
he has done to it, out of spite at me, because he once
suffered me to be called a lunatic in his Review. The

language he has altered throughout. Whatever inadequateness it had to its subject, it was, in point of composition, the prettiest piece of prose I ever writ : and so
my sister (to whom alone I read the MS.) said.   That
charm, if it had any, is all gone : more than a third of
the substance is cut away, and that not all from one
place, but *passim*, so as to make utter nonsense.   Every
warm expression is changed for a nasty cold one.

I have not the cursed alteration by me ; I shall never
look at it again ; but for a specimen, I remember I had
said the poet of the *Excursion* " walks through common
forests as through some Dodona or enchanted wood, and
every casual bird that flits upon the boughs, like that
miraculous one in Tasso, but in language more piercing
than any articulate sounds, reveals to him far higher
love-lays." It is now (besides half-a-dozen alterations in
the same half-dozen lines) " but in language more *intelli-
gent* reveals to him ;"—that is one I remember.

But that would have been little, putting his damn'd
shoemaker phraseology (for he was a shoemaker) instead
of mine, which has been tinctured with better authors
than his ignorance can comprehend ;—for I reckon myself
a dab at *prose ;*—verse I leave to my betters : God help
them, if they are to be so reviewed by friend and foe as
you have been this quarter ! I have read " It won't do."
But worse than altering words ; he has kept a few members only of the part I had done best, which was to
explain all I could of your " Scheme of Harmonies," as I
had ventured to call it, between the external universe
and what within us answers to it. To do this I had
accumulated a good many short passages, rising in length
to the end, weaving in the extracts as if they came in as
a part of the text naturally, not intruding them as specimens. Of this part a little is left, but so as, without
conjuration, no man could tell what I was driving at. A
proof of it you may see (though not judge of the whole
of the injustice) by these words. I had spoken something about " natural methodism ;" and after follows,

"and *therefore* the tale of Margaret should have been postponed" (I forget my words, or his words); now the reasons for postponing it are as deducible from what goes before as they are from the 104th Psalm. The passage whence I deduced it has vanished, but clapping a colon before a *therefore* is always reason enough for Mr. Baviad Gifford to allow to a reviewer that is not himself. I assure you my complaints are well founded. I know how sore a word altered makes one; but, indeed, of this review the whole complexion is gone. I regret only that I did not keep a copy. I am sure you would have been pleased with it, because I have been feeding my fancy for some months with the notion of pleasing you. Its imperfection or inadequateness in size and method I knew; but for the *writing part* of it I was fully satisfied; I hoped it would make more than atonement. Ten or twelve distinct passages come to my mind, which are gone; and what is left is, of course, the worse for their having been there; the eyes are pulled out, and the bleeding sockets are left.

I read it at Arch's shop with my face burning with vexation secretly, with just such a feeling as if it had been a review written against myself, making false quotations from me. But I am ashamed to say so much about a short piece. How are *you* served! and the labours of years turned into contempt by scoundrels!

But I could not but protest against your taking that thing as mine. Every *pretty* expression (I know there were many), every warm expression (there was nothing else), is vulgarised and frozen. But if they catch me in their camps again, let them spitchcock me! They had a right to do it, as no name appears to it; and Mr. Shoemaker Gifford, I suppose, never waived a right he had since he commenced author. God confound him and all caitiffs! C. L.

LETTER CLXXXIII.]   [1815.]

Dear Wordsworth—You have made me very proud with your successive book presents. I have been carefully through the two volumes, to see that nothing was omitted which used to be there. I think I miss nothing but a character in the antithetic manner, which I do not know why you left out,—the moral to the boys building the giant, the omission whereof leaves it, in my mind, less complete,—and one admirable line gone (or something come instead of it), "the stone-chat, and the glancing sand-piper," which was a line quite alive. I demand these at your hand. I am glad that you have not sacrificed a verse to those scoundrels. I would not have had you offer up the poorest rag that lingered upon the stript shoulders of little Alice Fell, to have atoned all their malice; I would not have given 'em a red cloak to save their souls. I am afraid lest that substitution of a shell (a flat falsification of the history) for the household implement, as it stood at first, was a kind of tub thrown out to the beast, or rather thrown out for him. The tub was a good honest tub in its place, and nothing could fairly be said against it. You say you made the alteration for the "friendly reader," but the "malicious" will take it to himself. Damn 'em, if you give 'em an inch, etc. The Preface is noble, and such as you should write. I wish I could set my name to it, *Imprimatur*, —but you have set it there yourself, and I thank you. I would rather be a doorkeeper in your margin, than have their proudest text swelling with my eulogies. The poems in the volumes which are new to me are so much in the old tone that I hardly received them as novelties. Of those of which I had no previous knowledge, the "Four Yew Trees," and the mysterious company which you have assembled there, most struck me— "Death the Skeleton and Time the Shadow." It is a sight not for every youthful poet to dream of; it is one of the last results he must have gone thinking on for

years for. " Laodamia " is a very original poem ; I mean
original with reference to your own manner. You have
nothing like it. I should have seen it in a strange
place, and greatly admired it, but not suspected its
derivation.

Let me in this place, for I have writ you several
letters naming it, mention that my brother, who is a
picture-collector, has picked up an undoubtable picture of
Milton. He gave a few shillings for it, and could get
no history with it, but that some old lady had had it for
a great many years. Its age is ascertainable from the
state of the canvas, and you need only see it to be sure
that it is the original of the heads in the Tonson editions,
with which we are all so well familiar. Since I saw you
I have had a treat in the reading way, which comes not
every day, the Latin Poems of V. Bourne, which were
quite new to me. What a heart that man had ! all laid
out upon town schemes, a proper counterpoise to *some
people's* rural extravaganzas. Why I mention him is,
that your " Power of Music " reminded me of his poem
of " The Ballad Singer in the Seven Dials." Do you
remember his epigram on the old woman who taught
Newton the A B C ? which, after all, he says, he hesi-
tates not to call Newton's " Principia." I was lately
fatiguing myself with going through a volume of fine
words by Lord Thurlow ; excellent words ; and if the
heart could live by words alone, it could desire no better
regales ; but what an aching vacuum of matter ! I don't
stick at the madness of it, for that is only a consequence
of shutting his eyes and thinking he is in the age of the
old Elizabeth poets. From thence I turned to Bourne.
What a sweet, unpretending, pretty-mannered, *matter-ful*
creature ! sucking from every flower, making a flower of
everything, his diction all Latin, and his thoughts all
English. Bless him ! Latin wasn't good enough for
him. Why wasn't he content with the language which
Gay and Prior wrote in ?

I am almost sorry that you printed extracts from

those first poems, or that you did not print them at length. They do not read to me as they do altogether. Besides, they have diminished the value of the original, which I possess as a curiosity. I have hitherto kept them distinct in my mind as referring to a particular period of your life. All the rest of your poems are so much of a piece, they might have been written in the same week; these decidedly speak of an earlier period. They tell more of what you had been reading. We were glad to see the poems "by a female friend." The one on the Wind is masterly, but not new to us. Being only three, perhaps you might have clapt a D. at the corner, and let it have past as a printer's mark to the uninitiated, as a delightful hint to the better instructed. As it is, expect a formal criticism on the poems of your female friend, and she must expect it. I should have written before, but I am cruelly engaged, and like to be. On Friday I was at office from ten in the morning (two hours dinner except) to eleven at night; last night till nine. My business and office business in general have increased so; I don't mean I am there every night, but I must expect a great deal of it. I never leave till four, and do not keep a holiday now once in ten times, where I used to keep all red-letter days, and some five days besides, which I used to dub Nature's holidays. I have had my day. I had formerly little to do. So of the little that is left of life, I may reckon two-thirds as dead, for time that a man may call his own is his life; and hard work and thinking about it taints even the leisure hours,—stains Sunday with work-day contemplations. This is Sunday: and the headache I have is part late hours at work the two preceding nights, and part later hours over a consoling pipe afterwards. But I find stupid acquiescence coming over me. I bend to the yoke, and it is almost with me and my household as with the man and his consort—

> "To them each evening had its glittering star,
>   And every Sabbath Day its golden sun"—

to such straits am I driven for the life of life, Time! O that from that superfluity of holiday leisure my youth wasted, "Age might but take some hours youth wanted not!" *N.B.*—I have left off spirituous liquors for four or more months, with a moral certainty of its lasting. Farewell, dear Wordsworth!

O happy Paris, seat of idleness and pleasure! from some returned English I hear that not such a thing as a counting-house is to be seen in her streets,—scarce a desk. Earthquakes swallow up this mercantile city and its "gripple merchants," as Drayton hath it—"born to be the curse of this brave isle!" I invoke this, not on account of any parsimonious habits the mercantile interest may have, but, to confess truth, because I am not fit for an office.

Farewell, in haste, from a head that is too ill to methodise, a stomach too weak to digest, and all out of tune. Better harmonies await you!   C. LAMB.

LETTER CLXXXIV.]

Excuse this maddish letter : I am too tired to write *in formâ.*

1815.

Dear Wordsworth—The more I read of your last two volumes, the more I feel it necessary to make my acknowledgments for them in more than one short letter. The "Night Piece," to which you refer me, I meant fully to have noticed ; but, the fact is, I come so fluttering and languid from business, tired with thoughts of it, frightened with the fears of it, that when I get a few minutes to sit down to scribble (an action of the hand now seldom natural to me—I mean voluntary pen-work) I lose all presential memory of what I had intended to say, and say what I can, talk about Vincent Bourne, or any casual image, instead of that which I had meditated (by the way, I must look out V. B. for you). So I meant to mention "Yarrow Visited," with that stanza, "But thou

that didst appear so fair;" than which I think no
lovelier stanza can be found in the wide world of poetry;
—yet the poem, on the whole, seems condemned to leave
behind it a melancholy of imperfect satisfaction, as if you
had wronged the feeling with which, in what preceded
it, you had resolved never to visit it, and as if the Muse
had determined, in the most delicate manner, to make
you, and *scarce make you,* feel it.   Else, it is far superior
to the other, which has but one exquisite verse in it, the
last but one, or the last two: this is all fine, except
perhaps that *that* of "studious ease and generous cares"
has a little tinge of the *less romantic* about it.   "The
Farmer of Tilsbury Vale" is a charming counterpart to
"Poor Susan," with the addition of that delicacy towards
aberrations from the strict path, which is so fine in the
"Old Thief and the Boy by his side," which always
brings water into my eyes.   Perhaps it is the worse for
being a repetition; "Susan" stood for the representative
of poor *Rus in Urbe.*   There was quite enough to stamp
the moral of the thing never to be forgotten; "bright
volumes of vapour," etc.   The last verse of Susan was
to be got rid of, at all events.   It threw a kind of
dubiety upon Susan's moral conduct.   Susan is a servant
maid.   I see her trundling her mop, and contemplating
the whirling phenomenon through blurred optics; but to
term her "a poor outcast" seems as much as to say that
poor Susan was no better than she should be, which
I trust was not what you meant to express.   Robin
Goodfellow supports himself without that *stick* of a moral
which you have thrown away; but how I can be brought
in *felo de omittendo* for that ending to the Boy-builders
is a mystery.   I can't say positively now,—I only know
that no line oftener or readier occurs than that "Light-
hearted boys, I will build up a Giant with you."   It
comes naturally, with a warm holiday, and the freshness
of the blood.   It is a perfect summer amulet, that I tie
round my legs to quicken their motion when I go out a
maying.   (*N.B.*) I don't often go out a *may*ing;—*must*

is the tense with me now. Do you take the pun? Young
Romilly is divine; the reasons of his mother's grief being
remediless. I never saw parental love carried up so
high, towering above the other loves. Shakspeare had
done something for the filial, in Cordelia, and, by implica-
tion, for the fatherly too, in Lear's resentment; he left
it for you to explore the depths of the maternal heart.
I get stupid, and flat, and flattering. What's the use of
telling you what good things you have written, or—I
hope I may add—that I know them to be good?
Apropos—when I first opened upon the just mentioned
poem, in a careless tone, I said to Mary, as if putting a
riddle, "*What is good for a bootless bene?*" To which,
with infinite presence of mind (as the jest-book has it),
she answered, "a shoeless pea." It was the first joke
she ever made. Joke the second I make. You distinguish well, in your old preface, between the verses of
Dr. Johnson, of the "Man in the Strand," and those
from "The Babes in the Wood." I was thinking, whether
taking your own glorious lines—

> "And from the love which was in her soul
> For her youthful Romilly,"

which, by the love I bear my own soul, I think have no
parallel in any of the best old ballads, and just altering
them to—

> "And from the great respect she felt
> For Sir Samuel Romilly,"

would not have explained the boundaries of prose expression, and poetic feeling, nearly as well. Excuse my
levity on such an occasion. I never felt deeply in my
life if that poem did not make me feel, both lately and
when I read it in MS. No alderman ever longed after a
haunch of buck venison more than I for a spiritual taste
of that "White Doe" you promise. I am sure it is
superlative, or will be when *drest, i.e.* printed. All things
read raw to me in MS.; to compare *magna parvis*, I
cannot endure my own writings in that state. The only

one which I think would not very much win upon me in print is " Peter Bell." But I am not certain. You ask me about your preface. I like both that and the supplement, without an exception. The account of what you mean by imagination is very valuable to me. It will help me to like some things in poetry better, which is a little humiliating in me to confess. I thought I could not be instructed in that science (I mean the critical), as I once heard old obscene, beastly Peter Pindar, in a dispute on Milton, say he thought that if he had reason to value himself upon one thing more than another, it was in knowing what good verse was. Who looked over your proof sheets and left *ordebo* in that line of Virgil ?

My brother's picture of Milton is very finely painted ; that is, it might have been done by a hand next to Vandyke's. It is the genuine Milton, and an object of quiet gaze for the half-hour at a time. Yet though I am confident there is no better one of him, the face does not quite answer to Milton. There is a tinge of *petit* (or *petite*, how do you spell it ?) querulousness about it ; yet, hang it ! now I remember better, there is not ; it is calm, melancholy, and poetical. *One* of the copies of the poems you sent has precisely the same pleasant blending of a sheet of second volume with a sheet of first. I think it was page 245 ; but I sent it and had it rectified. It gave me in the first impetus of cutting the leaves, just such a cold squelch as going down a plausible turning and suddenly reading " No thoroughfare !" Robinson's is entire : I wish you would write more criticism about Spenser, etc. I think I could say something about him myself ; but, Lord bless me ! these " merchants and their spicy drugs," which are so harmonious to sing of, they limetwig up my poor soul and body, till I shall forget I ever thought myself a bit of a genius ! I can't even put a few thoughts on paper for a newspaper. I " engross " when I should " pen " a paragraph. Confusion blast all mercantile transactions, all traffic, exchange of commodities, intercourse between nations, all the consequent civilisation, and wealth, and amity, and link of society, and getting rid of prejudices, and getting a knowledge of the face of the globe ; and rotting the very firs of the forest, that look so romantic alive, and die into desks ! *Vale.*

Yours, dear W., and all yours,   C. LAMB.

To ROBERT SOUTHEY.

LETTER CLXXXV.]   *London, May* 6, 1815.

Dear Southey—I have received from Longman a copy of *Roderick,* with the Author's Compliments, for which I much thank you.   I don't know where I shall put all the noble presents I have lately received in that way : the *Excursion,* Wordsworth's two last vols., and now *Roderick,* have come pouring in upon me like some irruption from Helicon.   The story of the brave Maccabee was already, you may be sure, familiar to me in all its parts.   I have, since the receipt of your present, read it quite through again, and with no diminished pleasure. I don't know whether I ought to say that it has given me more pleasure than any of your long poems. *Kehama* is doubtless more powerful, but I don't feel that firm footing in it that I do in *Roderick :* my imagination goes sinking and floundering in the vast spaces of unopened-before systems and faiths ; I am put out of the pale of my old sympathies ; my moral sense is almost outraged ; I can't believe, or with horror am made to believe, such desperate chances against Omnipotence, such disturbances of faith to the centre ; the more potent the more painful the spell.   Jove, and his brotherhood of gods, tottering with the giant assailings, I can bear, for the soul's hopes are not struck at in such contests ; but your Oriental almighties are too much types of the intangible prototype to be meddled with without shuddering.   One never connects what are called the attributes with Jupiter.— I mention only what diminishes my delight at the wonder-workings of *Kehama,* not what impeaches its power, which I confess with trembling; but *Roderick* is a comfortable poem. It reminds me of the delight I took in the first reading of the *Joan of Arc*. It is maturer and better than *that*, though not better to me now than that was then. It suits me better than *Madoc*. I am at home in Spain and Christendom. I have a timid imagination, I am afraid. I do not willingly admit of strange beliefs, or out-of-the-way creeds or places. I never read books of travels, at least not farther than Paris or Rome. I can just endure Moors, because of their connection as foes with Christians; but Abyssinians, Ethiops, Esquimaux, Dervises, and all that tribe, I hate. I believe I fear them in some manner. A Mahometan turban on the stage, though enveloping some well-known face (Mr. Cook or Mr. Maddox, whom I see another day good Christian and English waiters, innkeepers, etc.), does not give me pleasure unalloyed. I am a Christian, Englishman, Londoner, *Templar*. God help me when I come to put off these snug relations, and to get abroad into the world to come! I shall be like *the crow on the sand*, as Wordsworth has it; but I won't think on it: no need, I hope, yet.

The parts I have been most pleased with, both on first and second readings, perhaps, are Florinda's palliation of Roderick's crime, confessed to him in his disguise—the retreat of the Palayos family first discovered—his being made king—" For acclamation one form must serve *more solemn for the breach* of *old observances*." Roderick's vow is extremely fine, and his blessing on the vow of Alphonso:

> 'Towards the troop he spread his arms,
> As if the expanded soul diffused itself,
> And carried to all spirits *with the act*
> Its affluent inspiration."

It struck me forcibly that the feeling of these last lines might have been suggested to you by the Cartoon of Paul at Athens. Certain it is that a better motto or guide to that famous attitude can nowhere be found. I shall adopt it as explanatory of that violent but dignified motion.

I must read again Landor's *Julian*. I have not read it some time. I think he must have failed in Roderick, for I remember nothing of him, nor of any distinct character as a character—only fine-sounding passages. I remember thinking also he had chosen a point of time after the event, as it were, for Roderick survives to no use ; but my memory is weak, and I will not wrong a fine poem by trusting to it.

The notes to your poem I have not read again : but it will be a take-downable book on my shelf, and they will serve sometimes at breakfast, or times too light for the text to be duly appreciated. Though some of 'em— one of the serpent penance—is serious enough, now I think on't. Of Coleridge I hear nothing, nor of the Morgans. I hope to have him like a reappearing star, standing up before me some time when least expected in London, as has been the case whilere.

I am *doing* nothing (as the phrase is) but reading presents, and walk away what of the day hours I can get from hard occupation. Pray accept once more my hearty thanks, and expression of pleasure for your remembrance of me. My sister desires her kind respects to Mrs. S. and to all at Keswick.

Yours truly,   C. LAMB.

The next present I look for is the *White Doe*.

Have you seen Mat. Betham's *Lay of Marie?* I think it very delicately pretty as to sentiment, etc.

R. Southey, Esq.,
    Keswick, near Penrith,
        Cumberland.

LETTER CLXXXVI.]   *August* 9, 1815.

Dear Southey—Robinson is not on the circuit, as I erroneously stated in a letter to W. W., which travels with this, but is gone to Brussels, Ostend, Ghent, etc. But his friends, the Colliers, whom I consulted respecting your friend's fate, remember to have heard him say that Father Pardo had effected his escape (the cunning greasy rogue !), and to the best of their belief is at present in Paris. To my thinking, it is a small matter whether there be one fat friar more or less in the world. I have rather a taste for clerical executions, imbibed from early recollections of the fate of the excellent Dodd. I hear Buonaparte has sued his habeas corpus, and the twelve judges are now sitting upon it at the Rolls.

Your boute-feu (bonfire) must be excellent of its kind. Poet Settle presided at the last great thing of the kind in London, when the pope was burnt in form. Do you provide any verses on this occasion? Your fear for Hartley's intellectuals is just and rational. Could not the Chancellor be petitioned to remove him? His lordship took Mr. Betty from under the paternal wing. I think at least he should go through a course of matter-of-fact with some sober man after the mysteries. Could not he spend a week at Poole's before he goes back to Oxford? Tobin is dead. But there is a man in my office, a Mr. Hedges, who proses it away from morning to night, and never gets beyond corporal and material verities. He'd get these crack-brain metaphysics out of the young gentleman's head as soon as any one I know. When I can't sleep o' nights, I imagine a dialogue with Mr. Hedges, upon any given subject, and go prosing on in fancy with him, till I either laugh or fall asleep. I have literally found it answer. I am going to stand godfather ; I don't like the business ; I cannot muster up decorum for these occasions ; I shall certainly disgrace the font. I was at Hazlitt's marriage, and had like to have been turned out several times during the ceremony. Anything awful makes me laugh. I misbehaved once at a funeral. Yet I can read about these ceremonies with pious and proper feelings. The realities of life only seem the mockeries. I fear I must get cured along with

Hartley, if not too inveterate. Don't you think Louis the Desirable is in a sort of quandary?

After all, Buonaparte is a fine fellow, as my barber says, and I should not mind standing bareheaded at his table to do him service in his fall. They should have given him Hampton Court or Kensington, with a tether extending forty miles round London. Qu. Would not the people have ejected the Brunswicks some day in his favour? Well, we shall see. C. LAMB.

To WILLIAM WORDSWORTH.

LETTER CLXXXVII.] *August* 9, 1815.

Dear Wordsworth—We acknowledge with pride the receipt of both your handwritings, and desire to be ever had in kindly remembrance by you both and by Dorothy. Alsager, whom you call Alsinger (and indeed he is rather *singer* than *sager*, no reflection upon his naturals neither), is well, and in harmony with himself and the world. I don't know how he, and those of his constitution, keep their nerves so nicely balanced as they do. Or, have they any? Or, are they made of packthread? He is proof against weather, ingratitude, meat underdone, every weapon of fate. I have just now a jagged end of a tooth pricking against my tongue, which meets it half way, in a wantonness of provocation; and there they go at it, the tongue pricking itself, like the viper against the file, and the tooth galling all the gum inside and out to torture; tongue and tooth, tooth and tongue, hard at it; and I to pay the reckoning, till all my mouth is as hot as brimstone; and I'd venture the roof of my mouth, that at this moment, at which I conjecture my full-happiness'd friend is picking his crackers, not one of the double rows of ivory in his privileged mouth has as much as a flaw in it, but all perform their functions, and, having performed them, expect to be picked (luxurious steeds !), and rubbed down. I don't think he could be robbed, or have the house set on fire, or ever want money. I have heard him express a similar opinion of his own impassibility. I keep acting here Heautontimorumenos.

Mr. Burney has been to Calais, and has come a travelled Monsieur. He speaks nothing but the Gallic Idiom. Field is on circuit. So now I believe I have given account of most that you saw at our Cabin.

Have you seen a curious letter in the *Morning Chronicle*, by C. L. [Capell Lofft,] the genius of absurdity, respecting Buonaparte's suing out his Habeas Corpus ? That man is his own moon. He has no need of ascending into that gentle planet for mild influences.

Mary and I felt quite queer after your taking leave (you W. W.) of us in St. Giles's. We wish we had seen more of you, but felt we had scarce been sufficiently acknowledging for the share we had enjoyed of your company. We felt as if we had been not enough *expressive* of our pleasure. But our manners *both* are a little too much on this side of too-much-cordiality. We want presence of mind and presence of heart. What we feel comes too late, like an afterthought impromptu. But perhaps you observed nothing of that which we have been painfully conscious of, and are every day in our inter-course with those we stand affected to through all the degrees of love. Robinson is on the circuit. Our panegyrist I thought had forgotten one of the objects of his youthful admiration, but I was agreeably removed from that scruple by the laundress knocking at my door this morning, almost before I was up, with a present of fruit from my young friend, etc. There is something inex-pressibly pleasant to me in these *presents*, be it fruit, or fowl, or brawn, or *what not*. Books are a legitimate cause of acceptance. If presents be not the soul of friendship, undoubtedly they are the most spiritual part of the body of that intercourse. There is too much narrowness of thinking in this point. The punctilio of acceptance, methinks, is too confined and strait-laced. I could be content to receive money, or clothes, or a joint of meat from a friend. Why should he not send me a dinner as well as a dessert? I would taste him in the beasts of the field, and through all creation. Therefore did the basket of fruit of the juvenile Talfourd not displease me; not that I have any thoughts of bartering or reciprocating these things. To send him anything in return, would be to reflect suspicion of mercenariness upon what I know he meant a freewill offering. Let him overcome me in bounty. In this strife a generous nature loves to be overcome. You wish me some of your leisure. I have a glimmering aspect, a chink-light of liberty before me, which I pray God may prove not fallacious. My remonstrances have stirred up others to remonstrate, and altogether, there is a plan for separating certain parts of business from our department; which, if it take place, will produce me more time, *i.e.* my evenings free. It may be a means of placing me in a more conspicuous situation, which will knock at my nerves another way, but I wait the issue in submission. If I can but begin my own day at four o'clock in the afternoon, I shall think myself to have Eden days of peace and liberty to what I have had. As you say, how a man can fill three volumes up with an essay on the drama is wonderful; I am sure a very few sheets would hold all I had to say on the subject.

Did you ever read " Charron on Wisdom "? or " Patrick's Pilgrim "? If neither, you have two great pleasures to come. I mean some day to attack Caryl on Job, six folios. What any man can write, surely I may read. If I do but get rid of auditing warehousekeepers' accounts and get no worse-harassing task in the place of it, what a lord of liberty I shall be! I shall dance and skip, and make mouths at the invisible event, and pick the thorns out of my pillow, and throw 'em at rich men's night-caps, and talk blank verse, hoity-toity, and sing— " A clerk I was in London gay," " Ban, ban, Ca-Caliban," like the emancipated monster, and go where I like, up this street or down that alley.　Adieu, and pray that it may be my luck.

Good-bye to you all.　　　　　　　　C. LAMB.

To Miss HUTCHINSON.

LETTER CLXXXVIII.]　　　　　*Thursday, October* 19, 1815.

Dear Miss H.—I am forced to be the replier to your letter, for Mary has been ill, and gone from home these five weeks yesterday.　She has left me very lonely and very miserable.　I stroll about, but there is no rest but at one's own fireside, and there is no rest for me there now. I look forward to the worse half being past, and keep up as well as I can.　She has begun to show some favourable symptoms.　The return of her disorder has been frightfully soon this time, with scarce a six months' interval.　I am almost afraid my worry of spirits about the E. I. House was partly the cause of her illness, but one always imputes it to the cause next at hand; more probably it comes from some cause we have no control over or conjecture of.　It cuts sad great slices out of the time, the little time, we shall have to live together.　I don't know but the recurrence of these illnesses might help me to sustain her death better than if we had had no partial separations.　But I won't talk of death.　I will imagine us immortal, or forget that we are otherwise.　By God's blessing, in a few weeks we may be making our meal together, or sitting in the front row of the Pit at Drury Lane, or taking our evening walk past the theatres, to look at the outside of them, at least, if not to be tempted in.　Then we forget we are assailable; we are strong for the time as rocks;—"the wind is tempered to the shorn Lambs."　Poor C. Lloyd, and poor Priscilla!　I feel I hardly feel enough for him; my own calamities press about me, and involve me in a thick integument not to be reached at by other folks' misfortunes. But I feel all I can—all the kindness I can, towards you all—God bless you! I hear nothing from Coleridge.

Yours truly,

C. LAMB.

To THOMAS MANNING.

LETTER CLXXXIX.] *December* 25, 1815.

Dear old Friend and absentee—This is Christmas Day 1815 with us; what it may be with you I don't know, the 12th of June next year perhaps; and if it should be the consecrated season with you, I don't see how you can keep it. You have no turkeys; you would not desecrate the festival by offering up a withered Chinese bantam, instead of the savoury grand Norfolcian holocaust, that smokes all around my nostrils at this moment from a thousand firesides. Then what puddings have you? Where will you get holly to stick in your churches, or churches to stick your dried tea-leaves (that must be the substitute) in? What memorials you can have of the holy time, I see not. A chopped missionary or two may keep up the thin idea of Lent and the wilderness; but what standing evidence have you of the Nativity? 'Tis our rosy-cheeked, homestalled divines, whose faces shine to the tune of "Unto us a child was born," faces fragrant with the mince-pies of half a century, that alone can authenticate the cheerful mystery. I feel my bowels refreshed with the holy tide; my zeal is great against the unedified heathen. Down with the Pagodas—down with the idols—Ching-chong-fo—and his foolish priesthood! Come out of Babylon, O my friend! for her time is come; and the child that is native, and the Proselyte of her gates, shall kindle and smoke together! And in sober sense what makes you so long from among us, Manning? You must not expect to see the same England again which you left.

Empires have been overturned, crowns trodden into

dust, the face of the western world quite changed. Your friends have all got old—those you left blooming ; myself (who am one of the few that remember you), those golden hairs which you recollect my taking a pride in, turned to silvery and gray. Mary has been dead and buried many years : she desired to be buried in the silk gown you sent her. Rickman, that you remember active and strong, now walks out supported by a servant maid and a stick. Martin Burney is a very old man. The other day an aged woman knocked at my door, and pretended to my acquaintance. It was long before I had the most distant cognition of her ; but at last, together, we made her out to be Louisa, the daughter of Mrs. Topham, formerly Mrs. Morton, who had been Mrs. Reynolds, formerly Mrs. Kenney, whose first husband was Holcroft, the dramatic writer of the last century. St. Paul's Church is a heap of ruins ; the Monument isn't half so high as you knew it, divers parts being successively taken down which the ravages of time had rendered dangerous ; the horse at Charing Cross is gone, no one knows whither ; and all this has taken place while you have been settling whether Ho-hing-tong should be spelt with a ——, or a ——. For aught I see you might almost as well remain where you are, and not come like a Struldbrug into a world were few were born when you went away. Scarce here and there one will be able to make out your face. All your opinions will be out of date, your jokes obsolete, your puns rejected with fastidiousness as wit of the last age. Your way of mathematics has already given way to a new method, which after all is I believe the old doctrine of Maclaurin, new-vamped up with what he borrowed of the negative quantity of fluxions from Euler.

Poor Godwin ! I was passing his tomb the other day in Cripplegate churchyard. There are some verses upon it written by Miss ——, which if I thought good enough I would send you. He was one of those who would have hailed your return, not with boisterous shouts and clamours, but with the complacent gratulations of a

philosopher anxious to promote knowledge as leading to
happiness; but his systems and his theories are ten
feet deep in Cripplegate mould. Coleridge is just dead,
having lived just long enough to close the eyes of Wordsworth, who paid the debt to Nature but a week or two
before. Poor Col., but two days before he died he wrote
to a bookseller, proposing an epic poem on the "Wanderings of Cain," in twenty-four books. It is said he has
left behind him more than forty thousand treatises in
criticism, metaphysics, and divinity, but few of them in
a state of completion. They are now destined, perhaps,
to wrap up spices. You see what mutations the busy
hand of Time has produced, while you have consumed
in foolish voluntary exile that time which might have
gladdened your friends—benefited your country; but
reproaches are useless. Gather up the wretched reliques,
my friend, as fast as you can, and come to your old home.
I will rub my eyes and try to recognise you. We will
shake withered hands together, and talk of old things—
of St. Mary's Church and the barber's opposite, where
the young students in mathematics used to assemble.
Poor Crips, that kept it afterwards, set up a fruiterer's
shop in Trumpington Street, and for aught I know resides
there still, for I saw the name up in the last journey I
took there with my sister just before she died. I suppose
you heard that I had left the India House, and gone into
the Fishmongers' Almshouses over the bridge. I have a
little cabin there, small and homely, but you shall be
welcome to it. You like oysters, and to open them
yourself; I'll get you some if you come in oyster time.
Marshall, Godwin's old friend, is still alive, and talks of
the faces you used to make.

Come as soon as you can. C. LAMB.

LETTER CXC.] *December 26, 1815.*

Dear Manning—Following your brother's example, I
have just ventured one letter to Canton, and am now

hazarding another (not exactly a duplicate) to St. Helena.
The first was full of unprobable romantic fictions, fitting
the remoteness of the mission it goes upon ; in the present
I mean to confine myself nearer to truth as you come
nearer home. A correspondence with the uttermost parts
of the earth necessarily involves in it some heat of fancy ;
it sets the brain agoing, but I can think on the half-way
house tranquilly. Your friends then are not all dead or
grown forgetful of you through old age, as that lying
letter asserted, anticipating rather what must happen if
you kept tarrying on for ever on the skirts of creation, as
there seemed a danger of your doing ; but they are all
tolerably well and in full and perfect comprehension of
what is meant by Manning's coming home again. Mrs.
Kenney never lets her tongue run riot more than in
remembrances of you. Fanny expends herself in phrases
that can only be justified by her romantic nature. Mary
reserves a portion of your silk, not to be buried in (as the
false nuncio asserts), but to make up spick and span into
a bran-new gown to wear when you come. I am the
same as when you knew me, almost to a surfeiting
identity. This very night I am going to *leave off tobacco !*
Surely there must be some other world in which this
unconquerable purpose shall be realised. The soul hath
not her generous aspirings implanted in her in vain. One
that you knew, and I think the only one of those friends
we knew much of in common, has died in earnest. Poor
Priscilla ! Her brother Robert is also dead, and several
of the grown-up brothers and sisters, in the compass of a
very few years. Death has not otherwise meddled much
in families that I know. Not but he has his eye upon
us, and is whetting his feathered dart every instant, as
you see him truly pictured in that impressive moral
picture, " The good man at the hour of death." I have
in trust to put in the post four letters from Diss, and one
from Lynn, to St. Helena, which I hope will accompany
this safe, and one from Lynn, and the one before spoken
of from me, to Canton. But we all hope that these

letters may be waste paper.   I don't know why I have forborne writing so long ; but it is such a forlorn hope to send a scrap of paper straggling over wide oceans !   And yet I know, when you come home, I shall have you sitting before me at our fireside just as if you had never been away.   In such an instant does the return of a person dissipate all the weight of imaginary perplexity from distance of time and space !   I'll promise you good oysters.   Corry is dead that kept the shop opposite St. Dunstan's ; but the tougher materials of the shop survive the perishing frame of its keeper.   Oysters continue to flourish there under as good auspices.   Poor Corry ! but if you will absent yourself twenty years together, you must not expect numerically the same population to congratulate your return which wetted the sea-beach with their tears when you went away.   Have you recovered the breathless stone-staring astonishment into which you must have been thrown upon learning at landing that an Emperor of France was living in St. Helena ?   What an event in the solitude of the seas ! like finding a fish's bone at the top of Plinlimmon ; but these things are nothing in our western world.   Novelties cease to affect. Come and try what your presence can.

God bless you.—Your old friend,   C. LAMB.

To WILLIAM WORDSWORTH.

LETTER CXCI.]   *April* 9, 1816.

Dear Wordsworth—Thanks for the books you have given me and for all the books you mean to give me.   I will bind up the Political Sonnets and Ode according to your suggestion.   I have not bound the poems yet.   I wait till people have done borrowing them.   I think I shall get a chain and chain them to my shelves, *more Bodleiano,* and people may come and read them at chain's length.   For of those who borrow, some read slow ; some mean to read but don't read; and some neither read nor meant to read, but borrow to leave you an opinion of their sagacity. I must do my money-borrowing friends the justice to say that there is nothing of this caprice or wantonness of alienation in them. When they borrow my money they never fail to make use of it. Coleridge has been here about a fortnight. His health is tolerable at present, though beset with temptations. In the first place, the Covent Garden Manager has declined accepting his Tragedy, though (having read it) I see no reason upon earth why it might not have run a very fair chance, though it certainly wants a prominent part for a Miss O'Neil or a Mr. Kean. However, he is going to-day to write to Lord Byron to get it to Drury. Should you see Mrs. C., who has just written to C. a letter, which I have given him, it will be as well to say nothing about its fate, till some answer is shaped from Drury. He has two volumes printing together at Bristol, both finished as far as the composition goes; the latter containing his fugitive poems, the former his Literary Life. Nature, who conducts every creature, by instinct, to its best end, has skilfully directed C. to take up his abode at a Chemist's Laboratory in Norfolk Street. She might as well have sent a *Helluo Librorum* for cure to the Vatican. God keep him inviolate among the traps and pitfalls! He has done pretty well as yet.

Tell Miss H[utchinson] my sister is every day wishing to be quietly sitting down to answer her very kind letter, but while C. stays she can hardly find a quiet time; God bless him!

Tell Mrs. W. her postscripts are always agreeable. They are so legible too. Your manual-graphy is terrible, dark as Lycophron. "Likelihood," for instance, is thus typified . . . . I should not wonder if the constant making out of such paragraphs is the cause of that weakness in Mrs. W.'s eyes, as she is tenderly pleased to express it. Dorothy, I hear, has mounted spectacles; so you have deoculated two of your dearest relations in life

Well, God bless you, and continue to give you power to write with a finger of power upon our hearts what you fail to impress, in corresponding lucidness, upon our outward eye-sight !

Mary's love to all ; she is quite well.

I am called off to do the deposits on Cotton Wool ; but why do I relate this to you, who want faculties to comprehend the great mystery of deposits, of interests, of warehouse rent, and contingent fund ? Adieu !

C. LAMB.

A longer letter when C. is gone back into the country, relating his success, etc. — *my* judgment of *your* new books, etc. etc. — I am scarce quiet enough while he stays.

Yours again, C. L.

LETTER CXCII.] *Accountant's Office, April* 26, 1816.

Dear **W.**—I have just finished the pleasing task of correcting the revise of the poems and letter. I hope they will come out faultless. One blunder I saw and shuddered at. The hallucinating rascal had printed *battered* for *battened*, this last not conveying any distinct sense to his gaping soul. The Reader (as they call 'em) had discovered it, and given it the marginal brand, but the substitutory *n* had not yet appeared. I accompanied his notice with a most pathetic address to the printer not to neglect the correction. I know how such a blunder would " batter at your peace." With regard to the works, the Letter I read with unabated satisfaction. Such a thing was wanted—called for. The parallel of Cotton with Burns I heartily approve. Izaak Walton hallows any page in which his reverend name appears. " Duty archly bending to purposes of general benevolence " is exquisite. The poems I endeavoured not to understand, but to read them with my eye alone, and I think I succeeded. (Some people will do that when they come out, you'll say.) As if I were to luxuriate to-morrow at some picture gallery I was never at before, and going by to-day by chance, found the door open, and had but five minutes to look about me, peeped in; just such a *chastised* peep I took with my mind at the lines my luxuriating eye was coursing over unrestrained, not to anticipate another day's fuller satisfaction. Coleridge is printing " Christabel," by Lord Byron's recommendation to Murray, with what he calls a vision, " Kubla Khan," which said vision he repeats so enchantingly that it irradiates and brings heaven and elysian bowers into my parlour while he sings or says it; but there is an observation, " Never tell thy dreams," and I am almost afraid that " Kubla Khan " is an owl that won't bear daylight. I fear lest it should be discovered by the lantern of typography and clear reducting to letters no better than nonsense or no sense. When I was young I used to chant with ecstasy " MILD ARCADIANS EVER BLOOMING," till somebody told me it was meant to be nonsense. Even yet I have a lingering attachment to it, and I think it better than " Windsor Forest," " Dying Christian's Address," etc. Coleridge has sent his tragedy to D[rury] L[ane] T[heatre]. It cannot be acted this season; and by their manner of receiving, I hope he will be able to alter it to make them accept it for next. He is, at present, under the medical care of a Mr. Gillman (Killman?) a Highgate apothecary, where he plays at leaving off laud—m. I think his essentials not touched: he is very bad; but then he wonderfully picks up another day, and his face, when he repeats his verses, hath its ancient glory; an archangel a little damaged. Will Miss H. pardon our not replying at length to her kind letter? We are not quiet enough; Morgan is with us every day, going betwixt Highgate and the Temple. Coleridge is absent but four miles, and the neighbourhood of such a man is as exciting as the presence of fifty ordinary persons. 'Tis enough to be within the whiff and wind of his genius for us not to possess our souls in quiet. If I lived with him or the Author of the *Excursion,* I should, in a very little time, lose my own identity, and be dragged along in the current of other people's thoughts, hampered in a net. How cool I sit in this office, with no possible interruption further than what I may term *material !* There is not as much metaphysics in thirty-six of the people here as there is in the first page of Locke's "Treatise on the Human Understanding," or as much poetry as in any ten lines of the "Pleasures of Hope," or more natural "Beggar's Petition." I never entangle myself in any of their speculations. Interruptions, if I try to write a letter even, I have dreadful. Just now, within four lines, I was called off for ten minutes to consult dusty old books for the settlement of obsolete errors. I hold you a guinea you don't find the chasm where I left off, so excellently the wounded sense closed again and was healed.

N.B.—Nothing said above to the contrary, but that I hold the personal presence of the two mentioned potent spirits at a rate as high as any ; but I pay dearer. What amuses others robs me of myself : my mind is positively discharged into their greater currents, but flows with a willing violence. As to your question about work, it is far less oppressive to me than it was, from circumstances. It takes all the golden part of the day away, a solid lump, from ten to four ; but it does not kill my peace as before. Some day or other I shall be in a taking again. My head aches, and you have had enough. God bless you !   C. LAMB.

To Miss MATILDA BETHAM.

LETTER CXCIII.]   *East India House, June* 1, 1816.

Dear Miss Betham—All this while I have been tormenting myself with the thought of having been ungracious to you, and you have been all the while accusing yourself. Let us absolve one another, and be quiet. My head is in such a state from incapacity for business that I certainly know it to be my duty not to undertake the veriest trifle in addition. I hardly know how I can go on. I have tried to get some redress by explaining my health, but with no great success. No one can tell how ill I am because it does not come out to the exterior of my face, but lies in my skull, deep and invisible. I wish I was leprous, and black jaundiced skin over, and that all was as well within as my cursed looks. You must not think me worse than I am. I am determined not to be over-set, but to give up business rather, and get 'em to allow me a trifle for services past. Oh! that I had been a shoemaker, or a baker, or a man of large independent fortune! Oh! darling laziness! heaven of Epicurus! Saint's Everlasting Rest! that I could drink vast potations of thee thro' unmeasured Eternity—Otium *cum,* vel *sine* dignitate. Scandalous, dishonourable—any kind of *repose.* I stand not upon the dignified sort. Accursed, damned desks, trade, commerce, business! Inventions of the old original busy-body, brain-working Satan—Sabbathless, restless Satan! A curse relieves: do you ever try it?

A strange letter to write to a lady; but more honeyed sentences will not distil. I dare not ask who revises in my stead. I have drawn you into a scrape and am ashamed; but I know no remedy. My unwellness must be my apology. God bless you (tho' He curse the India House, and fire it *to the ground*), and may no unkind error creep into "Marie"*!* May all its readers like it as well as I do, and everybody about you like its kind author no worse! Why the devil am I never to have a chance of scribbling my own free thoughts, verse or prose, again? Why must I write of tea and drugs, and price goods and the bales of indigo? Farewell.   C. LAMB.

Mary goes to her place on Sunday—I mean your maid, foolish Mary; she wants a very little brains only to be an excellent servant; she is excellently calculated for the country, where nobody has brains.

Have you seen " Christabel " since its publication?

To H. DODWELL.

LETTER CXCIV.]   *July* 1816.

My dear fellow—I have been in a lethargy this long while, and forgotten London, Westminster, Marybone, Paddington—they all went clean out of my head, till happening to go to a neighbor's in this good borough of Calne, for want of whist players, we fell upon *Commerce:* the word awoke me to a remembrance of my professional avocations and the long-continued strife which I have been these 24 years endeavoring to compose between those grand Irreconcileables Cash and Commerce; I instantly called for an almanack, which with some difficulty was procured at a fortune-teller's in the vicinity (for the happy holyday people here having nothing to do, keep no account of time), and found that by dint of duty I must attend in Leadenhall on Wednesy. morning next, and shall attend accordingly. Does Master Hannah give macaroons still, and does he fetch the Cobbetts from my Attic? Perhaps it wouldn't be too much trouble for him to drop the inclosed up at my aforesaid Chamber, and any letters, etc., with it; but the inclosed should go without delay. *N.B.*—He isn't to fetch Monday's Cobbett, but it is to wait my reading when I come back. Heigh Ho! Lord have mercy upon me, how many does two and two make? I am afraid I shall make a poor clerk in future, I am spoiled with rambling among haycocks and cows and pigs. Bless me! I had like to have forgot (the air is so temperate and oblivious here) to say I have seen your brother, and hope he is doing well in the finest spot of the world. More of these things when I return. Remember me to the gentlemen,—I forget names. Shall

I find all my letters at my rooms on Tuesday? If you forgot to send 'em never mind, for I don't much care for reading and writing now; I shall come back again by degrees, I suppose, into my former habits. How is Bruce de Ponthieu, and Porcher and Co.?—the tears come into my eyes when I think how long I have neglected ——.

Adieu! ye fields, ye shepherds and—herdesses, and dairies and cream-pots, and fairies and dances upon the green.

I come, I come. Don't drag me so hard by the hair of my head, Genius of British India! I know my hour is come, Faustus must give up his soul, O Lucifer, O Mephistopheles! Can you make out what all this letter is about? I am afraid to look it over.   CH. LAMB.

Calne, Wilts, Friday,
July something, old style, 1816.

No new style here, all the styles are old, and some of the gates too for that matter.

[Addressed] H. Dodwell, Esq.,
India House, London.

In his absence may be opened by Mr. Chambers.

To JOHN RICKMAN.

LETTER CXCV.]   *December* 30, 1816.

Dear R.—Your goose found her way into our Larder with infinite discretion. Judging by her Giblets which we have sacrificed first, she is a most sensible Bird. Mary bids me say, first, that she thanks you for your remembrance, next that Mr. Norris and his family are no less indebted to you as the cause of his reverend and amiable visage being perpetuated when his Soul is flown. Finding nothing like a Subscription going on for the unhappy Lady, and not knowing how to press an actual Sum upon her, she hit upon the expedient of making believe that Mr. N. wanted his miniature (which his chops did seem to water after, I must confess, when 'twas first proposed, though with a *Nolo Pingier* for modesty), and the likeness being completed, your £5 is to go as from him. This I must confess is robbing Peter, or like the equitable distribution in Alexander's Feast, "Love was crowned" though somebody else "won the cause." And Love himself, smiling Love, he might have sat for, so complacent he sat as he used to sit when in his days of Courtship he ogled thro' his Spectacles. I have a shrewd suspicion he has an Eye upon his Spouse's picture after this, and probably some collateral branches may follow of the Norris or Faint Stock, so that your forerunner may prove a notable Decoy duck. The Colliers are going to sit. Item, her knightly Brother in Ireland is soon coming over, apprized of her difficulties, and I confidently hope an emergence for her. But G. Dyer Executor to a Nobleman! G. D. Residuary Legatee! What whirligig of Fortune is this? *Valet ima Summis.* Strange world, strange kings, strange composition!—I can't enjoy it sufficiently till I get a more active belief in it. You've seen the will of Ld. Stanhope. Conceive his old floor strew'd with *disjecta membra Poeseōs*, now loaden with codicils, deeds of Trust, Letters of attorney, Bonds, obligations, Forfeitures, Exchequer Bills, Noverint Universis. "Mr. Serjeant Best, pray take my arm-chair. My Lord Holland sit here, Lord Grantly will your Lordship take the other? Mr. Jekyll excuse my offering you the window seat—We'll now have that clause read over again."

B. and Fletcher describe a little French Lawyer spoilt by an accidental duel he got thrust into, from a Notable Counsellor turned into a Bravo. Here is G. D. more contra-naturally metamorphosed. My life on it, henceforth he explodes his old Hobby Horses. No more poring into Cambridge records—here are other Title deeds to be looked into—now can he make any Joan a Lady. And if he don't get too proud to marry, that long unsolved Problem of G. D. is in danger of being quickly melted. They can't choose but come and make offer of their coy wares. I see Miss H. prim up her chin, Miss B-n-j-o cock her nose.

He throws his dirty glove. G. D., *Iratis Veneribus*, marries, for my life on't.

And 'tis odds in that case but he leaves off making Love and Verses.

Indeed I look upon our friend as dead, dead to all his desperate fancies, pleasures,—he has lost the dignity of verse, the dignity of poverty, the dignity of digging on in desperation through mines of Literature that yielded nothing. Adieu! the wrinkled brow, the chin half shaved, the Ruined arm-chair, the wind-admitting and expelling screen, the fluttering Pamphlets, the lost Letters, the documents never to be found when wanting, the unserviceable comfortable Landress.

> G. D.'s occupation's o'er!
> Demptus per vim mentis gratissimus Error!

Hæc pauca de amico nostro antiquo accipe pro næniis, exequiis, et ejusdem generis aliis. Vale noster G. D.

From yours as he was, unchanged by Fortune.

C. L.

John Rickman, Esq.,
      New Palace Yard,
            Westminster.

NOTES.

CHAPTER I.

1796–1800.

THE Letters of this period are chiefly addressed to Coleridge, then at Bristol. They relate the sad fortunes of the Lamb family, arising out of the death of the mother in September 1796. They are also largely critical, and deal with Coleridge's first published poems, and the joint volume in which Lamb and Charles Lloyd made their earliest appearance in print.

LETTER I (p. 1).—Southey had just published his *Joan of Arc*, in quarto. He had produced two years before at Bristol, in conjunction with Robert Lovell, *Poems by Bion and Moschus*. Charles Valentine Le Grice, here mentioned, was schoolfellow with Lamb and Coleridge at Christ's Hospital, as also was James White. (For Le Grice, see *Dict. Nat. Biog.*) The latter published his *Original Letters of Sir John Falstaff* in this year. They were dedicated, in a manifestly satirical spirit, to "Master Samuel Irelaunde." The allusions in the letter to Coleridge's "Numbers" are to the weekly issue of his *Watchman*, which first appeared on March 1, 1796, and expired on May 13. *Conciones ad Populum*, or, Addresses to the People, appeared in November 1795.

LETTER II (p. 3).—*Poems on Various Subjects*, by S. T. Coleridge, late of Jesus College, Cambridge, was published this year, and it is to this volume, or the proof-sheets of it sent for inspection, that Lamb here refers as "your poems." The volume contained four sonnets signed C. L., and Coleridge's Preface announced that they "were written by Mr. Charles Lamb of the India House." The other sonnets by Lamb here submitted to Coleridge's opinion appeared in the second edition of Coleridge's Poems, in 1797. The story of the preparation of these small volumes of verse may be read, concurrently with these letters, in Joseph Cottle's *Recollections of Coleridge*, vol. i. *Moschus* was Robert Lovell, Southey's brother-in-law, several of whose sonnets were printed by Coleridge in his *Watchman*. He died of fever in this year. The "difference" which Lamb alludes to as having arisen between Coleridge and Southey was the split on the Pantisocratic Scheme which was to have been carried out by the young colonists on the banks of the Susquehanna.

LETTER III (p. 10).—The simile of the Laplander,

. . . "by Niemi lake,"

is from Coleridge's *Destiny of Nations*. The allusion to the "Monody on Henderson" in this letter needs explanation. John Henderson was a singular genius and precocious scholar, the son of a Bristol schoolmaster, an account of whom will be found in the appendix to the second volume of Cottle's *Recollections of Coleridge*. Cottle was also the author of the "Monody on Henderson" here referred to. It had appeared in a small volume of poems published, without Cottle's name, at Bristol in 1795. Coleridge had evidently forwarded this volume to Lamb for his opinion. The lines criticised by Lamb occur in the following passage :—

"As o'er thy tomb, my Henderson ! I bend,
Shall I not praise thee ? scholar, Christian, friend !
The tears which o'er a brother's recent grave
Fond nature sheds, those copious tears I gave ;
But now that Time her softening hues has brought
And mellowed anguish into pensive thought ;
Since through the varying scenes of life I've passed,
Comparing still the former with the last,
I prize thee more ! The *great*, the *learn'd* I see,
Yet memory turns from *little men* to *thee*."

The other "Monody" here criticised is that of Coleridge on Chatterton. The first symptoms of the subsequent coolness between Coleridge and Lamb may here be detected. It had its source in a delicate matter—Coleridge's alterations of Lamb's sonnets. The "Epitaph on an Infant" is the famous one—

"Ere sin could blight or sorrow fade ; "

at which Lamb never tired of laughing, up to the day when he applied it, in his "Essay on Roast Pig," to the infant grunter.

Dr. Forster was a popular corruption of Dr. Faustus in the old rhyme here alluded to :—

"Dr. Forster was a good man.
He whipped his scholars now and then,
And when he whipped them, he made them dance

> Out of Scotland into France,
> Out of France into Spain,
> And then he whipped them back again ! "

LETTER IV (p. 21).—*Your part of the " Joan of Arc."* "To the second book Coleridge contributed some four hundred lines, where Platonic philosophy and protests against the Newtonian hypothesis of æther are not very appropriately brought into connection with the shepherd-girl of Domremi. These lines disappeared from all editions after the first."—(Dowden's *Southey*, in the "Men of Letters Series.")

The verses on Lamb's grandmother are those afterwards entitled "The Grandame." See *Poems, Plays, and Essays*, vol. ii. of this edition, p. 8.

LETTER V (p. 23).—The *Salutation*. The inn near Christ's Hospital where Lamb and Coleridge used occasionally to meet and discuss poetry after Coleridge's departure from school. See Lamb's Preface to the 1818 edition of his works.

As curious a specimen of translation. A copy of this forgotten French novel is in my possession. It is entitled "Sentimental Tablets of the good Pamphile, written in the months of August, September, October, and November 1789, by M. Gorjy. Translated from the French by P. S. Dupuy, of the East India House, London, 1795." In the list of subscribers at the end of the volume appear many names connected with the India House, familiar to us through Lamb's correspondence, including Mr. Thomas Bye, Mr. Ball (afterwards of Canton), Charles and Frederick Durand, Mr. Evans, Mr. Savory (a brother of "Hester"), and "C. Lamb" himself.

LETTER VI (p. 26).—The Dactyls here parodied were by Southey, one stanza of them only being Coleridge's. They appear in Southey's Collected Poems as "The Soldier's Wife," and begin—

> "Weary way-wanderer ! languid and sick at heart,
>   Travelling painfully over the rugged road ;
>   Wild-visaged wanderer ! God help thee, wretched one."

It will be remembered as a curious coincidence that the same lines attracted the notice of the writers in the *Anti-Jacobin*, where a very humorous parody of them appears, which may be compared with Lamb's. Another like experiment in Latin metres by Southey was there transmuted into the more famous *Knife-Grinder*.

Your own lines, introductory to your poem on " Self," run smoothly and pleasurably. I am inclined to think that the reference is to a Fragment by Coleridge called "Melancholy," and to a poem addressed to Lamb, entitled "To a Friend, together with an Unfinished Poem." I believe that the unfinished poem was the Fragment just mentioned. Both were written as early as 1794, and the Fragment first appeared in the *Morning Chronicle.*

The poem referred to on the "Prince and Princess" was that bearing the title "On a Late Connubial Rupture in High Life," now first submitted to Lamb in manuscript.

Dyer stanza'd him. The first mention in these letters of George Dyer. See notes to "Oxford in the Vacation" (*Essays of Elia*).

LETTER VII (p. 28).—White's *Falstaff Letters* have been already referred to. Dr. Kenrick's *Falstaff's Wedding* was published in 1760. See notes in *Essays of Elia*, to "Oxford in the Vacation." Bürger's *Leonora*, translated by William Taylor of Norwich, first appeared in this year.

The Statute de Contumeliâ. See Coleridge's "Lines composed in a Concert Room." In most editions of Coleridge these lines are dated 1799, but it will be seen that Coleridge submitted them to Lamb three years before.

LETTERS VIII, IX, X, XI (pp. 32-39).—The following letters tell the sad story of the death of Lamb's mother. Whether the Mr. Norris of Christ's Hospital, here mentioned, is the Mr. Randal Norris, afterwards Sub-Treasurer of the Inner Temple, and to the end of his life Lamb's faithful friend, I cannot say. But I believe him to have been the same, and to have been thus designated because Coleridge would best remember Mr. Norris by his frequent visits to Charles Lamb when at Christ's Hospital. See "Christ's Hospital Five and Thirty Years Ago" in *Essays of Elia.*

Write as religious a letter as possible. Coleridge, we might be sure, obeyed this touching behest. In Gillman's unfinished *Life of Coleridge* there is given a letter by Coleridge addressed "To a friend in great anguish of mind on the sudden death of his mother." It is beyond all doubt the one addressed on this occasion to Lamb, for, as will be seen, it cites Lamb's particular request for "a religious letter." It runs as follows:—

"Your letter, my friend, struck me with a mighty horror. It rushed upon me and stupefied my feelings. You bid me write you a religious letter: I am not a man who would attempt to insult the greatness of your anguish by any other consolation. Heaven knows that in the easiest fortunes there is much dissatisfaction and weariness of spirit: much that calls for the exercise of patience and resignation; but in storms like these, that shake the dwelling and make the heart tremble, there is no middle way between despair and the yielding up of the whole spirit unto the guidance of faith. And surely it is a matter of joy that your faith in Jesus has been preserved : the Comforter that should relieve you is not far from you. But, as you are a Christian, in the name of that Saviour who was filled with bitterness and made drunken with wormwood, I conjure you to have recourse in frequent prayer to 'his God and your God,' the God of mercies and Father of all comfort. Your poor father is, I hope, almost senseless of the calamity : the unconscious instrument of Divine Providence knows it not, and your mother is in Heaven. It is sweet to be roused from a frightful dream by the song of birds, and the gladsome rays of the morning. Ah ! how infinitely more sweet to be awakened from the blackness and amazement of a sudden horror by the glories of God manifest, and the hallelujahs of angels.

"As to what regards yourself, I approve altogether of your abandoning what you justly call vanities. I look upon you as a man called by sorrow and anguish and a strange desolation of hopes into quietness, and a soul set apart and made peculiar to God : we cannot arrive at any portion of heavenly bliss without, in some measure, imitating Christ. And they arrive at the largest inheritance who imitate the most difficult parts of His character, and, bowed down and crushed under foot, cry in fulness of faith, 'Father, Thy will be done.'

"I wish above measure to have you for a little while here : no visitants shall blow on the nakedness of your feelings ; you shall be quiet, and your spirit may be healed. I see no possible objection, unless your father's helplessness prevent you, and unless you are necessary to him. If this be not the case, I charge you write me that you will come.

"I charge you, my dearest friend, not to dare to encourage gloom or despair : you are a temporary sharer in human miseries that you may be an eternal partaker of the Divine Nature. I charge you, if by any means it is possible, come to me" (Gillman's *Life of Coleridge*, vol. i. p. 338). See, afterwards, poor Lamb's comments on the concluding sentences of this letter.

LETTER XII (p. 41).—Lamb begins to find an interest in books once more. William Lisle Bowles's Poem, *Hope*, appeared this year in handsome quarto. *The Pursuits of Literature*, by T. J. Mathias, was also just published in its complete form, but anonymously.

LETTER XIII (p. 43).—Coleridge had removed about Christmas of this year to a cottage at Nether-Stowey near Bristol, in order to be near his friend Thomas Poole. A letter written to Joseph Cottle, shortly after his arrival, tells the same story of deep melancholy as he had also apparently confided to Lamb :—

"On the Saturday, the Sunday and ten days after my arrival at Stowey, I felt a depression too dreadful to be described,

> 'So much I felt my genial spirits droop,
> My hopes all flat : Nature within me seemed
> In all her functions, weary of herself.'

"Wordsworth's conversation aroused me somewhat, but even now I am not the man I have been, and I think never shall. A sort of calm hopelessness diffuses itself over my heart. Indeed every mode of life which has promised me bread and cheese, has been one after another torn away from me, but God remains."

The rest of Lamb's letter refers to the arrangements in progress for the publication of the second edition (1797) of Coleridge's Poems, with others by Lamb and Lloyd. The sonnet ending "So, for the mother's sake," is that entitled "To a Friend who asked how I felt when the Nurse first presented my Infant to me."

LETTER XIV (p. 46).—Coleridge dedicated the volume of 1797 to his brother, George Coleridge of Ottery St. Mary ; but the sonnets contained in the volume were prefaced by one addressed to Bowles, beginning—

> "My heart has thanked thee, Bowles ; "

and to this sonnet Lamb here alludes. The lines cited by Lamb, beginning—

> "When all the vanities of life's brief day,"

are unknown to me. His own motto, from Massinger, is from *A Very Woman, or The Prince of Tarent.* He quoted the scene in which it occurs, twelve years later, in his *Dramatic Specimens.*

LETTER XV (p. 49).—The forthcoming volume of 1797 is here under discussion. The numbers "40, 63," etc., refer to the pages in the first edition of Coleridge's Poems, 1796. "40" is "Absence, A Farewell Ode ; " "63" a sonnet, "To the Autumnal Moon ; " "84" "An Imitation from Ossian." In spite of Lamb's remonstrances these were omitted from the second edition. Of the "Epitaph on an Infant,"

> "Ere sin could blight or sorrow fade,"

Coleridge was indeed showing himself "tenacious." It had already appeared in the *Morning Chronicle,* and the *Watchman.* What lines of Lamb's are referred to, as beginning—

> "Laugh all that weep,"

I cannot say. They did not appear in the forthcoming volume. The sonnet on Mrs. Siddons was a joint composition of Lamb and Coleridge.

The lines "*Dear native brook*," published first in the *Watchman*, are the well-known sonnet "To the River Otter." No. "48" is the sonnet "To Priestley," beginning—

"Tho' roused by that dark Vizir Riot rude ; "

"52" the sonnet "To Kosciusko ;" and "53" that "To Fayette." *The last five lines of* 50 are those which conclude the sonnet to Sheridan. Sara Coleridge had a share in one poem in the edition of 1796,—that on page 129, here referred to, called "The Production of a Young Lady," on the subject of the loss of a silver thimble.

LETTER XVI (p. 52).—*The "divine chit-chat of Cowper"* was, as we learn from a sentence in the following letter, a phrase of Coleridge's own. Coleridge uses it again in a letter to John Thelwall of December 17 :—"But do not let us introduce an Act of Uniformity against poets. I have room enough in *my* brain to admire, aye, and almost equally, the *head* and fancy of Akenside and the *heart* and fancy of Bowles, the solemn lordliness of Milton, and the divine chit-chat of Cowper, and whatever a man's excellence is, that will be likewise his fault" (S. T. C. to J. Thelwall, Bristol, December 17, 1796. Mr. Cosens's MSS.)

LETTER XVII (p. 52).—"*The sainted growing woof*," etc. I have not traced this and the following quotation to their source. Coleridge's Lines on Burns, here referred to, were printed in a Bristol paper, and afterwards included in the poem, "To a friend who declared his intention of writing no more poetry."

LETTER XVIII (p. 55).—*The odd coincidence of two young men.* In the joint volume of 1797 Charles Lloyd republished a series of sonnets on the death of his grandmother, Priscilla Farmer. It will be remembered that Lamb's lines, "The Grandame," appeared in the same volume.

LETTER XIX (p. 58).—The lines to his sister were afterwards withdrawn by Lamb from the forthcoming volume, but were printed in the *Monthly Magazine* for October 1797, with the simple heading "Sonnet to a Friend." They will be found on page 4 of the second volume of this series. "David Hartley Coleridge" was now in his second year, having been born September 19, 1796. Priestley's "Examination of the Scotch Doctors" was, I presume, his reply to Dr. Jamieson and others who had criticised his *History of the Corruptions of Christianity.*

LETTER XX (p. 59).—Mention has been already made of Coleridge's contribution to Southey's *Joan of Arc* of certain lines in the second book. Coleridge in later years entirely endorsed his friend Lamb's opinion of the lines. On reading them again he says, " I was really astonished (1) at the school-boy, wretched, allegoric machinery ; (2) at the transmogrifica-tion of the fanatic virago into a modern novel-pawing proselyte of the Age of Reason—a Tom Paine in petticoats ; (3) at the utter want of all rhythm in the verse, the monotony and dead plumb-down of the pauses, and the absence of all bone, muscle, and sinew in the single lines."

The lines were omitted from all editions of Southey's Poem after the first, but were reprinted by Coleridge under the title of " The Destiny of Nations : a Vision," in his *Sibylline Leaves*, in 1817, and will be found in all complete editions of Coleridge's Poems. Lamb, with characteristic certainty of taste, selects for praise the finest lines of the whole composition—

> " For she had lived in this bad world
>   As in a place of tombs,
>   And touch'd not the pollutions of the dead."

Montauban dancing with Roubigné's tenants, is an incident in Mackenzie's *Julia de Roubigné*—the story which probably sug-gested to Lamb to attempt prose fiction.

The poem of Coleridge's here referred to as the " Dream " is that afterwards entitled " The Raven : a Christmas Tale told by a schoolboy to his little brothers and sisters," first printed in the *Morning Post* of March 10, 1798, and afterwards reprinted in *Annual Anthology*, and in *Sibylline Leaves*.

My poor old aunt. See Lamb's verses " Written on the Day of my Aunt's Funeral " (*Poems, Plays, and Essays*, p. 16).

No after friendship e'er can raise—from John Logan's poem " On the death of a young lady."

John Woolman. Readers of the *Essays of Elia* will remember the reference to the writings of John Woolman, the Quaker, in the essay " A Quaker's Meeting."

The poem in Southey's new volume which Lamb calls the " Miniature," was actually called " On my own miniature Picture," the " Robert " being of course Southey himself. " Spirit of Spenser ! was the wanderer wrong ? " is the last line of the poem.

Flocci-nauci-what-do-you-call-'em-ists ! may be deemed worthy of a note. " Flocci, nauci " is the beginning of a rule in the old Latin grammars, containing a list of words signifying " of no account," *floccus* being a lock of wool, and *naucus* a trifle. Lamb was recalling a sentence in one of Shenstone's Letters :—

" I loved him for nothing so much as his flocci-nauci-nihili-pili-fication of money."

Mr. Rogers is indebted for his story. In a note to "An Effusion on an Autumnal Evening," in the first edition of his Poems, Coleridge had asserted that the tale of Florio in Rogers's *Pleasures of Memory* was to be found in the *Lochleven* of Bruce. As the fruit of Lamb's remonstrance in this letter Coleridge introduced a handsome apology to Rogers in the next edition (1797), admitting that, on a re-examination of the two poems, he had not found sufficient resemblance to justify the charge.

LETTER XXI (p. 65).—*Did the wand of Merlin wave ?* Lamb refers to his sonnet, beginning " Was it some sweet delight of Fairy ?" In the 1796 edition of Coleridge's Poems the passage had run thus :—

> " Or did the wizard wand
> Of Merlin wave, impregning vacant air,
> And kindle up the vision of a smile
> In those blue eyes ?"

This, it seems, was an alteration of Coleridge's. In accordance with Lamb's instructions in this letter, the passage appeared in the 1797 edition without the "wizard wand of Merlin." See *Poems, Plays*, etc., by Ch. Lamb, p. 1. *Mr.* Merlin, the conjurer, of Oxford Street, was a well-known person at the end of the eighteenth century.

LETTER XXII (p. 69).—*Those very schoolboy-ish verses.* See the lines "To Sara and her Samuel," *Poems, Plays*, etc., of Ch. Lamb, p. 6.

LETTER XXIII (p. 71).—Compare with previous letter of January 5, 1797.

LETTER XXIV (p. 75).—Charles Lloyd, the son of a banker at Birmingham, lived under Coleridge's roof at Bristol, and at Nether-Stowey from the autumn of 1796 to the close of 1797. He was all his life subject to ill-health and persistent melancholia. The "Dedication" to which Lamb refers is the one to his sister, which introduced his portion of the volume of 1797. It ran thus :—" The few following poems, creatures of the Fancy and the Feeling, in life's more *vacant* hours ; produced for the most part by Love in Idleness, are, with all a brother's fondness, inscribed to Mary Ann Lamb, the author's best friend and sister."

LETTER XXV (p. 77).—*The above* was Lamb's poem, "A Vision of Repentance," published in an appendix to the volume of 1797. See *Poems, Plays*, etc., of Lamb, p. 13.

LETTER XXVI (p. 78).—"Gryll will be Gryll, and keep his hoggish mind."—Spenser, *Faëry Queen*.

Of my last poem. "The Vision of Repentance," mentioned in previous letter. *Riding behind in the basket* alludes to its being relegated to an appendix, with certain others by his two companions.

LETTER XXVII (p. 80).—*Life of John Buncle*, by Amory. See reference to this book, a great favourite of Lamb's, in the Essay on "Imperfect Sympathies."

LETTER XXVIII (p. 80).—*Our little book* was the volume of 1797, which now appeared with the following title-page :— "Poems, by S. T. Coleridge. Second edition. To which are now added Poems by Charles Lamb and Charles Lloyd," followed by the Latin motto of Coleridge, from the imaginary Epistles of Groscollias :—"Duplex nobis vinculum, et amicitiae et similium junctarumque Camenarum ; quod utinam neque mors solvat, neque temporis longinquitas."

The Richardson referred to in this and other letters was evidently some one in authority at the India House, who controlled the important matter of Lamb's occasional holidays.

LETTER XXIX (p. 81).—Written after Lamb's visit to Coleridge at Nether-Stowey. Talfourd placed this letter in the year 1800, and has been followed by all subsequent editors. Yet, strangely enough, the summer in which it was written is placed beyond all question by the letter itself. The visit to Coleridge of which it tells was for many reasons a memorable one. It was on the evening of Lamb's arrival that Coleridge met with the accident to his leg which prevented his accompanying him on a walk, and drew from him the well-known lines, entitled "This Lime-Tree Bower my Prison," containing the apostrophe to Lamb, "My gentle-hearted Charles," under which Lamb so often affected to wince. An allusion to Coleridge's injured leg, it will be seen, occurs in this letter ; and a further allusion to little Hartley cutting his teeth, adds a quite independent corroboration of the date.

That Inscription.—In all probability Wordsworth's lines "Left upon a Seat in a Yew-Tree," printed in the following year in the *Lyrical Ballads*.

LETTER XXX (p. 83).—*A little passage of Beaumont and Fletcher's.* The lines thus altered are from the "Maid's Tragedy" and run thus :—

> "And am prouder
> That I was once your love (though now refused),
> Than to have had another true to me."

When time drives flocks from field to fold. A noteworthy
instance of Lamb's random recollections. He has here blended
a line of "The Nymph's Reply to the Shepherd" in *England's
Helicon*, with another from the song in *Love's Labour's Lost.*

LETTER XXXI (p. 85).—*I had well-nigh quarrelled with
Charles Lloyd.* This sentence seems to throw light upon the
origin of Lamb's beautiful verses, composed in this very month,
"The Old Familiar Faces," and to suggest a different interpre-
tation of them from that usually given. In my Memoir of
Lamb ("Men of Letters Series"), I had supposed, in company
with many others, that the allusion in the lines—

> "I have a friend, a kinder friend has no man.
> Like an ingrate, I left my friend abruptly—
> Left him, to muse on the old familiar faces"—

was to Coleridge, between whom and Lamb the relations had,
as we have seen, for some time been rather strained. But it
has been pointed out to me by an obliging correspondent that
the reference in the lines just quoted is more probably to this
temporary rupture with Lloyd; and that the "Friend of my
bosom, thou more than a brother," in the last stanza but one, is
addressed to Coleridge. It is pleasant to think that this should
be the true explanation, and I gladly accept my correspondent's
correction.

Coleridge, as the address at the end of the letter shows, was
now at Shrewsbury, on a visit to the Unitarian minister, the Rev.
Mr. Rowe, whom he then proposed to succeed in that office.

LETTER XXXII (p. 87).—Lamb had been introduced to
Southey by Coleridge, as long back as 1795; but, according to
Talfourd, "no intimacy ensued until he accompanied Lloyd in
the summer of 1797 to the little village of Burton, near Christ
Church in Hampshire, where Southey was then residing, and
where they spent a fortnight as the poet's guests."

Sir R. Phillips was the proprietor of the *Monthly Magazine.*

Coleridge, in company with Wordsworth and his sister, left
England for Germany in September 1798. Coleridge was absent
a little less than a year. It was perhaps well for the future
relations between him and Lamb that this temporary separation
took place. Poetic rivalry and poetic criticism freely indulged
on both sides had left bitterness behind. The whole pitiable
story may be read, if it is worth reading, in the pages of Cottle's
Early Recollections of Coleridge. Cottle tells us that Coleridge
forwarded to him Lamb's letter, containing the sarcastic *Theses*
here propounded, adding "these young visionaries" (meaning
Lamb and Lloyd) "will do each other no good." The *Theses*

were prefaced by the following remarks :—" Learned Sir, my
friend, presuming on our long habits of friendship, and emboldened further by your late liberal permission to avail myself
of your correspondence in case I want any knowledge (which I
intend to do, when I have no Encyclopædia or Ladies' Magazine
at hand to refer to in any matter of science), I now submit to
your inquiries the above theological propositions, to be by you
defended or oppugned (or both) in the schools of Germany,
whither I am told you are departing, to the utter dissatisfaction
of your native Devonshire, and regret of universal England ;
but to my own individual consolation, if, through the channel
of your wished return, learned Sir, my friend, may be transmitted
to this our island, from those famous theological wits of Leipsic
and Gottingen, any rays of illumination, in vain to be derived
from the home growth of our English halls and colleges.
Finally wishing, learned Sir, that you may see Schiller, and
swing in a wood (*vide* Poems) and sit upon a tun, and eat fat
hams of Westphalia,—I remain your friend and docile pupil to
instruct,   CHAS. LAMB."

LETTER XXXIII (p. 90).—*Rosamund Gray*, by Charles
Lamb, was published in this year, 1798.

LETTER XXXIV (p. 91).—The Eclogue here criticised was that
entitled *The Ruined Cottage*. See note to "Rosamund Gray" in
Poems, Plays, etc., p. 388.

How does your Calendar prosper? There would seem to
have been an idea of calling the *Annual Anthology* a Calendar
or Almanack of the Muses. Southey thus opens his preface to
the first volume of the work :—" Similar collections to the
present have long been known in France and Germany under
the title of *Almanacks of the Muses*."

LETTER XXXV (p. 94).—The first of a remarkable series of
letters to Charles Lloyd's brother, Robert, first printed in
Charles Lamb and the Lloyds, a volume edited by Mr. E. V.
Lucas in 1898. The reader is referred to that volume for full
information as to the Lloyd family, and the remarkable discovery of these letters in 1894.

LETTER XXXVIII (p. 98).—Southey, who was now taking
Coleridge's place as Lamb's chief literary correspondent, had
sent two more Eclogues for his opinion— *The Wedding*, and
The Last of the Family.

LETTER XXXIX (p. 100).—The *Lyrical Ballads*, the joint
production of Wordsworth and Coleridge, had just made its
appearance, published by Joseph Cottle, at Bristol. It contained four poems by Coleridge, one being the " Ancient Mariner."

Lamb's pre-eminence as a critic, at this early age of three-and-twenty, appears wonderfully in his remarks upon this poem. "That last poem, which is yet one of the finest written," evidently refers to Wordsworth's "Lines written a few miles above Tintern Abbey," which come last in the little duodecimo volume. In the *Critical Review* for October 1798 Southey had reviewed the *Lyrical Ballads*. Of the *Ancient Mariner* he wrote, "We do not sufficiently understand the story to analyse it. It is a Dutch attempt at German sublimity. Genius has here been employed in producing a poem of little merit."

LETTER XLII (p. 104). — The lines entitled "Mystery of God," or "Living without God in the world," originally appeared in the first volume of Cottle's *Annual Anthology*, published this year, edited by Southey. They will be found in *Poems, Plays*, etc., p. 23. The sonnet referred to would seem to be the one to his sister, already given, "Friend of my earliest years." One of the titles proposed for the *Anthology* was "Gleanings." It was in fact a poetical miscellany to which Coleridge, Southey, Lloyd, and others, including the Cottles, contributed. Two volumes only were published. Pratt, the editor of Pratt's *Gleanings through Wales, Holland, and Westphalia* (1795), was a bookseller at Bath, who published novels and poems, as well as various compilations.

Southey continued to send his poems, as he wrote them, for Lamb's criticisms. The "Witch Ballad" was "The Old Woman of Berkeley," written in this year, as was also "Bishop Bruno." Lamb's "Witch" was the poem originally intended as an episode in *John Woodvil*, but afterwards withdrawn and printed separately. See *Poems, Plays*, etc., p. 66. The "Dying Lover" is the young Philip Fairford mentioned in the poem. George Dyer was at this time preparing a volume of poems. The lines criticised by Lamb occur in an ode "addressed to Dr. Robert Anderson" (*Poems*, by George Dyer : Longman and Co., 1801). Dyer did not accept his friend's correction. The line remains—

"Dark is the poet's eye—but shines his name."

The "two noble Englishmen" were of course Wordsworth and Coleridge. Coleridge, as is well known, parted from Wordsworth and his sister while they were still at Hamburg.

LETTER XLIII (p. 107). —*John May* was a gentleman whose acquaintance Southey had made during his first visit to Portugal, and who was thenceforth one of Southey's most intimate friends and frequent correspondents.

LETTER XLV (p. 110). —Most of Southey's poems here referred to will be found in vols. ii. and vi. of the ten-volume edition, collected by himself, 1837.   "The Parody" is the ballad called "The Surgeon's Warning."   "Cousin Margaret" is the poem "To Margaret Hill."

LETTER XLVI (p. 112).—See Southey's lines "To a Spider," vol. ii. of the edition just named.

Sam Le Grice. For some amusing particulars concerning him see *Leigh Hunt's Autobiography*, chap. iii. "He was the maddest of all the great boys in my time : clever, full of address, and not hampered by modesty. Remote rumours, not lightly to be heard, fell on our ears respecting pranks of his among the nurses' daughters. He had a fair handsome face, with delicate aquiline nose and twinkling eyes. I remember his astonishing me when I was 'a new boy,' with sending me for a bottle of water, which he proceeded to pour down the back of G., a grave Deputy Grecian. On the master asking him one day why he, of all the boys, had given up no exercise (it was a particular exercise that they were bound to do in the course of a long set of holidays) he said he had had a 'lethargy.' " He must, however, have had a good heart. See the previous letter of Lamb to Coleridge in which he tells of Sam Le Grice giving up every hour of his time to amuse the poor old father, in the sad period following the death of Lamb's mother.

LETTER XLIX (p. 117).—*I am much pleased with his poems in the Anthology.*" See C. Lloyd's poem, "Lines to a Brother and Sister" (*Annual Anthology*, vol. i. 192).
A sight of his novel—Edmund Oliver, published in 1798.

LETTER L (p. 118).—Lamb had been visiting his old haunts, near Blakesware in Herts. See note to "Blakesmoor in Hertfordshire ;" *Essays of Elia*, p. 409.
Gebor is Lamb's spelling of " Gebir "—Landor's poem, which was published in this year.

LETTER LI (p. 119).—Thomas Manning, whose name appears here for the first time as Lamb's correspondent, was so remarkable a man as to warrant my giving a few particulars of his life, taken from the Memoir prefixed to his "Journey to Lhasa," in 1811-12 (*George Bogle and Thomas Manning's Journey to Thibet and Lhasa*, by C. R. Markham, 1876).—" He was the second son of the Rev. William Manning, Rector of Diss in Norfolk, and was born at his father's first living of Broome, in the same county, on the 8th of November 1772. Owing to ill-health in early life he was obliged to forego the advantages of a public school ; but under his father's roof he was a close student of both classics and mathematics, and became an eager disciple of the philosophy of Plato. On his recovery he went to Caius College, Cambridge, and studied intensely, especially mathematics. While at Cambridge he published a work on Algebra, and a smaller book on Arithmetic. He passed the final examination, and was expected to be at least second wrangler, but his strong repugnance to oaths and tests debarred him from academic honours and preferments, and he left the university without a degree."

He continued to reside at Cambridge, as a private tutor at Caius, many years after the time when he should have graduated, and was there when Lamb first made his acquaintance, through the introduction of Charles Lloyd, in the autumn of 1799. " After he had lived at Cambridge for some years he began to brood over the mysterious empire of China, and devoted his time to an investigation of the language and arts of the Chinese, and the state of their country. He resolved to enter the Celestial Empire at all hazards, and to prosecute his researches till death stopped him, or until he should return with success. To enable him to undertake this hazardous enterprise he studied the Chinese language under the tuition of Dr. Hagar in France, and afterwards, with the aid of a Chinese, in London. When the English travellers were seized by Napoleon on the breaking out of war in 1803, Manning obtained leave to quit France entirely owing to the respect in which his undertaking was held by the learned men at Paris. His passport was the only one that Napoleon ever signed for an Englishman to go to England after war began."

The rest of Manning's adventures, and the result of his extraordinary expedition to Lhasa in 1811, as well as Manning's own Journal kept during his travels, will be found in Mr. Clements Markham's volume.

Manning was afterwards Chinese Interpreter to Lord Amherst's Embassy in 1817. He then "returned to England, after an absence of nearly twelve years, apparently a disappointed man. He was in Italy from 1827 to 1829, and then went to live in strict retirement at Bexley, whence he removed to a cottage near Dartford, called Orange Grove. He led a very eccentric life. It is said that he never furnished his cottage, but only had a few chairs, one carpet, and a large library of Chinese books. He wore a milky-white beard down to his waist." He died at Bath on the 2nd of May 1840, aged sixty-eight.

The Title of the Play.—Lamb had at first intended to call his play, *John Woodvil*, by a different name—*Pride's Cure*.

CHAPTER II.

1800–1809.

LETTER LIII (p. 122).—*Mr. Wyndham's unhappy composition.* Coleridge's criticism on Wyndham's note, contributed to the *Morning Post* in January 1800, is reprinted in the *Essays on his own Times* (i. 261).

Cottrellian grace. Doubtless an allusion to Sir Charles Cotterell, Master of the Ceremonies at the Court of Charles II.

LETTER LIV (p. 123).—*My Enemy's B—— is*, I am afraid, a variation upon "My enemy's dog" in a well-known speech from *King Lear.*

Mary Hayes. Mary Hayes was an intimate friend of Godwin and his wife, Mary Wollstonecraft. She wrote in the *Monthly Magazine*, also a novel called *Emma Courtenay.* "An uncommon book. Mary Hayes is an agreeable woman and a Godwinite." (Southey, *Life and Correspondence*, i. 305).

LETTER LV (p. 124).—"War, and Nature, and Mr. Pitt." Evidently some popular allegorical print of the day.

LETTER LVI (p. 126).—*Supposed manuscript of Burton.* See "Curious Fragments, extracted from a common-place book which belonged to Robert Burton" (*Poems, Plays, and Essays*, p. 197).

Olivia was Charles Lloyd's sister.

LETTER LVII (p. 127).—*Hetty died on Friday night.* Charles and Mary's one servant.

LETTER LIX (p. 128).—*To lodge with a friend in town.* John Mathew Gutch, a schoolfellow of Lamb's at Christ's Hospital, afterwards the editor of *Felix Farley's Bristol Journal.* He was in partnership with a law-stationer in Southampton Buildings, Holborn. Lamb lodged there occasionally for several years to come. See Letter to Coleridge, later on, p. 145.

LETTER LXII (p. 131).—*Lamb is quite enough.* There was evidently a disposition in the early days of Lamb's friendships to spell his name with a final *e.* I have seen it thus misspelt in magazines of the time.

By terming me gentle-hearted in print. See Coleridge's lines, "This Lime-Tree Bower my Prison," first published in the *Annual Anthology.*

I have hit off the following. See "A Ballad : Noting the Difference of Rich and Poor." *Poems, Plays, and Essays,* p. 68.

W.'s tragedy. "The Borderers." The second edition of the *Lyrical Ballads* was published this year.

LETTER LXIII (p. 134).—*His friend Frend.* The Rev. William Frend, who was expelled the University of Cambridge for tenets savouring of Unitarianism.

George Dyer. See note to the Elia Essay, "Oxford in the Vacation." *Essays of Elia,* p. 379.

LETTER LXIV (p. 136).—*Dr. Anderson.* James Anderson (1739-1808), writer on Agriculture and Politico-Economical subjects.

LETTER LXVII (p. 140).—The references to poems in this letter are to the second volume of the *Annual Anthology,* just published. "Blenheim" is, of course, Southey's well-known ballad ; "Lewti" and the "Raven" are by Coleridge.

Your 141st page refers to the poem " 'This Lime-Tree Bower my Prison,' a poem addressed to Charles Lamb, of the India House, London," in which Lamb was styled, "my gentle-hearted Charles."

LETTER LXIX (p. 145).—*On a visit to Grattan.* Lamb's own slip of the pen for *Curran.* See Mr. Kegan Paul's *Life of Godwin.*

LETTER LXX (p. 146).—John Mathew Gutch, when Lamb lodged with him in Southampton Buildings, Holborn, was in business there as a law-stationer. He was at the time engaged to a Miss Wheeley, the daughter of a coach-builder at Birmingham, and it was during one of his occasional visits to his fiancée in that city that Lamb played upon him the very harmless practical joke contained in this letter. Gutch married Miss Wheeley in the following year. The letter was kindly placed at my disposal by a niece of Mr. Gutch.

LETTER LXXI (p. 147).—*Helen.* These verses were by Mary Lamb.

Alfred, an epic poem by Joseph Cottle of Bristol, the book-seller and poet.

Hurlothrumbo.—For Samuel Johnson, author of this and other now forgotten extravagances, see *Dict. Nat. Biography.* The work referred to by Lamb is probably "A Vision of Heaven," published in 1738.

LETTER LXXII (p. 151).—*A " Conceit of Diabolic Possession."* See the lines afterwards entitled "Hypochondriacus" (*Poems, Plays, and Essays,* p. 204).

VOL. I.   2 O

LETTER LXXVI (p. 157).—*A pleasant hand, one Rickman.*
John Rickman (1771-1840), for many years Clerk-Assistant at the
Table of the House of Commons, an eminent statistician, and
author of the system for taking the population census, besides
many other inventions of greater or less utility.   He became
the intimate friend of Lamb, Southey, and others of that set.

Mr. Crisp was a barber over whose shop Manning lodged,
in St. Mary's Passage, Cambridge.

My Play.   "John Woodvil."

LETTER LXXIX (p. 162).—*How to abridge the Epilogue.*   The
epilogue Lamb was writing for Godwin's play, *Antonio.*   The
next two or three letters deal with the production and the failure
of the unfortunate drama.   See Mr. Kegan Paul's *Life of
Godwin.*

LETTER LXXXIII (p. 169).—*The Preface must be expunged.*
In the British Museum is Lamb's copy of Dyer's Poems.   It
contains the cancelled preface, and on the margin of advertisement, explaining how the book begins at p. lxix. instead of
p. i., Lamb has written, "One copy of this cancelled Preface,
snatched out of the fire, is prefixed to this volume."   The cancelled preface ran to sixty-six pages, not eighty, as Lamb says
to Manning.   Writing to G. C. Bedford, 22nd March 1817,
respecting one of his books then printing, Southey says, "Now,
pray, be speedy with the cancels.   On such an occasion Lamb
gave G. Dyer the title of *Cancellarius Magnus.*"   (*Letters of
R. S.* i. 428.)   For this interesting reference I am indebted to
my friend Mr. J. Dykes Campbell.

LETTER LXXXIV (p. 171).—*Miss Wesley.*   Daughter of
Samuel and niece of John Wesley.   "Eccentric but estimable,"
says H. Crabb Robinson in Diary, 27th May 1812.

One Miss Benjay.   Miss Elizabeth Benger, authoress of various poems and histories.   See *Dictionary of National Biography*,
iv. 221.

LETTER LXXXV (p. 174).—*Barbara Lewthwaite.*   The little
heroine of Wordsworth's poem "The Pet Lamb."

LETTER LXXXVI (p. 176).—The "second volume" that
Lamb had borrowed was the second volume of the *Lyrical
Ballads*, then just published.   The "Song of Lucy" is clearly
the famous lyric beginning—

"She dwelt among the untrodden ways."

Lamb's criticism on the second title of the "Ancient Mariner"
proved effectual in the end, but the title was retained until the

publication of the *Sibylline Leaves* in 1817. The stanzas referred to by Lamb as "The Mad Mother," are those beginning with the words, "Her eyes are wild." Wordsworth in later editions dropped the original title.

I totally differ from your idea. Wordsworth had appended a note to the second edition of the *Lyrical Ballads* (vol. i.), expressing his opinion on the *Ancient Mariner*, and the probable causes of its failure to please. The note is of such singular interest, and so little known, that I make no apology for giving it in full.

"*Note to the Ancient Mariner*, p. 155.—I cannot refuse myself the gratification of informing such Readers as may have been pleased with this Poem, or with any part of it, that they owe their pleasure in some sort to me; as the Author was himself very desirous that it should be suppressed. This wish had arisen from a consciousness of the defects of the Poem, and from a knowledge that many persons had been much displeased with it. The Poem of my Friend has indeed grave defects; first, that the principal person has no distinct character, either in his profession of mariner, or as a human being who, having been long under the control of supernatural impressions, might be supposed himself to partake of something supernatural; secondly, that he does not act, but is continually acted upon; thirdly, that the events, having no necessary connection, do not produce each other; and, lastly, that the imagery is somewhat too laboriously accumulated. Yet the Poem contains many delicate touches of passion, and indeed the passion is everywhere true to nature; a great number of the stanzas present beautiful images, and are expressed with unusual felicity of language; and the versification, though the metre is itself unfit for long poems, is harmonious and artfully varied, exhibiting the utmost powers of that metre, and every variety of which it is capable. It therefore appeared to me that these several merits (the first of which, namely, that of the passion, is of the highest kind) gave to the Poem a value which is not often possessed by better Poems. On this account I requested of my Friend to permit me to republish it."

The coarse epithet of "pin-point." In the first version of the *Poet's Epitaph*, the line to which we are now accustomed—

"Thy ever-dwindling soul away,"

ran thus:—

"Thy pin-point of a soul away."

LETTER LXXXVIII (p. 180).—The greater portion of this letter was in earlier editions printed in the Notes. It is now included in the Text, and a delightful paragraph about George Dyer is now restored.

LETTER LXXXIX (p. 183).—*George Dyer's Poems:* Longman and Rees, 1801. The passage about Shakspeare from the long poem called "Poetic Sympathies" in this volume, beginning—

"Yet, muse of Shakspeare, whither wouldst thou fly
With hurried step, and dove-like, trembling eye?"

is hardly worth quoting further, but may be referred to by the curious.

John Stoddart, Esq. John, afterwards Sir John, Stoddart, was the brother of Mrs. William Hazlitt (the *first* W. H.). He was a writer in the *Times*—quarrelled with Walter, and set up the *New Times*, a short-lived venture, and went to Malta, where he was Chief Justice. While there he invited S. T. Coleridge to visit him, and the invitation was accepted.

My back tingles from the northern castigation. This alludes, of course, to the letter from Wordsworth referred to in the letter to Manning of Feb. 15, 1801.

I am going to change my lodgings. The Lambs were now about to leave Southampton Buildings (see Letter LXIX) for Mitre Court Buildings, in the Temple, destined to be their home for the next eight years.

LETTER XCI (p. 189).—Baron Maseres, Cursitor Baron of the Exchequer. See the Elia Essay, "The Old Benchers of the Inner Temple."

LETTER XCV (p. 194).—*Walter Wilson,* bookseller, and afterwards writer, best known as the author of the *Memoirs of Defoe,* to which Lamb was later to contribute some interesting critical matter.

LETTER XCVI (p. 195).—See Lamb's Essay on "Newspapers Thirty-five Years Ago," and the note upon it in this edition. He there tells us that this epigram gave the unfortunate *Albion* its *coup de grâce.*

LETTER XCVIII (p. 199).—*Your story.* The story of Godwin's later play of *Faulkener* would seem to be indicated here. That play was built upon Defoe's *Roxana,* and Lamb here suggests that the strange history of Richard Savage's parentage might advantageously be borrowed. *Faulkener* was not produced till 1807, and then unsuccessfully. A subsequent letter (No. C.) evidently refers to the plot of the same proposed drama.

LETTER XCIX (p. 201).—The first of a series of letters to Rickman here printed for the first time. Rickman had gone to Dublin as secretary to Charles Abbot (afterwards Lord Colchester) who was made Chief Secretary for Ireland this year. Abbot held the office for only six months, being elected to the Speakership of the House of Commons in January 1802. Rickman remained his secretary after the return to London, and rose to being First Clerk Assistant at the House of Commons.

George Burnett. The son of a farmer in Somersetshire. He was sent to Balliol College, Oxford, and there made the acquaintance of Southey, who was at the same college. He subsequently joined Southey and Coleridge in their "Pantisocracy" scheme. Through these two friends he made the acquaintance of Lamb. He figures largely in these letters to Rickman, where he is commonly styled George the Second, in distinction from Dyer, George the First.

The Professor is courting. Godwin married Mrs. Clairmont in December of this year. She was a widow with two children. The daughter came to play an important part in the lives of Shelley and Byron. *Abbas, King of Persia*, was the title of Godwin's second tragedy, which was not destined to be performed.

LETTER CIV (p. 212).—*The Goul and Gouless* are Godwin and his new wife. "So am not I, said the foolish fat scullion." —*Tristram Shandy.*

LETTER CV (p. 215).—*Letter with the broad seal.* Rickman was Deputy Keeper of the Privy Seal at the Castle.

Earl of Buchan was only sixty years of age at this date. This eccentric nobleman, it will be remembered, was the owner of Dryburgh Abbey, and bestowed its sepulchral aisle upon Walter Scott in order that he might be there buried with his Haliburton ancestors.

LETTER CVII (p. 219).—*Lord Stanhope.* George Burnett had been chosen as tutor to Lord Stanhope's two sons.

LETTER CVIII (p. 220).—*The sweet girl.* See Note to Letter CXXVI. The young lady's name was Mary Druitt.

His two young lords. This would seem to be a fairly accurate account of what happened. After the *escapade* of the two sons, Lord Stanhope paid Burnett a year's salary. Burnett did not long remain an inmate of Lord Stanhope's house, and became later a regimental surgeon.

LETTER CXI (p. 225).—*My Play,* "John Woodvil." The copy sent to Manning, mainly in the handwriting of Mary Lamb, with various omissions marked and corrections added in the handwriting of Charles, is before me, kindly lent by Mr. C. R. Manning of Diss. In the inside cover of the MS. is pasted a sheet of paper, on which Lamb has written as follows :—

Mind this goes for a letter. (Acknowledge it *directly*, if only in ten words.)

Dear Manning—(I shall want to hear this comes safe.) I have scratched out a good deal, as you will see. Generally, what I have rejected was either *false* in *feeling*, or a violation of character—mostly of the first sort. I will here just instance in the concluding few lines of the "Dying Lover's Story," which completely contradicted his character of *silent* and *unreproach-ful*. I hesitated a good deal what copy to send you, and at last resolved to send the worst, because you are familiar with it, and can make it out ; and a stranger would find so much difficulty in doing it, that it would give him more pain than pleasure.

This is compounded precisely of the two persons' hands you requested it should be.—Yours sincerely,   C. LAMB.

I will now transcribe the "Londoner." I have printed this letter, with the accompanying note by Talfourd, but in point of fact the "Londoner" was never published in the *Reflector*. See *Poems, Plays, and Essays*, p. 301.

LETTER CXIV (p. 228).—This letter is written to Coleridge on the return of Charles and Mary from paying him a holiday visit at Keswick. Thomas Clarkson was then residing in a cottage on Ulswater. See following letter to Manning.

LETTER CXVI (p. 229).—*Fenwick is a ruined man.* See *Elia Essays*, "The Two Races of Men," and "Newspapers Thirty-five Years Ago."

Fell, my other drunken companion. Mr. Ralph Fell, author of a *Tour through the Batavian Republic*—according to Southey, a "dull book."

LETTER CXVII (p. 233).—The first of several letters in this correspondence written in Latin ; and in the present instance, as would appear, in reply to a challenge from Coleridge. The letter as hitherto printed is full of certain mistakes for which Lamb is clearly not responsible. These I have ventured to correct, but I have not thought it desirable to amend the Latinity otherwise in passages where it is certainly not im-maculate. The grammar and idiom are frequently so lax as to jeopardise the writer's meaning, but with the assistance of my friend Dr. Calvert of Shrewsbury, I hope I have disen-tangled most of Lamb's somewhat involved allusions. The letter is interesting as bearing reference to several events of interest in the lives of both Coleridge and Wordsworth. It bears date October 9, 1802. A few days earlier, on October 2, Wordsworth had been married to Mary Hutchinson. On the same day (possibly by mere coincidence) Coleridge had printed in the *Morning Post* the first version of his splendid Ode, entitled "Dejection." In this version the person addressed throughout is a certain "Edmund," and not, as in the later revision of the poem, the "Lady," addressed in the often quoted lines—

> "O Lady, we receive but what we give,
> And in *our* Life alone does Nature live."

That "Edmund," the writer's dearest friend and a great poet, could be no other than Wordsworth we might be sure from internal evidence, even if we had not in this letter a curious confirmation. The *Carmina Chamouniana* refer to Coleridge's "Hymn before Sunrise, in the Vale of Chamouni," then recently printed for the first time in the *Morning Post*. Lamb's allusions will be intelligible to those who recall the passage beginning—

> "Who bade the sun
> Clothe you with rainbows? Who with living flowers
> Of loveliest blue, spread garlands at your feet?
> God! God! the torrents, like a shout of nations,
> Utter! the ice-plain bursts, and answers God!"

Although hitherto printed by Lamb's editors, *Tod, Tod*, the reading, I am convinced, should be *Dodd, Dodd*. There is a mountain near Skiddaw called *Skiddaw Dodd*, which Lamb doubtless remembered. Furthermore, the crime and punishment of "the unhappy Doctor," bearing the same name, was fresh in the memory of many persons then living.

The comparisons of the First Consul with the Roman Emperors refer to a series of Essays then recently published by Coleridge in the *Morning Post*. They are reprinted in the *Essays on his own Times:* Pickering, 1850 (vol. ii. pp. 478-514). The allusion to the *Ludus Americanus* must perhaps remain unsolved. The "Flying Opossum" was little Derwent Coleridge, then just entering his third year. The child's vain attempts to pronounce the name of this creature in his picture-book, to which he never attained nearer than "Pi-pos," had fastened this nickname upon the little fellow. "Pi-pos" will recur in many of the succeeding letters.

I. append a translation, partly paraphrased, of the entire letter :—

My very dear Friend—"Pay the post, and go to——" you say ; *i.e.* to Tartarus. Nay ! but have *you* not rather caught a Tartar ? Here have I, for all these years, used my vernacular with (for a writing-clerk) passable elegance ; and yet you are bent on goading me on with your neat and masterly letter, to yelp an answer in such dog-Latin as I may. However, I will try, though afraid my outlandish and far-fetched barbarisms will bring disgrace upon Christ's Hospital, the school still so proud of its learned Barnes and Markland, where in days gone by a wrong-headed master perseveringly drenched me with classical lore. But I must go on as best I can. Come then at my call, all ye troops of conjugations or declensions ! horrible spectres ! and come first and foremost thou—mightiest shadow and image of the Rod—now thank Heaven a thing of the past, the thought of which makes me howl as though I were a boy again !

Your lines written at Chamouni I certainly think very noble, but your English rendering of the echo among the Grisons (*God! God!*) rather jars upon me. I cannot forget that in your own Cumbrian mountains I heard you rouse the echo (Dodd ! Dodd !) of the unfortunate Doctor's name, a sound by no means divine ! As to the rest, I entirely approve.

Your comparisons also I recognise fully as witty and wise. But how about their truth ? I find you asserting in one breath quite inconsistently, merely for comparison's sake, that the First Consul is endowed with the "irritable mind" of Julius Cæsar, as well as with a "constitutional coolness and politic craft" more appropriate to Augustus : and then in the third place you have taken much trouble to extract a resemblance to Tiberius. Why deal with one or two Cæsars when the whole Twelve are only too ready to offer you their services for comparison ? Besides I respect antiquity too much not to detest unfair parallels.

I am wonderfully pleased to have your account of the marriage of Wordsworth, or perhaps I should say of a certain "Edmund" of yours. All blessings rest on thee, Mary ! too happy in thy lot. . . . I wish thee also joy in this new alliance, Dorothy —truly so named, that other "gift of God."

The American "Ludus" of which you prattle so much, Coleridge, I pass over, as utterly abhorrent from a "Ludus" (as such things go). For tell me, what "fun" is there in estranging from ourselves, sprung from the same stock (for the sake of one miserable *jeu d'esprit*), the whole of the Columbian nation. I ask you for a subject for something "Sportive," and you offer me "Bloody Wars."

To wind up, good-bye, and let me know what you think of my Latin style ; and wish for me all health and beauty to my "Flying Opossum," or as you prefer to call him the "Odd Fish." Best greetings to your wife and my good Hartley. We are well, self and sister, who desires her best wishes. No more at present. My time is not my own.

I had almost forgotten to tell you that I have two volumes of John Milton's Latin Works, which (*D. V.*) I will have sent with the rest of your books sooner or later by Mary. You know, however, that in such matters I am by no means in the habit of hurrying; and I plead guilty. I have only to say further that they are handsome volumes, containing all J. M.'s Latin works. I am just now myself engaged and deeply interested in his very spirited Apology for the People of England.

I will carefully observe your instructions about Stuart. Good-bye, once more; and O remember me.

LETTER CXVIII (p. 235).—*Your offer about the German poems.* Coleridge was to translate some of the best German lyrics into literal prose, and Lamb was then to turn them into verse. One experiment of the kind is Lamb's version of Thekla's Song in "Wallenstein." See *Poems, Plays, and Essays*, p. 69.

Your "Epigram on the Sun and Moon." An epigram of Coleridge's contributed this month to the *Morning Post :*—"On the curious circumstance that in the German language the sun is feminine and the moon masculine."

Allen. The schoolfellow of Coleridge and Lamb at Christ's Hospital. Robert Allen went to University College, Oxford, in 1792—the year after Coleridge went to Jesus College, Cambridge. Coleridge visited Allen at Oxford in June 1794, and was introduced by him to Southey. Allen was one of the original Pantisocrats. He was very handsome. See anecdote of him in the Elia Essay, "Christ's Hospital five and thirty years ago."

LETTER CXIX (p. 237).—"*Once a Jacobin.*" An essay of Coleridge's in the *Morning Post* for October 1802. "Once a Jacobin, always a Jacobin." *Essays on his own Times*, ii. p. 542.

Sam Le Grice. Lamb's schoolfellow at Christ's Hospital. See Elia Essay, "Christ's Hospital five and thirty years ago," and my notes thereon.

LETTER CXX (p. 239).—S. T. C.'s first letter to Mr. Fox was published in the *Morning Post* of Thursday, November 4, 1802. A second followed on November 9. Both are included in the *Essays on his own Times*, vol. ii.

LETTER CXXI (p. 241).—Joseph Cottle, the bookseller and publisher, was also, like his brother Amos, a poet. He produced *Malvern Hills* in 1798.

Alfred, an epic poem, in 1801.

LETTER CXXII (p. 242).—*A merry natural captain.* Captain,

afterwards Admiral Burney, who sailed with Captain Cook in two of his voyages.

LETTER CXXIII (p. 244).—*On the death of a young Quaker.* See the beautiful verses entitled "Hester" (*Poems, Plays,* etc., p. 69). Miss Emma Savory of Blackheath, a niece of Hester Savory, has kindly supplied me with a few biographical details. "She (Hester) was the eldest sister of my father, A. B. Savory, and lived with him and his sisters, Anna and Martha, at Pentonville. She married Charles Stoke Dudley, and died, eight months after her marriage, of fever. I possess a miniature portrait of her which I greatly value. My mother used to say that her beauty consisted more in expression than in regularity of features." I may add that I have seen this miniature which, even after reading Lamb's tender and beautiful lyric, is anything but disappointing. It is a bright-eyed gypsy face such as we know so well from the canvas of Reynolds. Miss Savory adds, "I do not think our mother was aware of Charles Lamb's attachment to Hester Savory. Perhaps she did not know it herself."

LETTER CXXIV (p. 245).—This letter refers to the third edition (1803) of Coleridge's Poems, which he had placed in Lamb's hands for revision. The poem called "The Silver Thimble" is that already referred to, in which Sara Coleridge had some small share. The verses on "Flicker and Flicker's Wife" were entitled simply, "Written after a Walk before Supper." They open thus—

"Tho' much averse, dear Jack, to flicker,
To find a likeness for friend V—ker,
I've made this Earth and air and sea
A voyage of Discovery !
And let me add (to ward off strife),
For V—ker, and for V—ker's wife."

Lamb's habitual inaccuracy comes out here also. As for the omission of this *jeu d'esprit* in the forthcoming edition, no one will be found to dissent from his judgment.

LETTER CXXVI (p. 248).—This letter is addressed to "Mr. T. Manning, Maison Magnan, No. 342 Boulevard Italien, Paris." *An epitaph scribbled upon a poor girl.* Written upon a young lady of the name of Mary Druitt, at Wimborne, Dorsetshire. This was done at the request of John Rickman. Lamb was not personally acquainted with the girl, but wrote the lines on Rickman's description. The late Mr. J. P. Collier gives a slightly different version of the lines in his "Old Man's Diary" (privately printed). Mr. Collier says that the girl died at the age of nineteen, of smallpox, and that the lines were engraved upon the tomb ; but I learn from members of the Druitt family still living at Wimborne that this latter statement is not correct. (See Letter CVIII.)

LETTER CXXXI (p. 255). — Lamb's animadversions upon Godwin's lengthy *Life of Chaucer* are as usual admirably just. The work consisted of four-fifths ingenious guessing to one-fifth of material having any historic basis.

Schoolboy copy of verses for Merchant Taylors' boys. The boys were allowed to get help from outside in the composition of their weekly epigrams. In later years we find him making some for the late Archdeacon Hessey and his brother, when at that school.

LETTER CXXXVIII (p. 266). — *Farewell to my "Friendly Traitress."* The "Farewell to Tobacco." First published in Leigh Hunt's *Reflector* in 1811, and afterwards in Lamb's collected works in 1818. See *Poems, Plays*, etc., p. 70.

LETTER CXXXIX (p. 269). — *Mr. Dawe.* See the paper by Lamb, written long afterwards, "Recollections of a late Royal Academician." (*Mrs. Leicester's School*, etc., p. 307.)

Lord Nelson, died October 21, 1805.

Luck to Ned Search. The Light of Nature, by Edward Search, Esq., was a work by Abraham Tucker, which Hazlitt was at this time engaged in abridging and editing. His abridgment appeared in 1807.

The American Farmer. Letters from an American Farmer, Philadelphia, 1774, by Hector St. John Crevecœur.

LETTER CXLI (p. 272). — *Life of Fawcett.* "Report was rife that a life of the Rev. Joseph Fawcett, Mr. Hazlitt's early friend, might be expected from the same quarter ; but such was not the fact" (*Memoir of Hazlitt*, by his Grandson). Fawcett was a dissenting minister at Walthamstow, who published various *Sermons, Poems*, etc.

LETTER CXLVI (p. 278). — Addressed :—"Mr. Manning, Passenger on Board the *Thames*, East Indiaman, Portsmouth." A short postscript to this letter was omitted by Talfourd :— "One thing more, when you get to Canton you will most likely see a young friend of mine, Inspector of Teas, named Ball. He is a very good fellow, and I should like to have my name talked of in China. Give my kind remembrances to the same Ball."

LETTER CXLVIII (p. 281). — *The good news of Mrs. W.* Wordsworth's son Thomas was born on the 16th of June 1806.

Mr. H.—See *Poems, Plays*, etc., p. 348 and note.

A young gentleman of my office. We shall have occasion here-after to mention this fellow-clerk of Lamb's. For an account of Coleridge's early passion for Evans's sister Mary, see Gillman's *Life of Coleridge* and Cottle's *Reminiscences.*

LETTER CLIII (p. 292).—*The Tales from Shakspeare.* The plates referred to by Lamb were designed (as is believed) by William Mulready, then a young man of twenty, and engraved by William Blake. The "bad Baby" was a familiar nickname for Mrs. Godwin. The subject from the *Merchant of Venice* was lettered, Gratiano and Nerissa desire to be married;" the illustration to the *Midsummer Night's Dream* bore for title "Nic Bottom and the Fairies." In spite of Lamb's objection to this latter, it is by far the best of all the illustrations, both in design and drawing, and indicates very clearly the hand of Blake. The "giants and giantesses" of whom Lamb complains are certainly too frequent in these illustrations.

LETTER CLIV (p. 293).—The story of William Hazlitt's disappearance, which caused anxiety to his family, will be found in the *Memoir of Hazlitt*, by his grandson (chapter xi.).

LETTER CLV (p. 294).—Talfourd omitted a few sentences from this letter, which may as well be restored. "Godwin keeps a shop in Skinner Street, Cornhill; he is termed children's bookseller, and sells penny, twopenny, threepenny, and fourpenny books. Sometimes he gets an order for the dearer sort of books (mind, all that I tell you in this letter is true)."

As the boys followed Tom the Piper. Edward FitzGerald, in a letter to Mr. Aldis Wright of March 1878, writes, apropos of this passage: "I had not thought who Tom was: rather acquiesced in some idea of the 'pied Piper of Hamelin'; and not half an hour after, chancing to take down Browne's *Britannia's Pastorals*, found Tom against the Maypole with a ring of Dancers about him. I suppose Tom survived in folk-lore till dear Lamb's time; but how he, a Cockney, knew of it, I don't know."

LETTER CLVI (p. 298).—The passage about the "giant's vomit" was from the story of Polyphemus in Lamb's version of the *Odyssey.*

LETTER CLVIII (p. 300).—Coleridge's *Friend* made its first appearance on the 1st of June 1809, and its last on March 15, 1810.

CHAPTER III.

1809–1816.

LETTER CLX (p. 302). — *Mrs. Clarke.* The mistress of the Duke of York, second son of George III., and Commander-in-Chief of the Forces. "It was established beyond the possibility of doubt that the Duke had permitted Mrs. Clarke to interfere in military promotions ; that he had given commissions at her recommendation ; and that she had taken money for the recommendations." In consequence of the public excitement and indignation on the subject, the Duke resigned his office on the 20th of March of this year.

Godwin's little book. Godwin, *On Sepulchres.*

LETTER CLXI (p. 304). — *Wordsworth's book.* The Convention of Cintra. "Concerning the relations of Great Britain, Spain, and Portugal to each other, and to the common enemy at this crisis, and specifically as affected by the Convention of Cintra," etc. etc., by W. Wordsworth. Longmans. May 20, 1809.

Daniel, enriched with manuscript notes. These are printed in *Notes and Queries,* 1st Series, vi. 117.

Two volumes of Juvenile Poetry. "Poetry for Children, entirely original." By the Author of *Mrs. Leicester's School.* In two volumes. London. Printed for M. J. Godwin at the Juvenile Library, No. 44, Skinner Street. 1809.

Cœlebs. "Cœlebs in Search of a Wife," by Hannah More, published in 1809.

LETTER CLXII (p. 307). — For full information about Charles Lloyd, the father of Lamb's friends, Charles and Robert Lloyd, see Mr. E. V. Lucas's *Charles Lamb and the Lloyds.*

LETTER CLXIII (p. 309). — *The rich Auditors in Albemarle Street.* The audience at the Lectures by Coleridge, given at the Royal Institution the year before.

My admiration of the pamphlet. Evidently refers to Wordsworth's pamphlet on the Convention of Cintra, mentioned in a preceding letter (No. CLXI).

LETTER CLXV (p. 311). — *Dr. Tuthill,* afterwards Sir

George L. Tuthill, M.D., Physician to Bethlehem, Bridewell, and Westminster Hospitals.

Hazlitt has written a grammar. "A new and improved grammar of the English tongue for the use of schools . . . to which is added a new guide to the English tongue, in a letter to Mr. W. F. Mylius, author of the School Dictionary, by Edward Baldwin, Esq. (Godwin)." 1810.

LETTER CLXVII (p. 316).—See Lamb's Essay "On the Poetical Works of George Wither" (*Poems, Plays, and Essays*, p. 295, and note upon it, p. 397). The annotated volume is now in the possession of Mr. A. C. Swinburne, who has published a full and very interesting account of it (see *Nineteenth Century*, Jan. 1886).

LETTER CLXVIII (p. 317).—*Winterslow, near Sarum.* The residence of William Hazlitt, on the border of Salisbury Plain. Charles and Mary Lamb spent their summer holiday with Mr. and Mrs. Hazlitt this year. Basil Montagu had written to Lamb suggesting to him to revise a MS. treatise on the subject of Capital Punishment.

LETTER CLXIX (p. 318).—*H. Robinson.* Henry Crabb Robinson. See his delightful *Diaries* for frequent mention of Charles and Mary Lamb.

LETTER CLXX (p. 319).—*Cram monsters in the voids of the maps.* Lamb was thinking of Swift's lines (in the "Ode to Poetry") about the geographers who—

> "On Afric downs
> Place elephants for want of towns."

LETTER CLXXI (p. 319).—*Your continuation of the Essay on Epitaphs.* Wordsworth had published the first part of this essay in Coleridge's *Friend*, February 22, 1810. He published it later in separate form with additions. The "turgid epitaph" referred to was one from a churchyard in Westmoreland, of the year 1693, of which Wordsworth thought it worth while to compose a simpler version in prose.

LETTER CLXXIII (p. 322).—*Your reply to the Edinburgh Review.* "Reformist's reply to the Edinburgh Review," 1810. "A pamphlet," says Hunt in his *Autobiography*, "which I wrote in defence of the *Review's* own reforming principles, which it had lately taken into its head to renounce as impracticable."

LETTER CLXXIV (p. 323).—John Lamb's brochure has at length come to light, and an account of it was first published by Mr. L. S. Livingston in the New York *Bookman* for January 1899. It is entitled, "A Letter to the Right Hon. William Windham on his opposition to Lord Erskine's Bill for the Prevention of Cruelty to Animals, London, 1810." Mr. Windham had taken the line, in the House of Commons, that the subject was one not fitted for legislation. John Lamb, in his protest, expressly insists on man's cruelty to *eels*, and dilates on the theme with much rhetorical effusiveness.

LETTER CLXXV (p. 324).—The letter congratulates William Hazlitt on the birth of his first child, or at least the first which survived.

H. Bunbury, Esq. (1750-1811). The caricaturist, friend of Johnson, Goldsmith, and Garrick.

Martin and the card-boys. Martin Burney and the rest of the little whist-coterie.

LETTER CLXXVI (p. 325).—*To give your vote to-morrow.* H. Crabb Robinson, under date, March 16, 1811, writes: "C. Lamb stepped in to announce Dr. Tuthill's defeat as candidate for the post of physician to St. Luke's Hospital." The contest, Mrs. Procter informed me, was very severe, and many friends of the candidates bought governorships at £50 for the sake of votes. Basil Montagu bought one for Lamb.

LETTER CLXXVII (p. 326).—*The Well-bred Scholar.* I do not find any work of this name assigned to W. F. Mylius, who was a diligent compiler of school-books. He was a master at Christ's Hospital. Dr. Southey was a brother of the poet.

Going to eat turbot. At the annual dinner of old Christ's Hospital boys.

LETTER CLXXVIII (p. 328).—*The noblest conversational poem.* Wordsworth's *Excursion*, just published.

The whole surface of Hyde Park is dry crumbling sand. Early in August 1814, the three London Parks were thrown open to the public, in celebration of the Peace between England and France. There were fireworks and illuminations; Chinese Pagodas and "Temples of Concord" were erected; and the Parks were, in fact, converted into a vast Fair. It was two years before they recovered their usual verdure.

"*At the coming of the milder day.*" See Wordsworth's Poem, "Hart-Leap Well"—

> "She leaves these objects to a slow decay,
> That what we are, and have been, may be known;
> But at the coming of the milder day
> These monuments shall all be overgrown."

LETTER CLXXIX (p. 331).—"*Remorse.*" Coleridge's tragedy, which, owing to the good offices of Lord Byron, had been brought out at Drury Lane, January 23, 1813, with a Prologue by Lamb. It ran twenty nights.

Old Jimmy Boyer. Rev. James Boyer, the former Head-Master of Christ's Hospital, while Lamb and Coleridge were at the school.

LETTER CLXXX (p. 333).—*Time enough for the Quarterly.* Lamb's forthcoming Review of the *Excursion.* See the Review, and notes thereupon, in *Mrs. Leicester's School and other Writings,* etc., pp. 210 and 395.

LETTER CLXXXI (p. 335).—*Your experience about tailors.* Wordsworth may have told Lamb a story of some tailor in his neighbourhood who had thrown himself over a precipice. If so, it is possible that James Hogg, in his volume of Parodies (the *Poetic Mirror*), published a year or more later, having heard the same story, called his Parody of the *Excursion,* the "Flying Tailor." Another explanation is possible. Lamb may already have seen Hogg's Parody in MS., and in this case the opening paragraph of this letter may be simple, and rather mischievous, *badinage.* The reference to Burton is obviously to Lamb's paper "On the Melancholy of Tailors," signed "Burton Junior," which appeared first in the *Champion,* Dec. 4, 1814.

W. H. is William Hazlitt, who had lately reviewed Wordsworth's *Excursion* in the *Examiner.* This Review was partially reprinted by Hazlitt in the *Round Table,* 1817.

The melancholy Jew. A Jew of the name of Levi had lately flung himself from the monument in Fish Street Hill.

Another Hylas. "An interesting little love-adventure which he (Hazlitt) met with down at the Lakes while he was on his first experimental trip in search of sitters, is so distinctly alluded to in a letter from Lamb to Wordsworth, that I shall just give what Lamb says about it, premising that Patmore had heard in his time of some story of my grandfather being struck by the charms of a village beauty in Wordsworth's neighbourhood, and of having narrowly escaped being ducked by the swains for his ill-appreciated attentions. Wordsworth had evidently described the whole affair in a letter to Lamb" (*Memoirs of William Hazlitt,* by W. C. Hazlitt, i. 105, 106).

LETTER CLXXXII (p. 337).—*I have read "It won't do."* The first words of Jeffrey's famous Review of the *Excursion* in the *Edinburgh,* November 1814, "This will never do!"

LETTER CLXXXIII (p. 340).—*Your successive book presents.* In 1815 Wordsworth published a New Edition of his Poems with the following title :—*Poems by William Wordsworth: including Lyrical Ballads, and the Miscellaneous Pieces of the Author. With Additional Poems, a new Preface, and a Supplementary Essay. In two Volumes.* Among the poems that appeared for the first time in this edition were " Yarrow Visited," "The Force of Prayer ; or, The Founding of Bolton Abbey," "The Farmer of Tilsbury Vale," "Laodamia," "Yew Trees," "A Night Piece," and others. It was naturally on these that Lamb made his comments. He also refers to the various changes of text made since the appearance of the previous edition in 1807. Some of the former readings were restored in later editions, perhaps in consequence of Lamb's remonstrances. The admirable line—

" The stone-chat and the glancing sand-piper "

(as Lamb truly says, "a line quite alive ") is one of these. It occurs in the beautiful poem " Lines left upon a Seat in a Yew-tree," and in the 1815 edition had given place to the far inferior—

"The stone-chat, or the sand-lark, restless Bird,
    Piping along the margin of the lake."

The "substitution of a shell" to which Lamb alludes was in the poem "The blind Highland Boy," where the vessel in which the poor boy embarked was originally a washing-tub, but which was now exchanged (at the request of friends whose self-respect was wounded) for a turtle-shell.

The Preface is noble. The allusion in the words that follow is to a mention Wordsworth had made of Lamb, in citing a sentence from his Essay on Hogarth. He there speaks of Lamb as one of his "most esteemed friends." The "printed extracts from those first poems" refers to the extracts from an " Evening Walk " and " Descriptive Sketches," early poems first published in 1793.

The poems "by a female friend" were by Dorothy Wordsworth. "Three short pieces (now first published)," we read in the Preface, "are the work of a Female Friend, and the Reader to whom they may be acceptable is indebted to me for his pleasure."

An undoubtable picture of Milton. This picture, which came into Charles Lamb's possession after his brother's death, was given by him to Emma Isola.

The Latin Poems of V. Bourne. Cowper's friend, and Master at Westminster School. Lamb, as well as Cowper, wrote and printed various translations from Bourne's Latin Poems.

" To them each evening had its glittering star "—from the *Excursion*, Book V. "The man and his consort" are the

matron and her husband on whose industrious lives these lines are a comment.

LETTER CLXXXIV (p. 343).—"*Yarrow Visited.*" The lovely stanza referred to I would almost hope there is no need to cite, but it is a pleasure to repeat it :—

> "But thou that didst appear so fair
>   To fond imagination,
> Dost rival in the light of day
>   Her delicate creation."

The poem called by Lamb the "Boy-builders" is that better known as "Rural Architecture." It was first printed in 1800, and had a final stanza, omitted in 1815, ending with the lines—

> "Then, light-hearted boys, to the top of the crag,
> And I'll build up a giant with you."

I don't often go out a "may"ing ;—"must" is the tense with me now. It is interesting to remember that Hood uses this antithesis with exquisite effect in his "Ode to Melancholy" :—

> "Even as the blossoms of the *May,*
> Whose fragrance ends in *must.*"

"*What is good for a bootless bene?*" The first line of the poem on Bolton Abbey :—

> "'What is good for a bootless bene?'
>   With these dark words begins my tale ;
> And their meaning is, whence can comfort spring
>   When Prayer is of no avail?"

Who looked over your proof-sheets and left "ordebo" in that line of Virgil? Wordsworth had cited in his preface Virgil's lines in the first Eclogue about the shepherd and the goats :—

> "Non ego vos posthac viridi projectus in antro
> Dumosa pendere procul de rupe *videbo.*"

LETTER CLXXXV (p. 347).—Southey's *Roderick, The Last of the Goths,* was published in quarto, in 1814.

LETTER CLXXXVI (p. 349).—*Hartley's intellectuals.* Hartley Coleridge, now just nineteen years of age, was at Oxford.

Spend a week at Poole's. Thomas Poole, a gentleman whose name has occurred already as the friend of Coleridge and Lamb. Poole succeeded to his father's business as a tanner at Nether-Stowey. Coleridge made his acquaintance, through friends in

Bristol, as early as 1794 ; and it was to be near Poole that he went to live at Stowey in the winter of 1796-97. It was thus that Nether-Stowey became, as Mrs. Henry Sandford, Poole's relative, truly says, "a centre of the leading intellectual impulses of the time." Among other friends of Poole's were Sir Humphry Davy, the Wedgwood brothers, and John Rickman ; and in a less intimate degree Wordsworth, Southey, and Clarkson. Poole retired from business about the year 1804, and thenceforth devoted himself to the interests of his native place, and to all questions affecting the welfare of the labouring classes. He died in 1837. An admirable memoir of Poole has been written by Mrs. Henry Sandford in her book *Thomas Poole and his Friends* (Macmillan and Co.).

LETTER CLXXXVII (p. 351).— *Alsager.* Thomas Massa Alsager. For twenty-eight years attached to the *Times* newspaper, in which he wrote the city and money articles. He further controlled the musical department of the paper. He did more than perhaps any man of his time to promote the study and performance of classical chamber music, especially Beethoven's Quartettes. Hence Lamb's allusion to the propriety of varying the spelling of his name. He died in 1846.

Heautontimorumenos. "The Self-tormentor," the title of a comedy of Terence.

Capell Lofft (1751-1824). The Whig lawyer, writer on legal and political subjects, and poet. He was a native of Bury St. Edmunds, and brought into notice the Suffolk poet, Bloomfield. He sometimes printed sonnets with his initials C. L., to the disgust of Lamb, who bore the same.

The juvenile Talfourd. This first mention of one who was afterwards to be Lamb's biographer deserves a word of comment. He was at this time a young man of twenty, living in chambers in Inner Temple Lane, and reading with Mr. Joseph Chitty, the Special Pleader. Talfourd had just before this been introduced to Lamb at the house of Mr. William Evans, of the India House, and editor of the *Pamphleteer.* I shall have occasion hereafter to mention this latter gentleman in connection with Lamb and Joseph Cottle.

LETTER CLXXXVIII (p. 354). — *Miss Hutchinson,* Mrs. Wordsworth's sister.

LETTER CXCI (p. 359).—*The Political Sonnets and Ode.* The ode was evidently Wordsworth's Thanksgiving Ode, composed on the morning of the day appointed for a General Thanksgiving, January 18, 1816.

The Covent Garden Manager has declined accepting his Tragedy. Coleridge's play *Zapolya.* Though Byron's good offices were ineffectual in getting this second tragedy accepted by the managers, Byron introduced Coleridge to John Murray, which was the means (according to Moore) of its publication as *A Christmas Tale* a year later.

At a Chemist's Laboratory in Norfolk Street. This was probably Lamb's joke. He assumes that Coleridge would naturally choose a chemist's laboratory as being handy for opium purchases.

LETTER CXCII (p. 361).—*The revise of the poems and letter.* The letter referred to was Wordsworth's *Letter to a Friend of Burns*, London, 1816. Wordsworth had been consulted by a friend of Burns as to the best mode of vindicating the reputation of the poet which, it was alleged, had been much injured by the publication of Dr. Currie's *Life and Correspondence of Burns.*

Morgan is with us every day. John Morgan, Coleridge's old Bristol friend, and through life one of his kindest and staunchest supporters. He had a house at Calne, in Wiltshire, where Coleridge lived with him for many months at a time. Lamb was in all probability staying with Morgan when he wrote the letter that follows, dated from that town.

LETTER CXCIII (p. 363).—*Marie.* Miss Betham's "Lay of Marie" (1816).

LETTER CXCIV (p. 365). Henry Dodwell was a fellow-clerk of Lamb's in the India House. This exquisite letter was first printed by me in the Eversley Edition. I quoted a portion of it in the Notes to a previous volume of this edition. The "Cobbetts" are of course the "Political Registers."

LETTER CXCV (p. 366).—*The unhappy lady.* Matilda Betham, who painted miniatures as well as writing poems and compiling histories. "Her knightly brother" was Sir William Betham, at this time in Ireland, Deputy to the Ulster King of Arms.

G. Dyer, Executor to a Nobleman. Dyer was one of Lord Stanhope's ten executors. In company with his colleagues he was bequeathed a share of the Earl's disposable property.

END OF VOL. I

Printed by R. & R. CLARK, LIMITED, *Edinburgh.*

The Eversley Series—*Continued.*

Globe 8vo.   Cloth.   4s. net per volume.

French Poets and Novelists. By HENRY JAMES.

Partial Portraits. By HENRY JAMES.

Modern Greece. Two Lectures. By Sir RICHARD JEBB.

Letters of John Keats to his Family and Friends. Edited by SIDNEY COLVIN.

The Works of Charles Kingsley. 13 Vols.
WESTWARD HO! 2 Vols.
HYPATIA. 2 Vols.
YEAST. 1 Vol.
ALTON LOCKE. 2 Vols.
TWO YEARS AGO. 2 Vols.
HEREWARD THE WAKE. 2 Vols.
POEMS. 2 Vols.

The Works of Charles Lamb. Edited, with Introduction and Notes, by Canon AINGER. 6 Vols.
THE ESSAYS OF ELIA.
POEMS, PLAYS, AND MISCELLANEOUS ESSAYS.
MRS. LEICESTER'S SCHOOL, and other Writings.
TALES FROM SHAKESPEARE. By CHARLES and MARY LAMB.
THE LETTERS OF CHARLES LAMB. 2 Vols.

Life of Charles Lamb. By Canon AINGER.

Historical Essays. By J. B. LIGHTFOOT, D.D.

The Poetical Works of John Milton. Edited, with Memoir, Introduction, and Notes, by DAVID MASSON, M.A. 3 Vols.
VOL. 1. THE MINOR POEMS.
VOL. 2. PARADISE LOST.
VOL. 3. PARADISE REGAINED, AND SAMSON AGONISTES.

Collected Works of John Morley. 11 Vols.
VOLTAIRE. 1 Vol.
ROUSSEAU. 2 Vols.
DIDEROT AND THE ENCYCLOPÆDISTS. 2 Vols.
ON COMPROMISE. 1 Vol.
MISCELLANIES. 3 Vols.
BURKE. 1 Vol.
STUDIES IN LITERATURE. 1 Vol.

Essays by F. W. H. Myers. 3 Vols.
SCIENCE AND A FUTURE LIFE, AND OTHER ESSAYS.
CLASSICAL ESSAYS.
MODERN ESSAYS.

Records of Tennyson, Ruskin, and Browning. By ANNE THACKERAY RITCHIE.

Works by Sir John R. Seeley, K.C.M.G., Litt.D. 5 Vols.
THE EXPANSION OF ENGLAND. Two Courses of Lectures.
LECTURES AND ESSAYS.
ECCE HOMO. A Survey of the Life and Work of Jesus Christ.
NATURAL RELIGION.
LECTURES ON POLITICAL SCIENCE.

The Works of Shakespeare. 10 Vols. With short Introductions and Footnotes by Professor C. H. HERFORD.
VOL. 1. LOVE'S LABOUR'S LOST—COMEDY OF ERRORS—TWO GENTLEMEN OF VERONA—MIDSUMMER-NIGHT'S DREAM.
VOL. 2. TAMING OF THE SHREW—MERCHANT OF VENICE—MERRY WIVES OF WINDSOR—TWELFTH NIGHT—AS YOU LIKE IT.
VOL. 3. MUCH ADO ABOUT NOTHING—ALL'S WELL THAT ENDS WELL—MEASURE FOR MEASURE—TROILUS AND CRESSIDA.
VOL. 4. PERICLES—CYMBELINE—THE WINTER'S TALE—THE TEMPEST.
VOL. 5. HENRY VI.: First Part—HENRY VI.: Second Part—HENRY VI.: Third Part—RICHARD III.
VOL. 6. KING JOHN—RICHARD II.—HENRY IV.: First Part—HENRY IV.: Second Part.
VOL. 7. HENRY V.—HENRY VIII.—TITUS ANDRONICUS—ROMEO AND JULIET.
VOL. 8. JULIUS CÆSAR—HAMLET—OTHELLO.
VOL. 9. KING LEAR—MACBETH—ANTONY AND CLEOPATRA.
VOL. 10. CORIOLANUS—TIMON OF ATHENS—POEMS.

Works by James Smetham.
LETTERS. With an Introductory Memoir. Edited by SARAH SMETHAM and WILLIAM DAVIES. With a Portrait.
LITERARY WORKS. Edited by WILLIAM DAVIES.

Life of Swift. By Sir HENRY CRAIK, K.C.B. 2 Vols. New Edition.

Selections from the Writings of Thoreau. Edited by H. S. SALT.

Essays in the History of Religious Thought in the West. By Bishop WESTCOTT, D.D.

The Works of William Wordsworth. Edited by Professor KNIGHT. 10 Vols.
POETICAL WORKS. 8 Vols.
PROSE WORKS. 2 Vols.

The Journals of Dorothy Wordsworth. 2 Vols.

MACMILLAN AND CO., LTD., LONDON.

10.8.02

The Eversley Series.

Globe 8vo. Cloth. 4s. net per volume.

The Works of Matthew Arnold. 8 vols.
ESSAYS IN CRITICISM. First Series.
ESSAYS IN CRITICISM. Second Series.
EARLY AND NARRATIVE POEMS.
LYRIC AND ELEGIAC POEMS.
DRAMATIC AND LATER POEMS.
AMERICAN DISCOURSES.
LETTERS. Edited by G. W. E.
RUSSELL. 2 Vols.

The Holy Bible. Arranged in paragraphs, with an Introduction by J. W.
MACKAIL, M.A. In 8 volumes. Vol. 1.
GENESIS—NUMBERS. Vol. 2. DEUTERO-
NOMY—2 SAMUEL. Vol. 3. 1 KINGS—
ESTHER. Vol. 4. JOB—SONG OF SOLO-
MON. Vol. 5. ISAIAH—LAMENTATIONS.
Vol. 6. EZEKIEL—MALACHI. Vol. 7.
MATTHEW—JOHN. Vol. 8. ACTS—
REVELATION.

Essays by George Brimley. Third
Edition.

Chaucer's Canterbury Tales. Edited by
A. W. POLLARD. 2 Vols.

**Miscellaneous Writings of Dean
Church.** Collected Edition. 9 Vols.
MISCELLANEOUS ESSAYS.
DANTE : and other Essays.
ST. ANSELM. | SPENSER. | BACON.
THE OXFORD MOVEMENT. Twelve
Years, 1833-1845.
THE BEGINNING OF THE MIDDLE
AGES. (Included in this Series by
permission of Messrs. LONGMANS
& Co.)
OCCASIONAL PAPERS. Selected from
The Guardian, The Times, and *The
Saturday Review,* 1846-1890. 2 Vols.

Life and Letters of Dean Church.
Edited by his Daughter, MARY C.
CHURCH.

**Lectures and Essays by W. K. Clifford,
F.R.S.** Edited by LESLIE STEPHEN
and Sir F. POLLOCK. New Edition.
2 Vols.

Collected Works of Emerson. 6 Vols.
With Introduction by JOHN MORLEY.
MISCELLANIES. | ESSAYS. | POEMS.
ENGLISH TRAITS AND REPRESENTA-
TIVE MEN.
THE CONDUCT OF LIFE, AND SOCIETY
AND SOLITUDE.
LETTERS AND SOCIAL AIMS.

Letters of Edward FitzGerald. Edited
by W. A. WRIGHT. 2 Vols.

More Letters of Edward FitzGerald.

**Letters of Edward FitzGerald to
Fanny Kemble, 1871-1883.** Edited by
W. A. WRIGHT.

Pausanias and other Greek Sketches.
By J. G. FRAZER, M.A.

Goethe's Maxims and Reflections.
Translated, with Introduction, by T. B.
SAUNDERS.
*** *The Scientific and Artistic
Maxims were selected by Professor
Huxley and Lord Leighton respectively.*

**Collected Works of Thomas Gray in
Prose and Verse.** 4 Vols. Edited by
EDMUND GOSSE. Vol. 1. Poems, Jour-
nals, and Essays. Vols. 2 and 3. Letters.
Vol. 4. Notes on Aristophanes and Plato.

Works by John Richard Green. 14 Vols.
HISTORY OF THE ENGLISH PEOPLE.
8 Vols.
THE MAKING OF ENGLAND. With
Maps. In 2 Vols.
THE CONQUEST OF ENGLAND. With
Maps. In 2 Vols.
STRAY STUDIES FROM ENGLAND AND
ITALY.
OXFORD STUDIES.

Guesses at Truth. By TWO BROTHERS.

**The Choice of Books, and other Liter-
ary Pieces.** By FREDERIC HARRISON.

Earthwork out of Tuscany. Third
Edition. By MAURICE HEWLETT.

Poems of Thomas Hood. Edited, with
Prefatory Memoir, by Canon AINGER.
In 2 Vols. Vol. 1. SERIOUS POEMS.
Vol. 2. POEMS OF WIT AND HUMOUR.
With Vignettes and Portraits.

Collected Essays of R. H. Hutton. 6 Vols.
LITERARY ESSAYS.
ESSAYS ON SOME OF THE MODERN
GUIDES OF ENGLISH THOUGHT IN
MATTERS OF FAITH.
THEOLOGICAL ESSAYS.
CRITICISMS ON CONTEMPORARY
THOUGHT AND THINKERS. 2 Vols.
ASPECTS OF RELIGIOUS AND SCIEN-
TIFIC THOUGHT. Selected from *The
Spectator,* and Edited by his Niece,
E. M. ROSCOE. With Portrait.

**Life and Works of Thomas Henry
Huxley.** 12 Vols. Vol. 1. METHOD AND
RESULTS. Vol. 2. DARWINIANA. Vol. 3.
SCIENCE AND EDUCATION. Vol. 4.
SCIENCE AND HEBREW TRADITION.
Vol. 5. SCIENCE AND CHRISTIAN
TRADITION. Vol. 6. HUME. With Helps
to the Study of Berkeley. Vol. 7. MAN'S
PLACE IN NATURE : and other An-
thropological Essays. Vol. 8. DIS-
COURSES, BIOLOGICAL AND GEOLOGI-
CAL. Vol. 9. EVOLUTION AND ETHICS,
AND OTHER ESSAYS. Vols. 10, 11, and 12.
LIFE AND LETTERS OF T. H. HUXLEY.
By LEONARD HUXLEY.

MACMILLAN AND CO., LTD., LONDON.